IMAGES of America
20TH-CENTURY RETAILING IN DOWNTOWN DETROIT

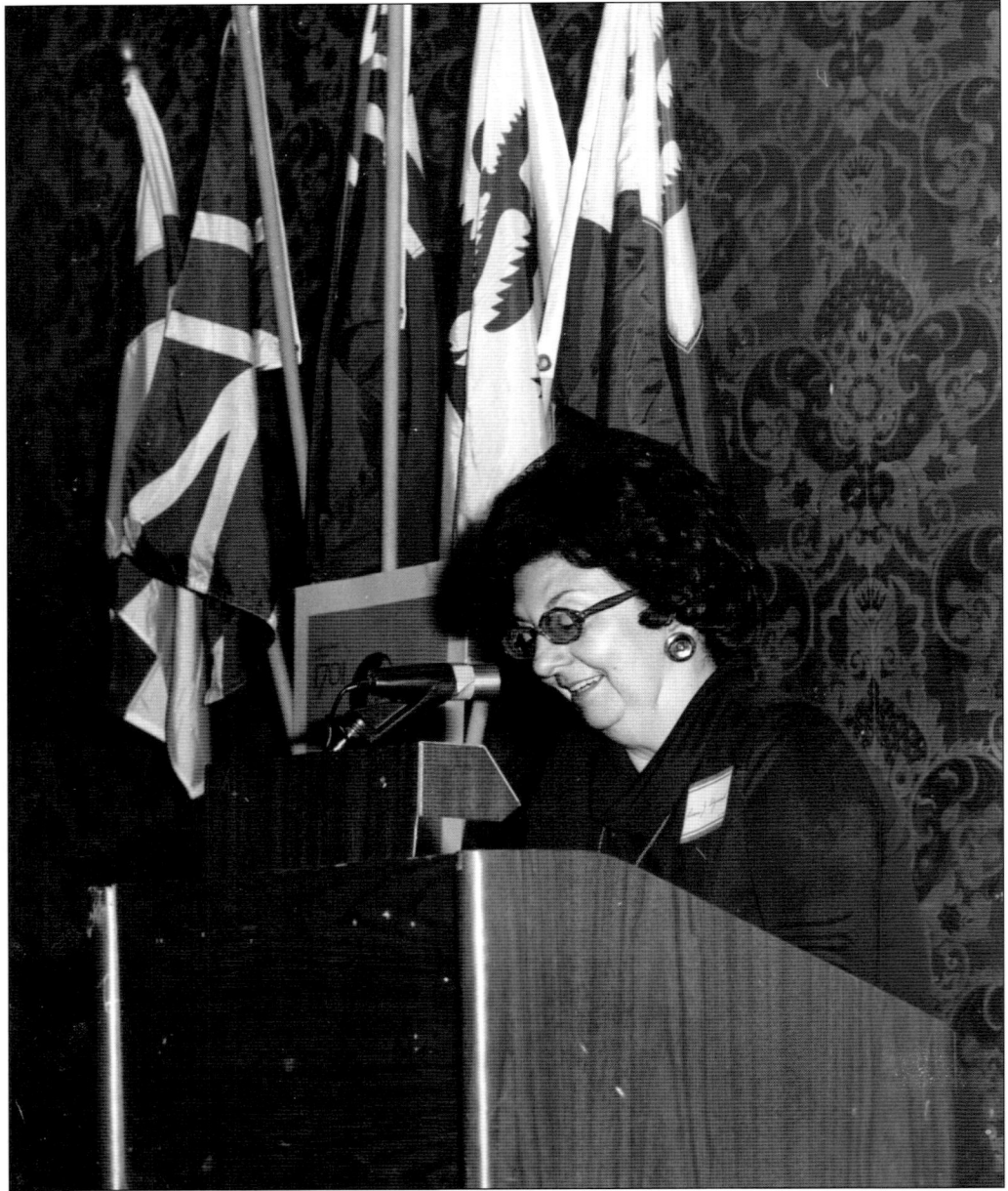

DIANE EDGECOMB ADDRESSING BICENTENNIAL COMMITTEE, 1976. Many Detroiters only know Diane Edgecomb as the promotions guru for the Central Business District Association. Her peers know her as a strong executive who is well versed in taxes, transportation, and land use as they relate to urban issues. (Courtesy Central Business District Foundation.)

On the cover: Please see page 22. (Courtesy Central Business District Foundation.)

IMAGES of America

20TH-CENTURY RETAILING IN DOWNTOWN DETROIT

Michael Hauser and Marianne Weldon

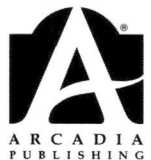

Copyright © 2008 by Michael Hauser and Marianne Weldon
ISBN 978-0-7385-6190-5

Published by Arcadia Publishing
Charleston SC, Chicago IL, Portsmouth NH, San Francisco CA

Printed in the United States of America

Library of Congress Catalog Card Number: 2008928991

For all general information contact Arcadia Publishing at:
Telephone 843-853-2070
Fax 843-853-0044
E-mail sales@arcadiapublishing.com
For customer service and orders:
Toll-Free 1-888-313-2665

Visit us on the Internet at www.arcadiapublishing.com

Dedicated to Diane Edgecomb, whose leadership and tenacity paved the way for future generations to discover, appreciate, and prosper in downtown Detroit

Contents

Acknowledgments		6
Introduction		7
1.	Evolution of Woodward Avenue and Environs	9
2.	Central Business District Association Revives Retail	15
3.	Central Business District Association Holiday Events	31
4.	The J. L. Hudson Company	45
5.	Crowley Milner and Company	65
6.	The Ernst Kern Company	73
7.	Specialty Stores and Services	87
8.	Value Merchants	115

ACKNOWLEDGMENTS

We gratefully acknowledge the assistance of the following individuals: Alyn Thomas of the Manning Brothers Historical Collection, Thomas Featherstone of the Walter P. Reuther Library at Wayne State University, the staff of the Burton Historical Collection at the Detroit Public Library, the Detroit Historical Museum, Diane Edgecomb of the Central Business District Foundation, Rebecca Binno Savage, Cynthia Young, and Patience Nauta. We also wish to thank our editor, Anna Wilson, for her guidance and perseverance.

INTRODUCTION

Among the most venerable aspects of city life were the department stores. They provided the city its character and held it together through prosperous periods and tumultuous times. These emporiums of commerce also became the sites of memorable family traditions. It would be difficult to come across an individual who did not have memories of the legendary Hudson's department store, meeting for lunch under the Kern's clock, riding Crowley's wooden escalators, savoring a hot fudge sundae at Sanders, or having lunch at Kresge's or Woolworth's. Personal milestones such as a first back-to-school outfit, a prom dress, a family portrait, or a visit to the bridal registry shaped lives and created lasting memories of bustling downtown Detroit retailers.

The diversity of the downtown shopping experience was a microcosm of the community, employing thousands of people on the selling floor, in nonselling areas, and in corporate offices. These stores catered to the needs of all socioeconomic demographics, from high-end department and specialty stores, to value merchants and dime stores, to moderately priced clothing retailers and merchants who relied on credit customers. Homegrown institutions like Hudson's, Crowley's, Kern's, Kresge's, Siegel's, Himelhoch's, and Winkelman's, to name a few, were more than just a store. Shoppers and visitors could enjoy fashion shows, explore community exhibits, purchase stamps and pay bills, attend lectures, plan vacations, and get items repaired. The leaders of these firms lived and invested in Detroit.

For years, downtown Detroit was envied by other cities. It featured over 400 merchants, encompassing four million square feet of space. Just imagine, the equivalent of four Somerset Collection malls could fit into the amount of space that was formerly devoted to retail shopping downtown.

With the rise of suburban shopping centers, downtown retailers like Hudson's began competing with their own branch locations. The loss of Detroit's streetcar and interurban train network, along with the opening of freeways, advanced the push to suburban areas. By the end of the 1950s, downtown Detroit retail sales dropped by almost a third, while the volume for the metropolitan area rose by almost 50 percent.

The Central Business District Association (originally the Downtown Property Owners Association) was founded in 1922 by Oscar Webber of the J. L. Hudson Company and other downtown retailers for the purpose of joining together to fight taxes. When the organization changed its name in 1954, its purpose was redefined to building a strong central city by improving and increasing business downtown.

Northland Center was a wake-up call for many merchants who had become complacent. In 1954, Diane Edgecomb was hired as promotions director for the Central Business District Association to revive retail by implementing fresh ideas and promotions as a way to entice suburbanites downtown. Her ideas were legendary, and many are still with the community today. She was the driving force behind the ethnic festivals, the Downtown Development Authority, Detroit Aglow holiday lighting activities, Downtown Detroit Days, the lighting of the Ambassador Bridge, the concept and leadership that created the People Mover, the restoration of the Wayne County Courthouse, a master plan for downtown lighting, the Ideas Before Dawn speaker series, and countless other programs. Edgecomb refused to give up on Detroit, even during the bleakest periods.

Times have changed dramatically since Northland Center paved the way for suburban growth and doomed urban retailing as Detroiters once knew it. The days of spending a leisurely afternoon shopping downtown, dining in a department store tearoom or at a dime store lunch counter, or catching a first-run film in a movie palace are long gone, as are the holiday windows and spectacular displays.

We have attempted to provide you, our readers, with a glimpse of the golden years of Woodward Avenue retailing. Many of the images in this book have not been seen publicly for decades. There are some omissions, as we obviously could not include all your favorites. We have also included some of the individuals and events that made Woodward Avenue a memorable destination for many Detroiters. Sit back, relax, and let the memories unfold.

One
EVOLUTION OF WOODWARD AVENUE AND ENVIRONS

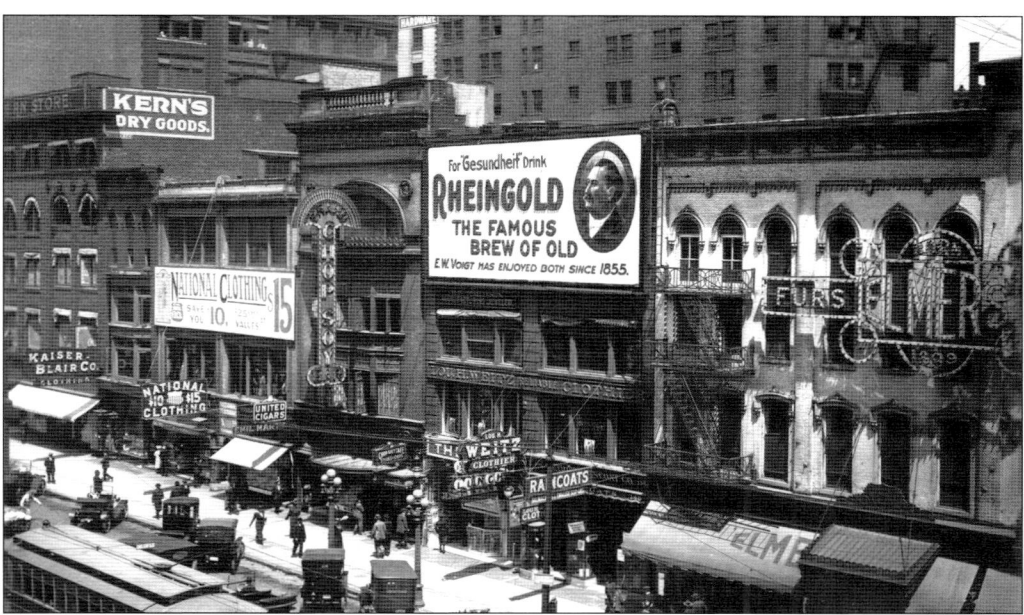

WOODWARD AVENUE AT GRATIOT AVENUE, 1914. By 1914, Detroit's retail district that began on Jefferson Avenue migrated to Campus Martius. Little did anyone at the time realize that the Campus Martius area would become one of the busiest crossroads in America. The image above depicts Kern's in its modest four-story structure, with Hudson's towering in the background. (Courtesy Manning Brothers Historical Collection.)

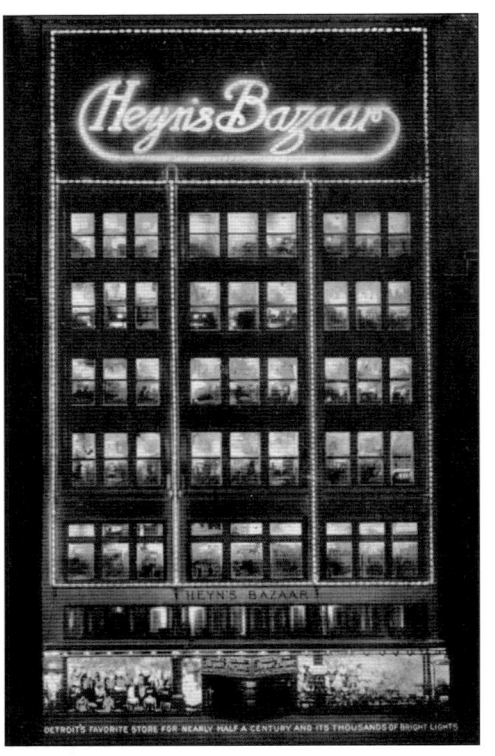

POSTCARD VIEW OF HEYN'S BAZAAR, 1241 WOODWARD AVENUE, 1912. Heyn's Bazaar was established in 1873 on Woodward Avenue, just north of Campus Martius. Its building was a beacon for traffic, as it was outlined with thousands of lightbulbs. Business was booming, and in 1919, the firm constructed a 10-story emporium at 1200 Woodward Avenue, on the former site of Fyfe's Shoes. In 1936, New York–based Lerner Shops leased the building and remained there until the mid-1980s. (Courtesy Michael Hauser.)

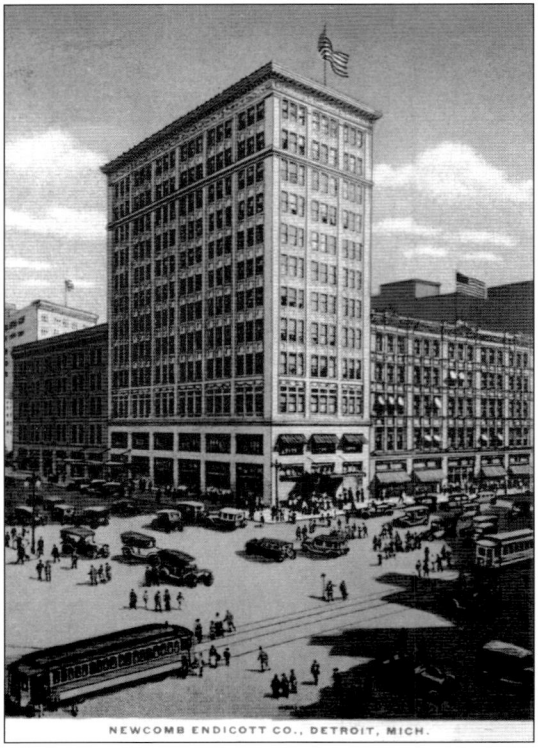

POSTCARD VIEW OF NEWCOMB ENDICOTT COMPANY, 1920. The Newcomb Endicott Company was founded in 1868 by C. A. Newcomb and Charles Endicott near Woodward and Jefferson Avenues. The firm prospered and in 1869 moved to the Detroit Opera House on Campus Martius. By 1881, it was in a five-story structure near Woodward and Grand River Avenues and in 1902 acquired an adjacent two-story structure. That building was demolished in 1918 to erect a 12-story addition. (Courtesy Michael Hauser.)

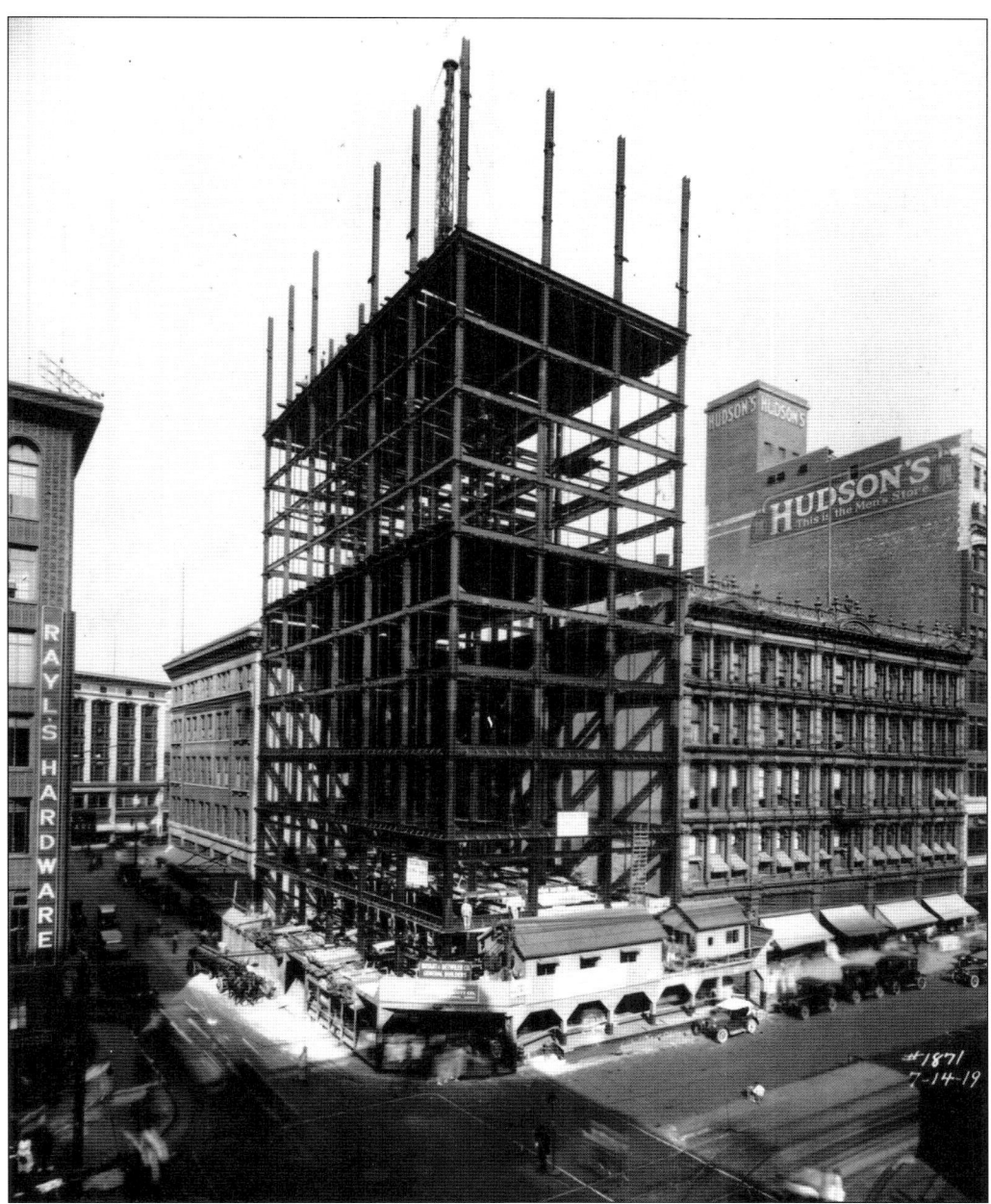

CONSTRUCTION OF NEWCOMB'S 12-STORY ADDITION, 1919. Newcomb's was responsible for a number of retail firsts in Michigan, including being the first department store, the first retailer to adopt motorized delivery, the first store to open an economy basement (1910), and the first to publish its own home magazine. During the holidays, families would line up in Newcomb's toy land to see Santa, who was accompanied by six live reindeer. The J. L. Hudson Company acquired Newcomb's in 1927 and announced plans to demolish the store and erect a 16-story addition to Hudson's. (Courtesy Burton Historical Collection, Detroit Public Library.)

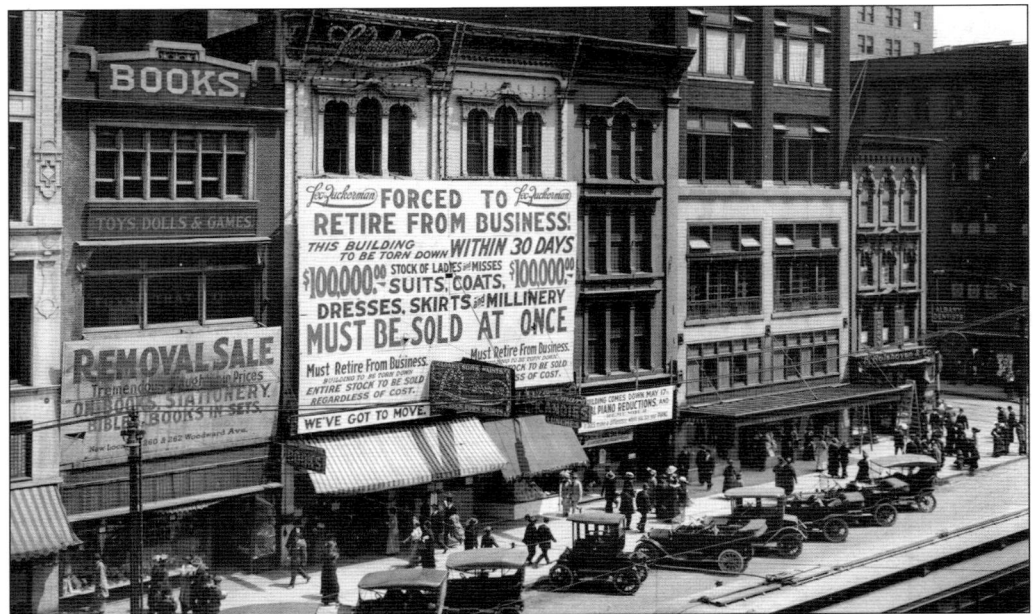

Woodward Avenue between Gratiot and Grand River Avenues, 1914. The retailers in the image above are being forced to vacate for the massive expansion of the J. L. Hudson Company. At this time, Hudson's only presence on Woodward Avenue was the tall, slender building on the right. The bulk of the store's operations were on Farmer Street. Note the angled parking that was permitted on Woodward Avenue at the time. (Courtesy Manning Brothers Historical Collection.)

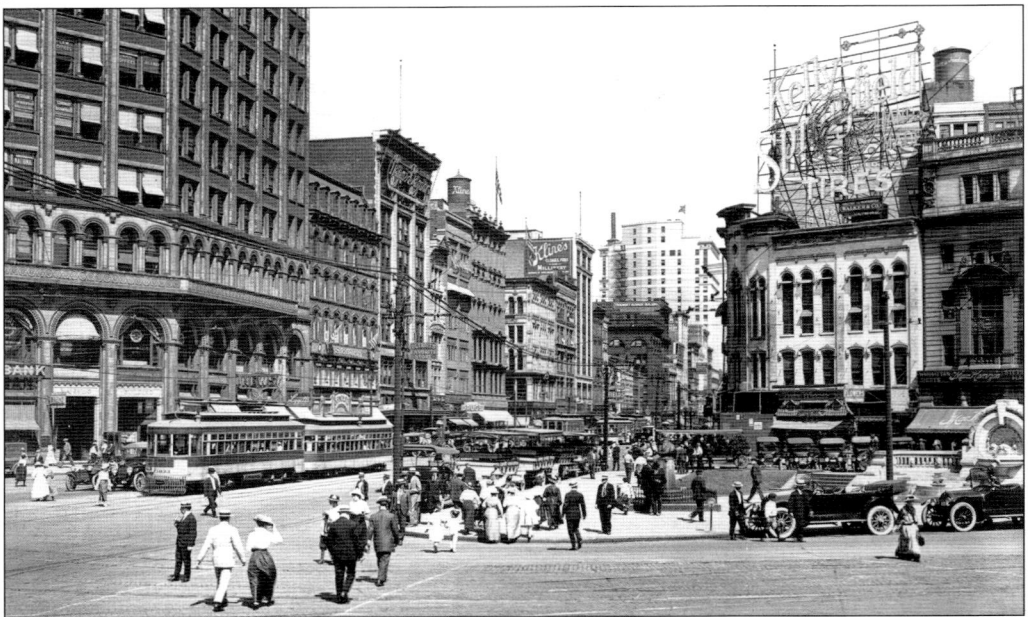

Woodward Avenue at Campus Martius, 1916. By 1916, Campus Martius had become the retail and entertainment hub of Detroit. Kline's women's clothing and Heyn's Bazaar are visible on the left and the Detroit Opera House on the right. Adjacent Monroe Street was filled with shops, restaurants, and a dozen motion picture theaters. (Courtesy Manning Brothers Historical Collection.)

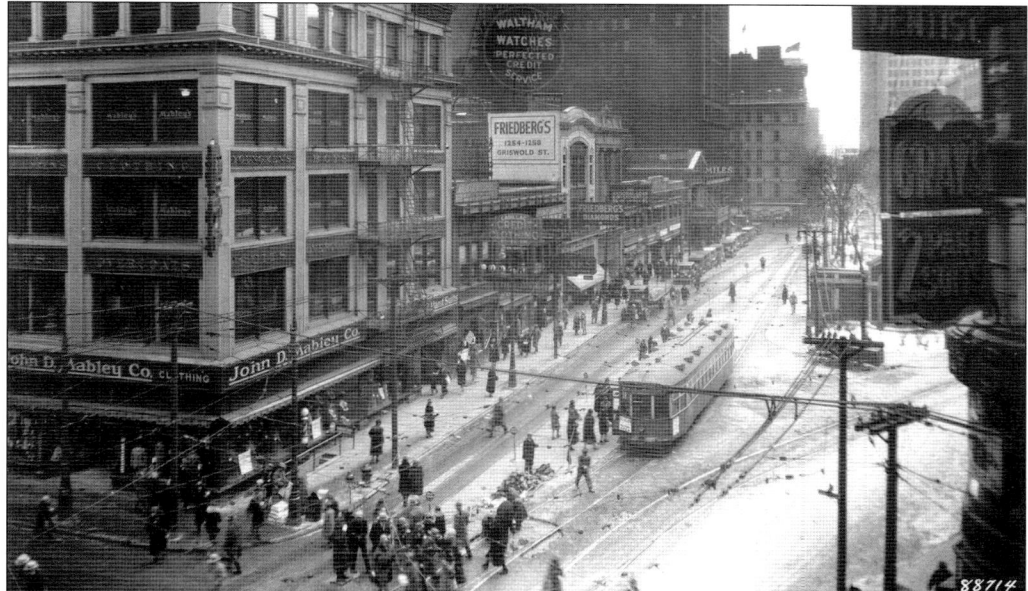

GRISWOLD STREET AT CAPITOL PARK, 1928. One block to the west of Woodward Avenue was another retail hub situated around Capitol Park. This district was anchored by Mabley's Clothing, Friedberg's Jewelers, the Miles Theatre, and People's Outfitting. A number of credit clothing stores also existed in the neighborhood as well as eateries. (Courtesy Manning Brothers Historical Collection.)

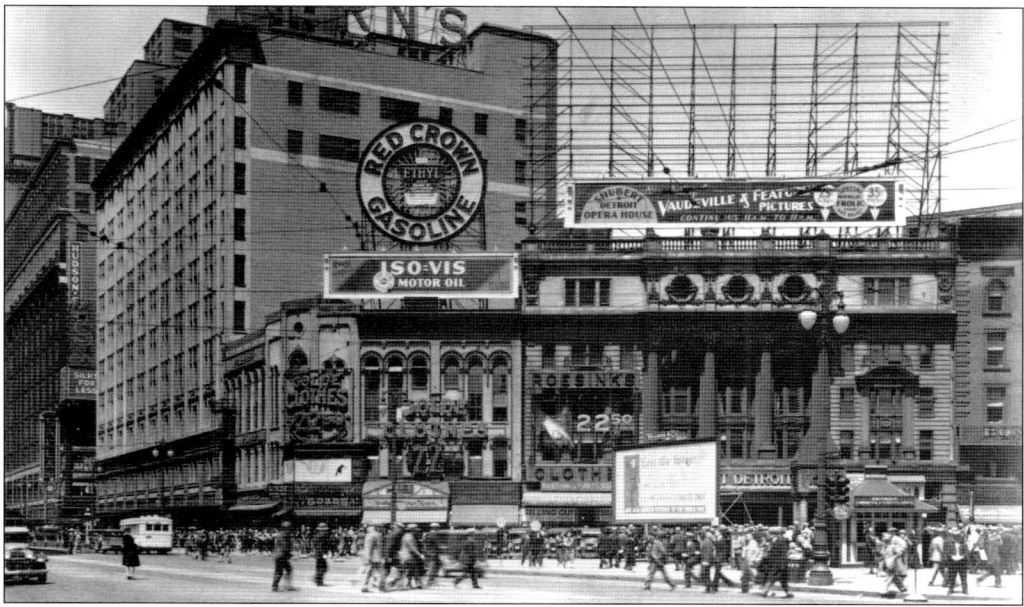

BUSTLING CAMPUS MARTIUS, 1930. Campus Martius had become Detroit's version of Times Square with towering electric signs and a transportation hub with the convergence of streetcars, motor coach, and automobile traffic. The area was also the gathering spot for parades, speeches, and other public spectacles. Note the convention and visitor's bureau kiosk on the right. (Courtesy Manning Brothers Historical Collection.)

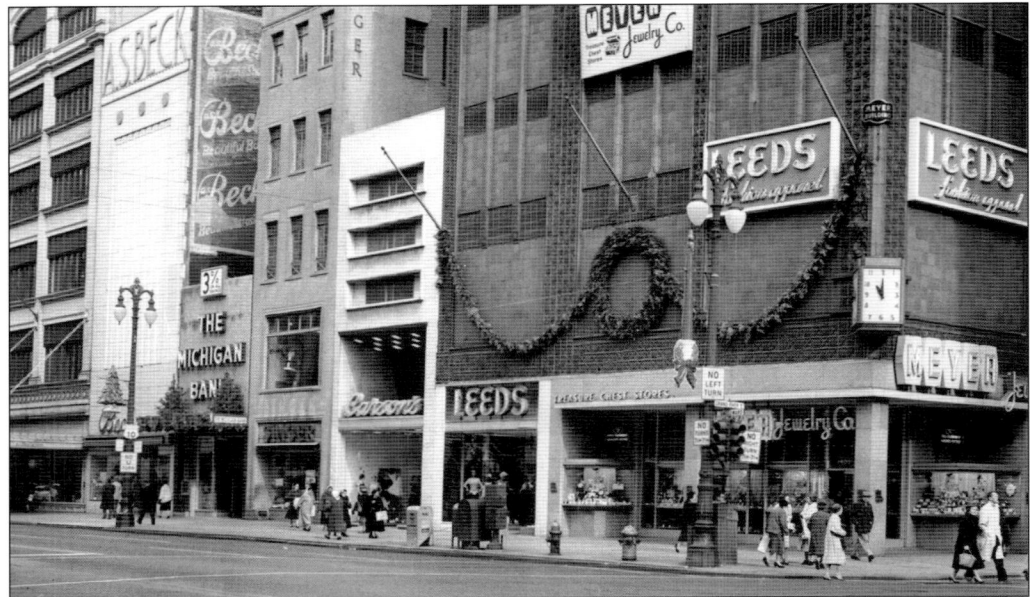

WOODWARD AND GRAND RIVER AVENUES, 1958. In the mid-1950s, this block was improved with large investments by Meyer Jewelry Company, which relocated its downtown store and corporate headquarters to this block, and Winkelman Brothers, which opened its first downtown store. Leed's Fashions opened in 1957, joining mainstays A. S. Beck Shoes, Singer Sewing Center, and D. J. Healy Shops. (Courtesy Central Business District Foundation.)

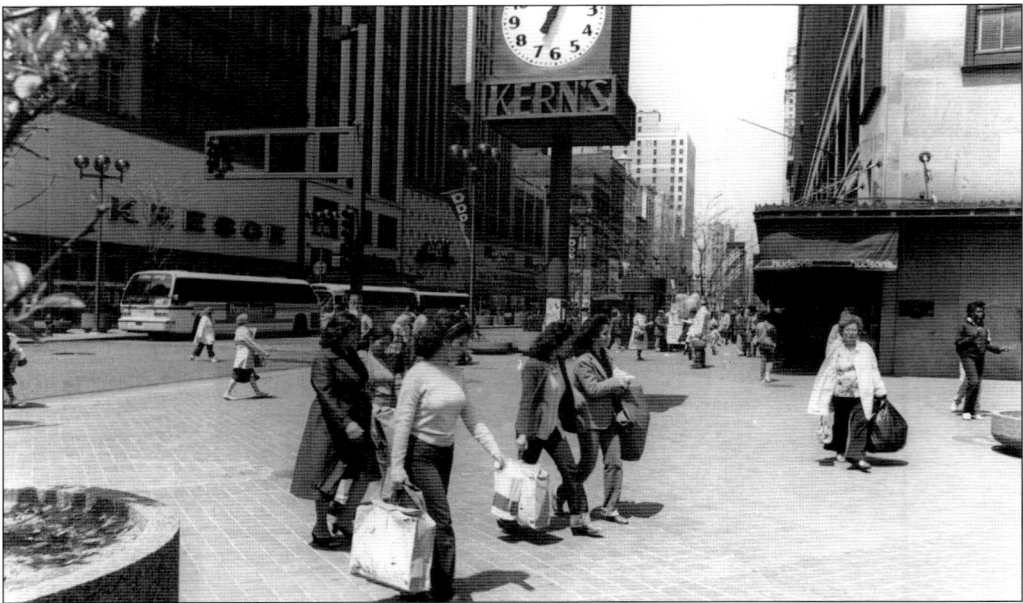

FINAL DOWNTOWN DETROIT DAYS WITH HUDSON'S, 1982. The October 1982 version of Downtown Detroit Days was bittersweet, as Detroiters knew this event would never be the same without Hudson's. Besides being downtown's last department store, Hudson's was the event's largest financial contributor. Once the store closed in January 1983, the other retailers on Woodward Avenue fell like dominoes. (Courtesy Central Business District Foundation.)

Two
CENTRAL BUSINESS DISTRICT ASSOCIATION REVIVES RETAIL

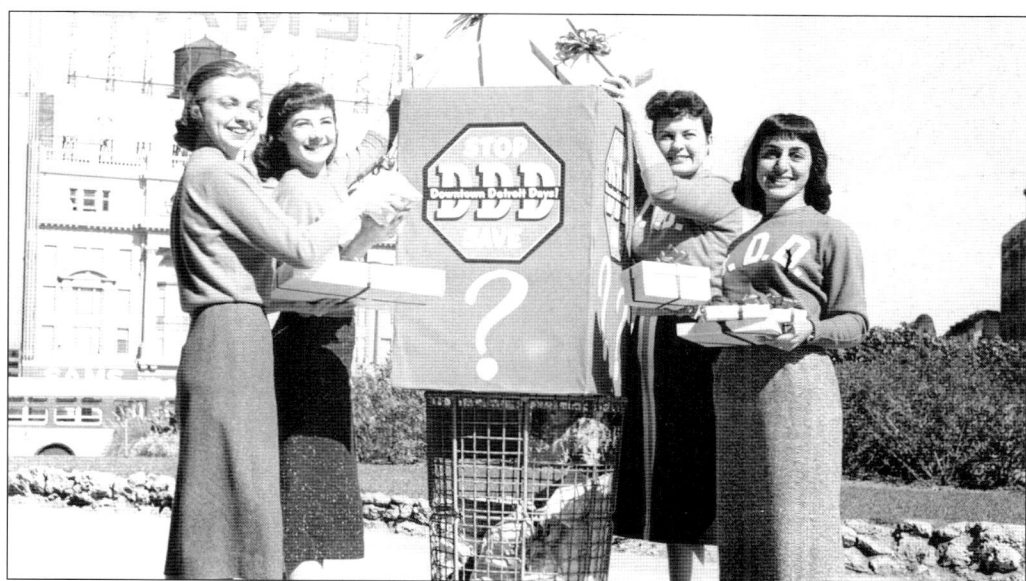

PROMOTING DOWNTOWN DETROIT DAYS ON CAMPUS MARTIUS, 1950S. Downtown Detroit Days was a powerhouse when it came time to promote this fun-filled event. Print advertisements appeared in the *Detroit Free Press*, the *Detroit News*, the *Detroit Times*, and the *Detroit Shopping News*. There were radio, television, movie trailers, window banners, interior displays, contests, bus cards, table tents, and flags and banners for all downtown lampposts. (Courtesy Central Business District Foundation.)

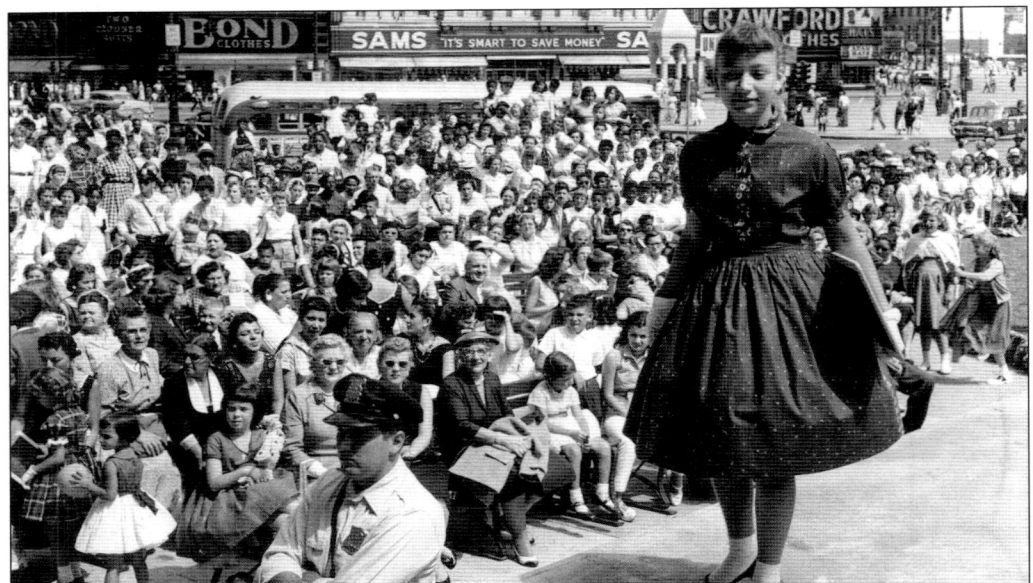

BACK-TO-SCHOOL KICKOFF AT CAMPUS MARTIUS, 1957. Each August, the Central Business District Association staged a highly anticipated week of events for the back-to-school season. Detroit students modeled the latest fashions. Also included were receptions, concerts, student arts and crafts demonstrations, prizes, and television personalities. A life-size schoolhouse was erected each year in front of the old Detroit City Hall with grandstand seating for 1,500. (Courtesy Central Business District Foundation.)

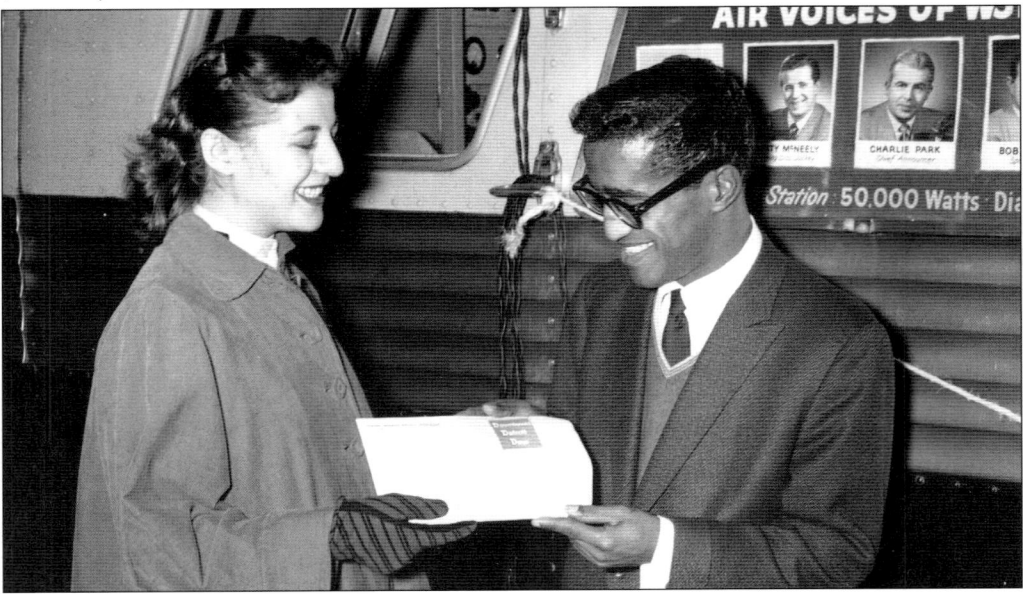

SAMMY DAVIS JR. PROMOTES DOWNTOWN DETROIT DAYS, 1955. Many of the promotions sponsored by the Central Business District Association included personalities from radio, stage, and screen. Above, recording and television star Sammy Davis Jr. helps promote Downtown Detroit Days. Besides performing on Washington Boulevard, Davis launched hundreds of balloons containing parking passes and movie tickets. (Courtesy Central Business District Foundation.)

SPRUCING UP WOODWARD AVENUE WITH SOME GREENERY, 1955. As part of the Central Business District Association's Fall Fashion Festival, Woodward Avenue was transformed into a tree-lined avenue, providing a European flair. Over 100 elms and maples adorned the sidewalks. Outdoor cafés were set up, serving tea and cookies. The idea was warmly received and permanent planters were erected. (Courtesy Central Business District Foundation.)

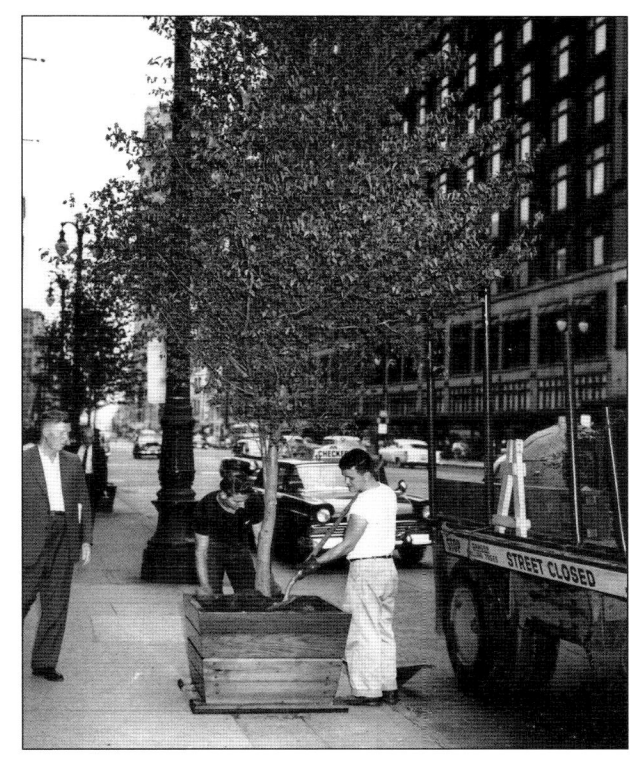

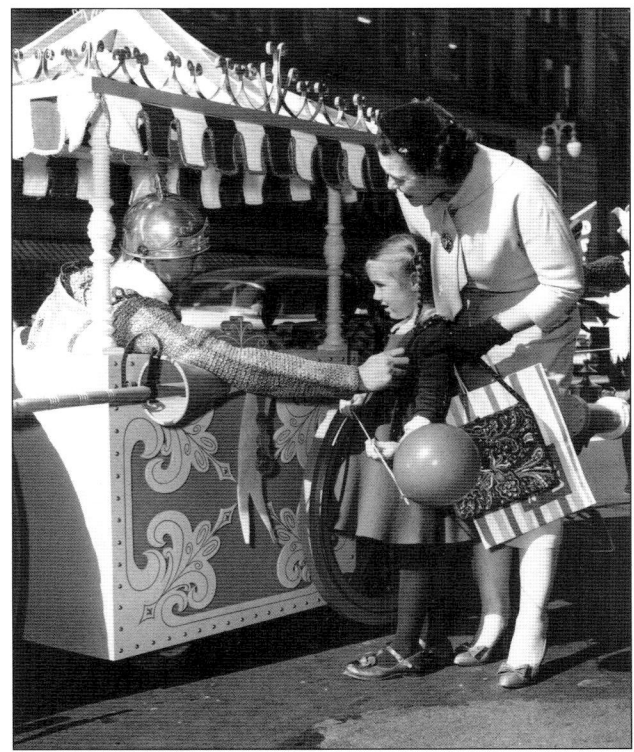

DOWNTOWN DETROIT DAYS CONTEST WINNER, 1958. Mary Ellen Courtney, shown here when she was five years of age, won a trip to Disneyland with her mother. The knight in armor greeting Courtney was accompanied by a red-eyed green dragon that spit fire and was pulled by 12 elves up Woodward Avenue from the Detroit Civic Center to Grand Circus Park. (Courtesy Central Business District Foundation.)

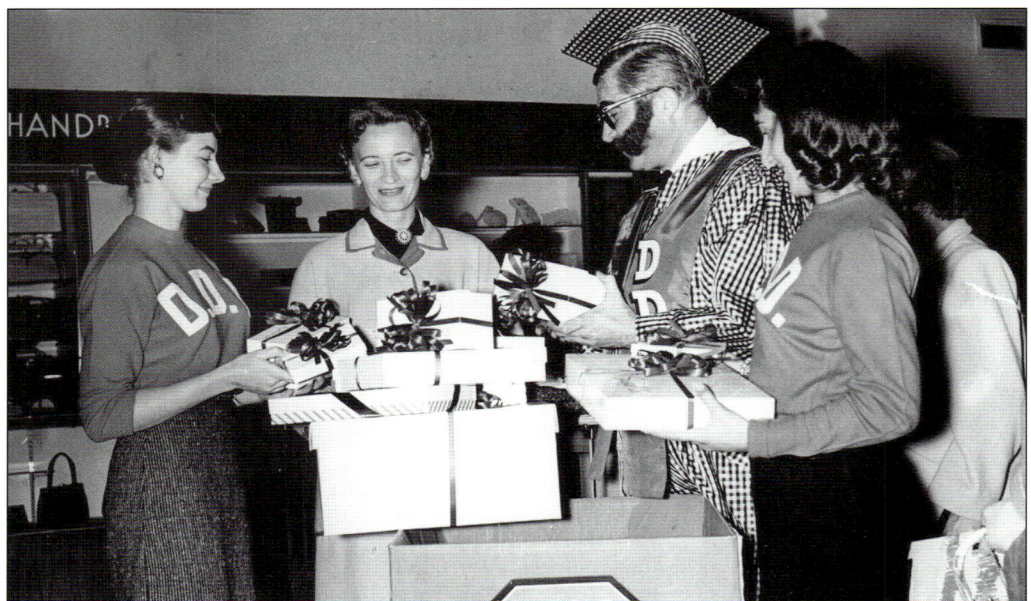

PROFESSOR DOWNTOWN PERSONAL APPEARANCE, 1956. The Central Business District Association created Professor Downtown as a marketing personality to bolster retail sales. He appeared at downtown stores with the world's largest blackboard, to quiz young folks who visited him, and give away surprises. Many times, Professor Downtown (Fred Wolf of WXYZ Radio) was teamed with visiting national personalities. (Courtesy Central Business District Foundation.)

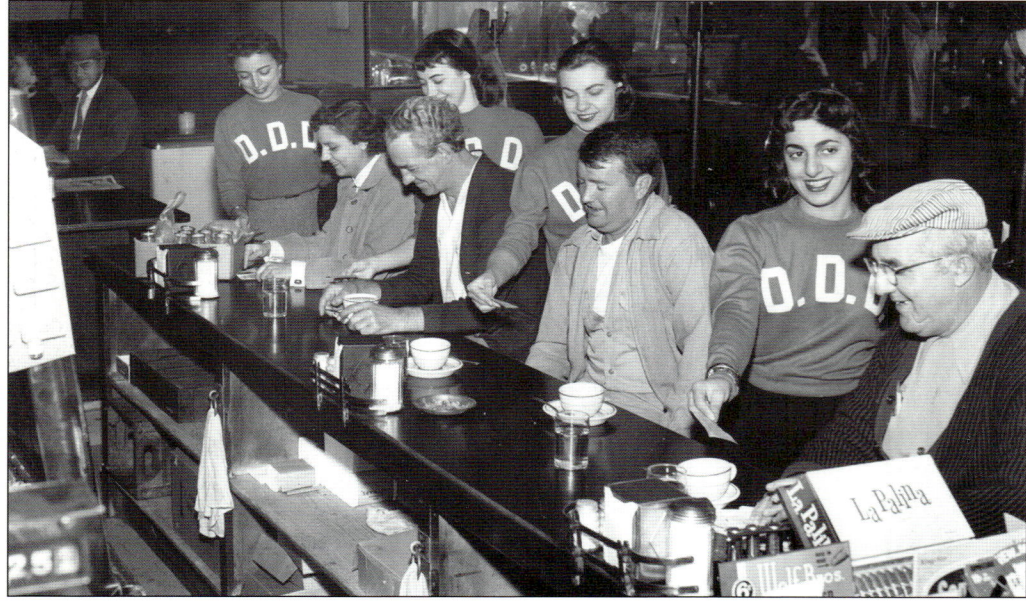

MYSTERY SHOPPERS PICKING UP THE TAB FOR THE GUYS, 1957. Downtown Detroit Days did not forget about the gents who were a part of the crowd that thronged downtown. The lovely ladies above are distributing food and beverage vouchers, informing these patrons that their meals were complimentary. In the 1960s, a Mr. Downtown Detroit Days was selected. (Courtesy Central Business District Foundation.)

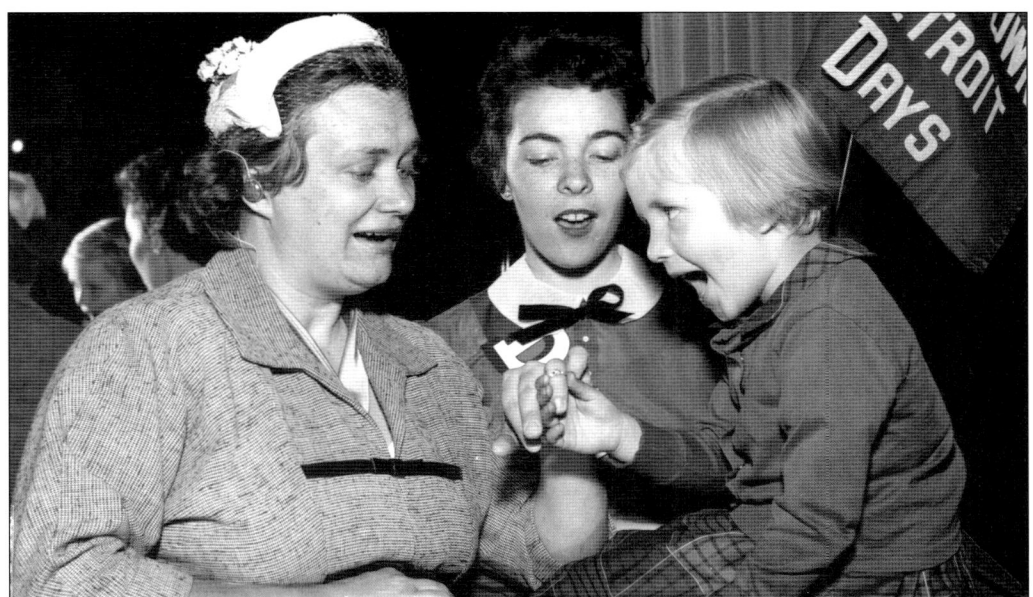

EVERYONE WAS A WINNER DURING DOWNTOWN DETROIT DAYS, 1958. Mrs. Lester Wade and her daughter Emma are surprised at winning a diamond ring from the popular Treasure Chest of Fun. Other winners received wardrobes, trips, or household appliances. Thousands of gift certificates for movies, restaurants, and parking were also distributed by mystery shoppers. (Courtesy Central Business District Foundation.)

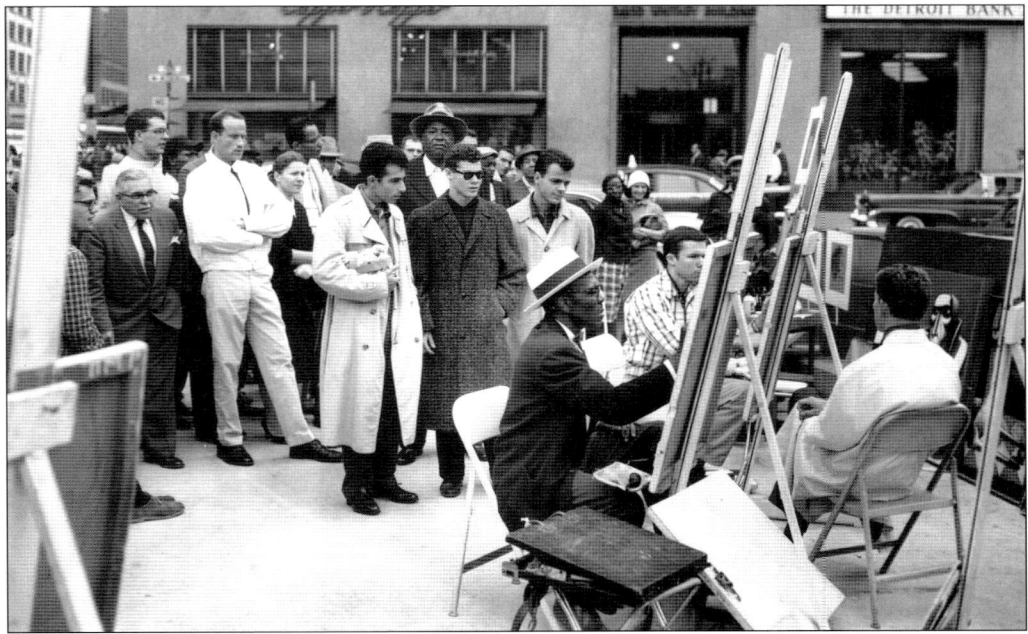

ARTISTS IN GRAND CIRCUS PARK, 1958. The annual Fall Fashion Festival also included art shows in Grand Circus Park and on Campus Martius. There were portrait artists and sketch artists from the Palette and Brush Guild, Bloomfield Art Association, Society of Women Painters, and Associated Art School. (Courtesy Central Business District Foundation.)

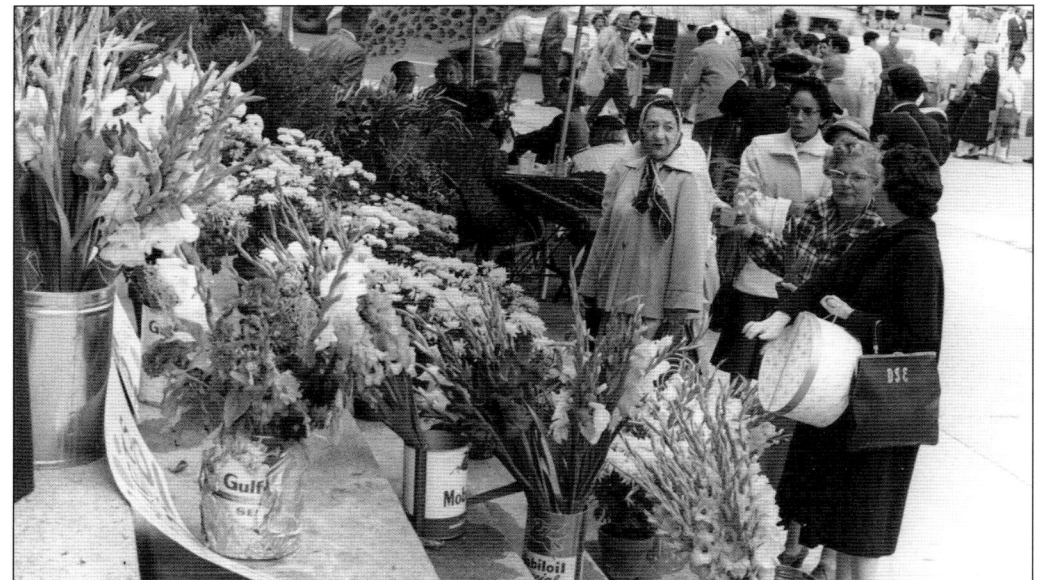

FLOWER STALLS FOR DOWNTOWN DETROIT DAYS, 1959. The premise for Downtown Detroit Days was to showcase extraordinary values—not markdowns, not clearance, and not month-end items. The combination of real values, unexpected special events, and visually pleasing touches such as the flower stalls beside the old Detroit City Hall made the biannual promotion the extraordinary event it became. (Courtesy Central Business District Foundation.)

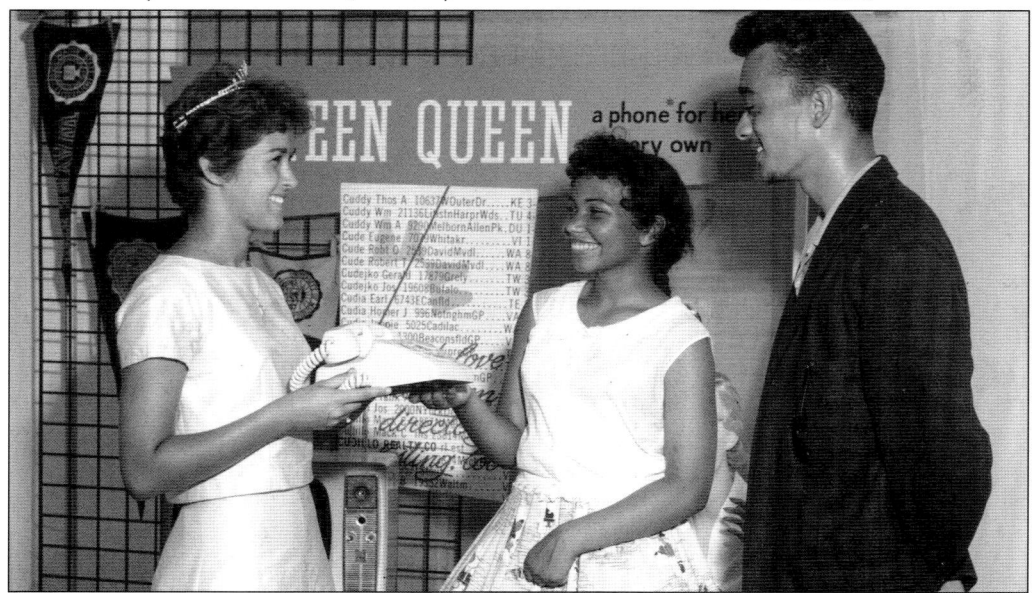

BACK-TO-SCHOOL TEEN QUEEN CONTEST, 1959. As part of the Central Business District Association's effort to attract young consumers, a Teen Queen contest was launched. Applicants between the ages of 15 and 19 competed for a back-to-school wardrobe, a $100 bank account, a $300 scholarship, and a chance to audition with the Vanguard Playhouse. Fred Weiss of WXYZ Radio emceed the contest on the lawn at the old Detroit City Hall. (Courtesy Central Business District Foundation.)

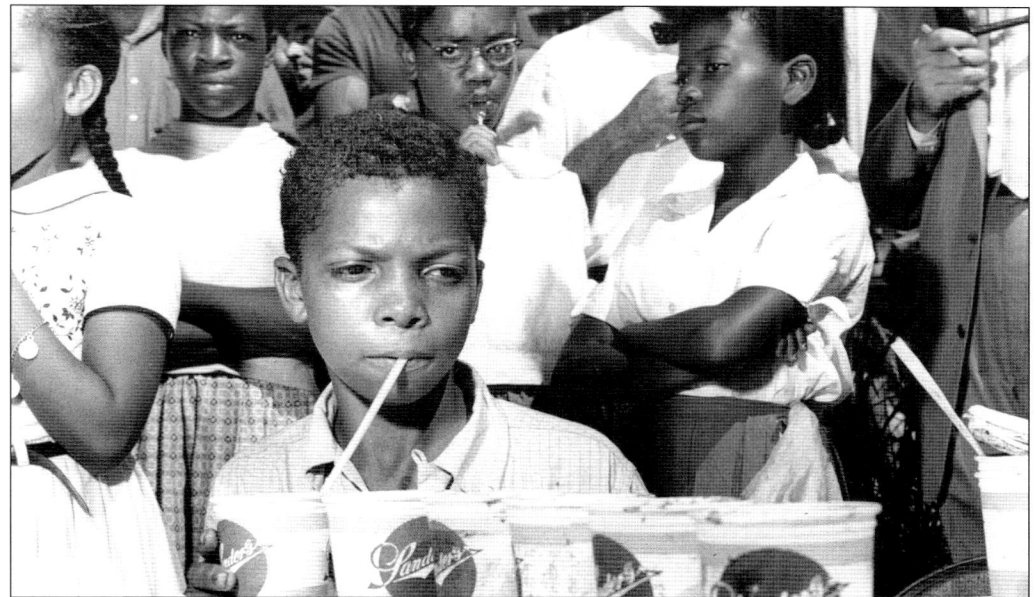

SODA-DRINKING CONTEST ON CAMPUS MARTIUS, 1959. The Central Business District Association teamed up with Detroit-based Sanders Confectionery each summer for a soda-drinking contest. Young folks had 30 minutes to stow away all the chocolate ice-cream sodas they could drink. The prize was either a new bicycle or free soda for every day of the year. Winner Darnell Dawsey, above, opted for a bicycle. (Courtesy Central Business District Foundation.)

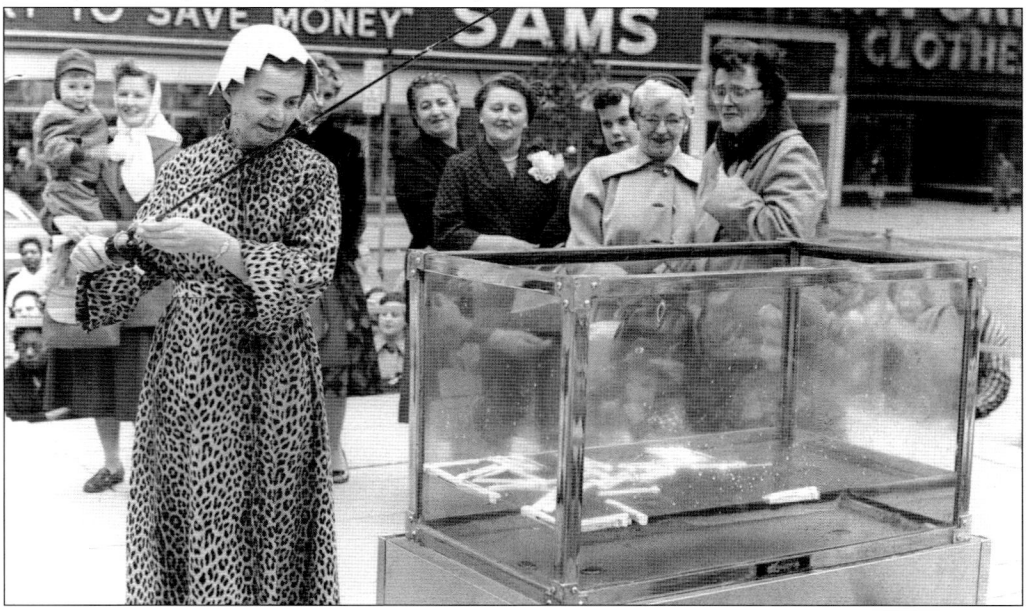

FISHING FOR BARGAINS ON CAMPUS MARTIUS, 1959. The Central Business District Association mystery shoppers distributed cards to passersby during Downtown Detroit Days. Those lucky folks were provided the opportunity to reel in gifts of their choice, with the aid of Chuck Daughtery of WXYZ Radio. Prizes included silver dollars, televisions, and household items (Courtesy Central Business District Foundation.)

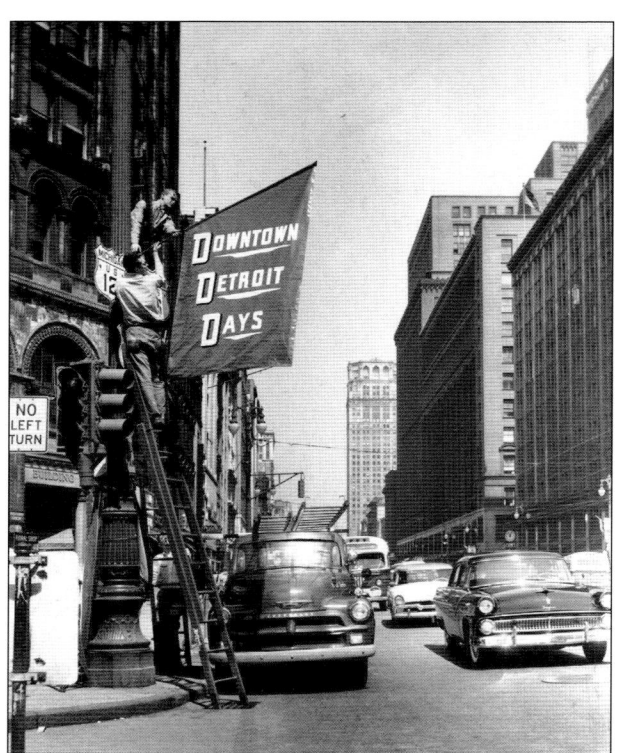

INSTALLING BANNERS AT WOODWARD AND MICHIGAN AVENUES, 1955. The Central Business District Association made sure that shoppers and visitors alike knew that Downtown Detroit Days was special. Streets and stores were adorned with 14,000 colorful flags and banners. Over 500 balloons were launched containing gift certificates. The Department of Street Railways also cooperated by offering 15¢ fares on streetcars and buses. (Courtesy Central Business District Foundation.)

HERALDING THE ARRIVAL OF DOWNTOWN DETROIT DAYS, 1957. These exuberant young ladies (from left to right, Donna Kaye, Sandra Krygier, and Josephine Kachadourian) stroll West Fort Street dispensing information and prizes. Even Miss Dougall, the pooch on the leash, got into the act. The customized hatboxes with the DDDays inscription were created by the visual merchandising department at Hudson's. (Courtesy Central Business District Foundation.)

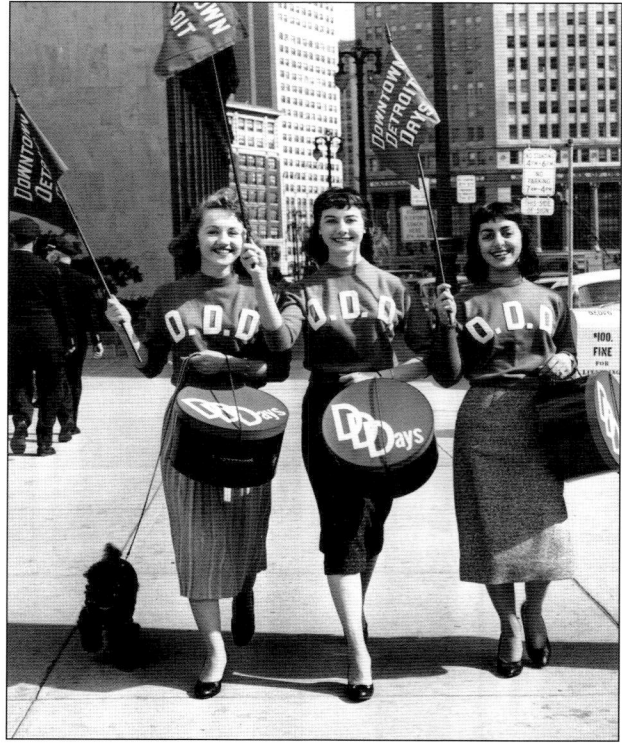

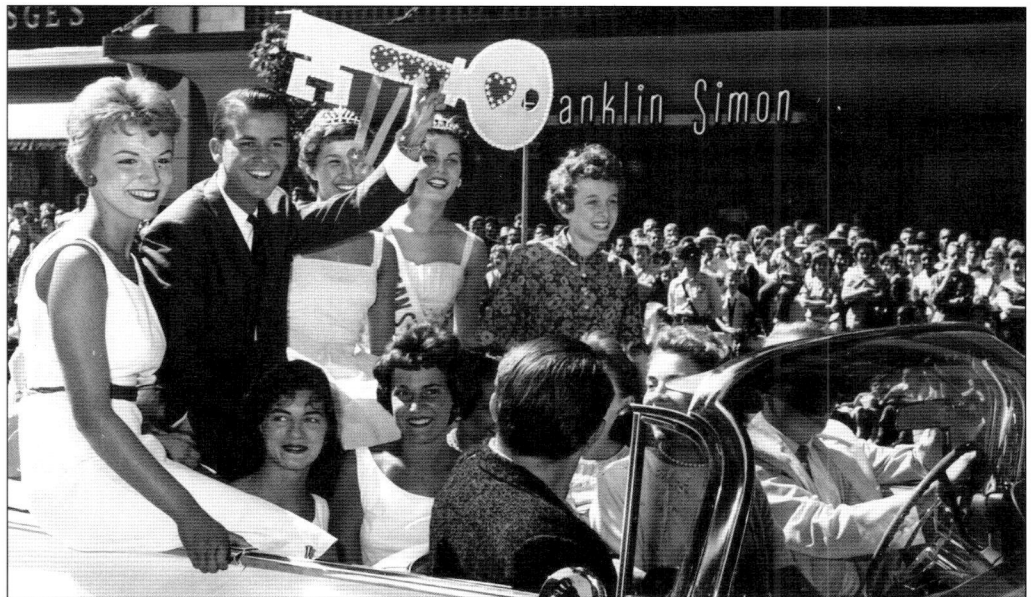

TELEVISION PERSONALITY DICK CLARK ON WOODWARD AVENUE, 1959. America's oldest teenager was presented the key to the city by the back-to-school Teen Queen and members of her court on behalf of the Central Business District Association. Clark appeared in the Michigan State Fair Parade, which was comprised of 110 units and 3,500 participants. This parade was second in size only to Hudson's Thanksgiving Day parade. (Courtesy Central Business District Foundation.)

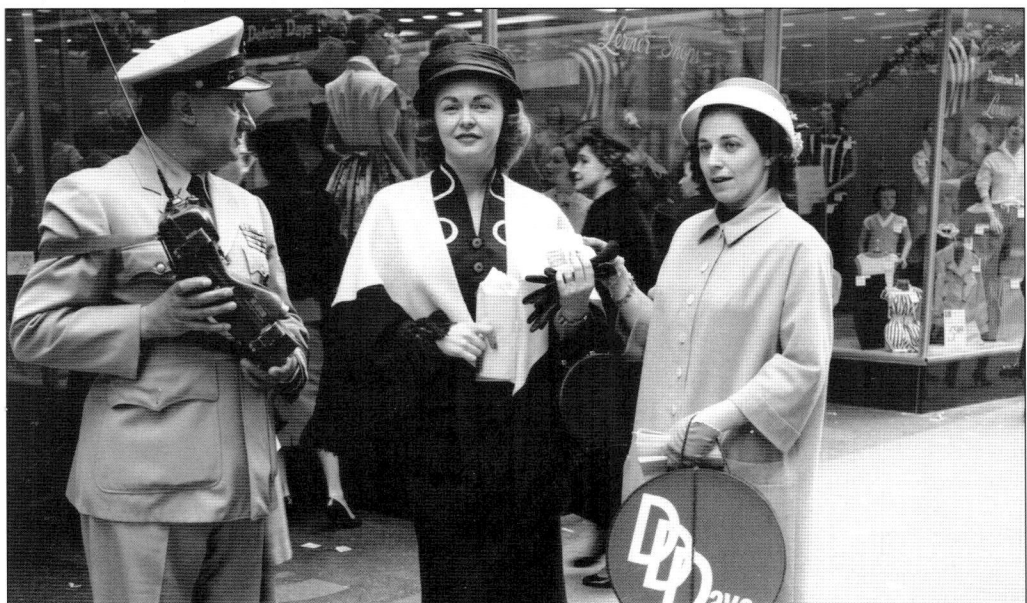

COLLABORATING WITH ARMED FORCES WEEK, 1957. These stylish goodwill ambassadors for the Central Business District Association stop a serviceman dead in his tracks to present him with several gift certificates good at downtown retailers. (Technology certainly has downsized gadgets such as this enormous two-way radio!) In conjunction with Armed Forces Week, there were demonstrations, exhibits, and window displays. (Courtesy Central Business District Foundation.)

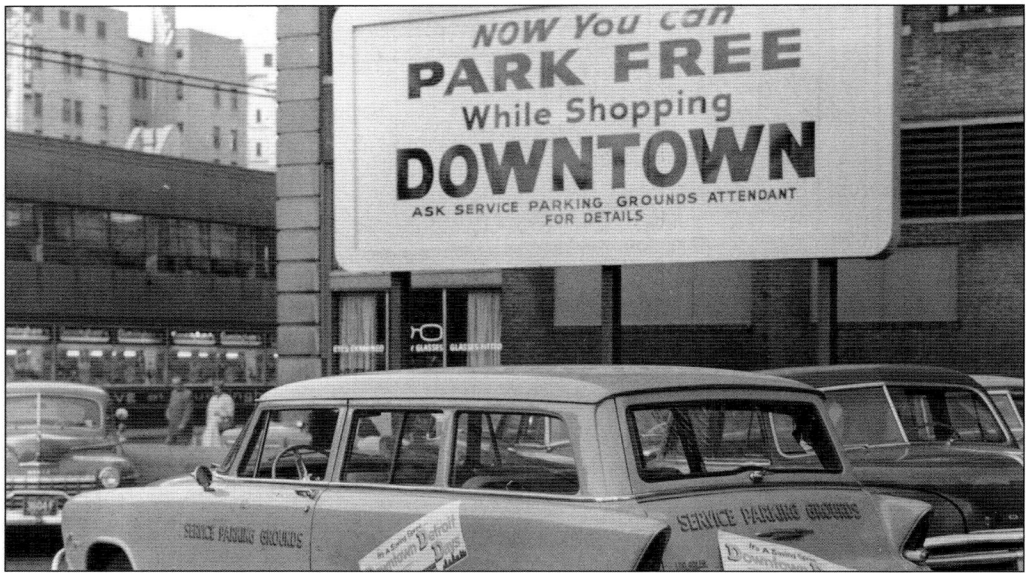

TACKLING TRANSPORTATION AND PARKING ISSUES, 1955. The Central Business District Association was at the forefront of parking and mass transit issues as far back as the 1920s, offering the earliest proposals for a Detroit subway. The association consistently worked with the Department of Street Railways to provide discounted bus and streetcar fares during major events. In later years, the Central Business District Association assisted with parking promotions to draw folks downtown. (Courtesy Central Business District Foundation.)

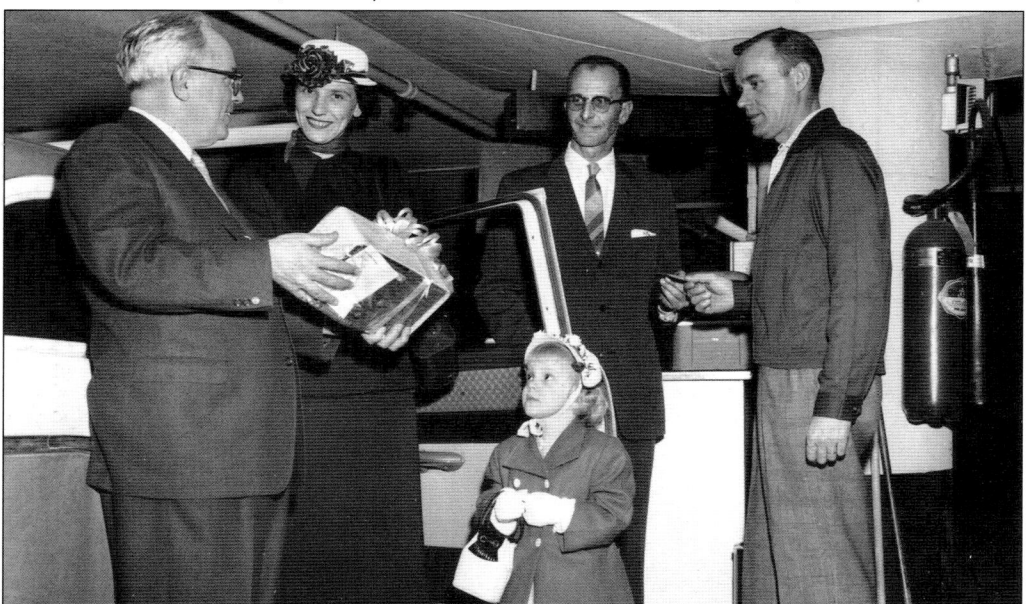

CELEBRATING THE GRAND CIRCUS UNDERGROUND GARAGE, 1958. Less than a year after it opened, the Grand Circus Park garage greeted its 500,000th customer, Mr. and Mrs. Barney Wasoiorcz, who received a clock radio. Foster Winter (left), board chair of the Central Business District Association, made the presentation. This parking garage project was 15 years in the making due to bitter politics. (Courtesy Central Business District Foundation.)

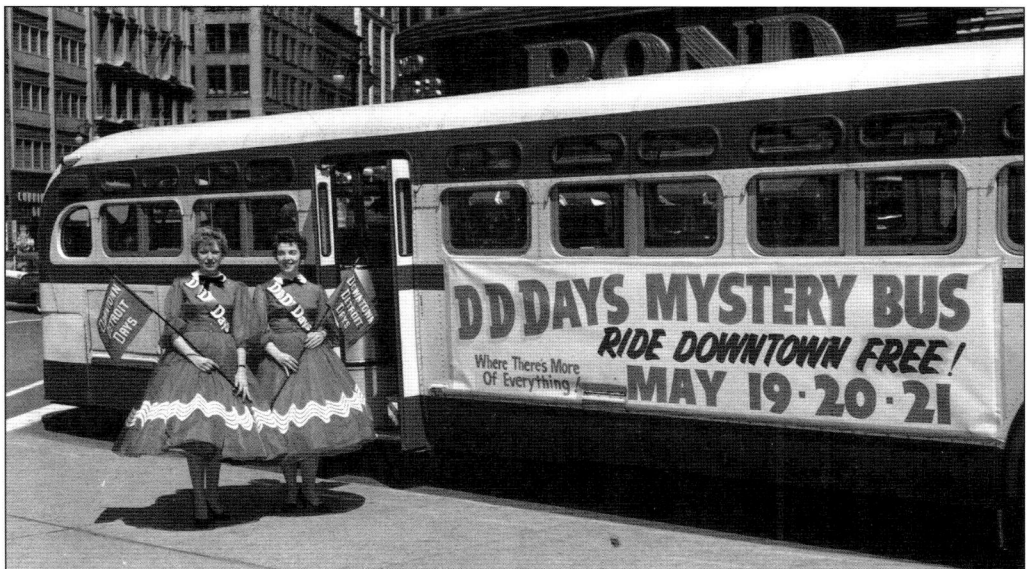

HOP ABOARD THE DETROIT DOWNTOWN DAYS MYSTERY BUS AND SAVE, 1960S. The Central Business District Association worked closely with the Department of Street Railways on cross-promotions. A mystery bus operated as an express ride to downtown for shoppers on four different routes. Upon boarding the coach, a passenger was greeted by a costumed hostess who distributed free gifts of imported fragrance, movie tickets, and restaurant passes. (Courtesy Central Business District Foundation.)

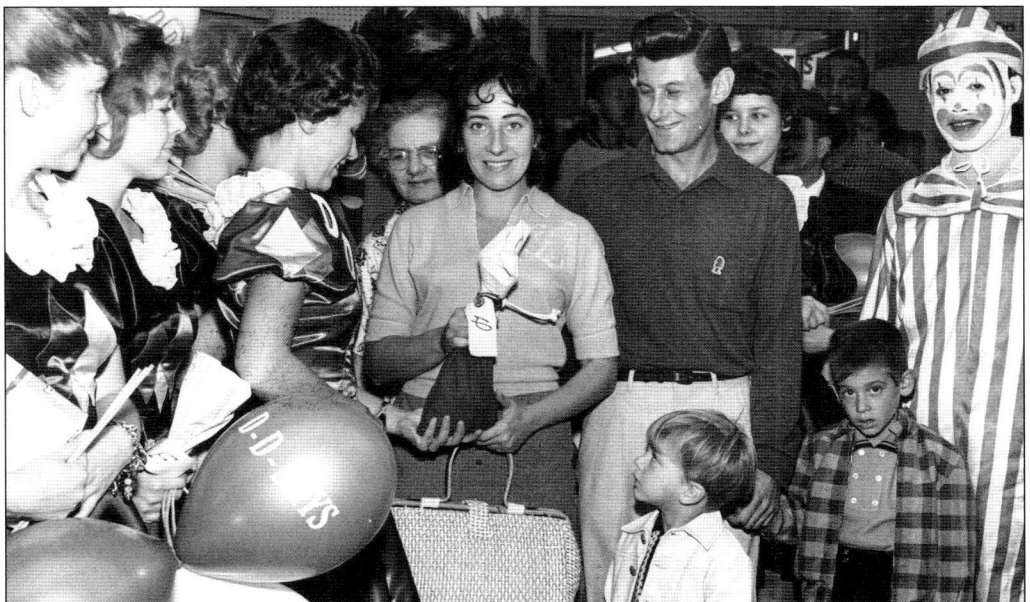

FAMILY ACTIVITIES DURING DOWNTOWN DETROIT DAYS, 1960. Another entertaining aspect of the Central Business District Association's Downtown Detroit Days was the annual Name the Clown contest on Campus Martius. Contestants were encouraged to dress as their interpretation of a happy clown. Metropolitan area boys and girls judged the winners, and each received 50 silver dollars. (Courtesy Central Business District Foundation.)

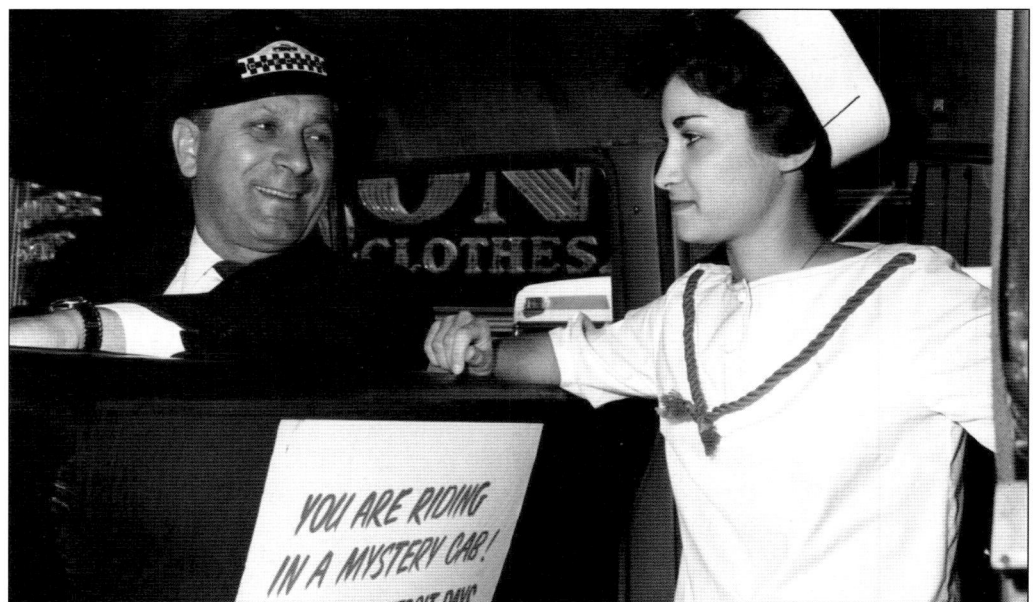

MYSTERY SHOPPER CONFERS WITH A CHECKER CABBIE, 1961. In the 1960s, Downtown Detroit Days expanded the mystery shopper program by dispatching mystery taxicabs operated by Checker Cab. Drivers would inform passengers upon entry that their ride home was free. Another popular mystery shopper feature was the Courtesy Is Contagious program. (Courtesy Central Business District Foundation.)

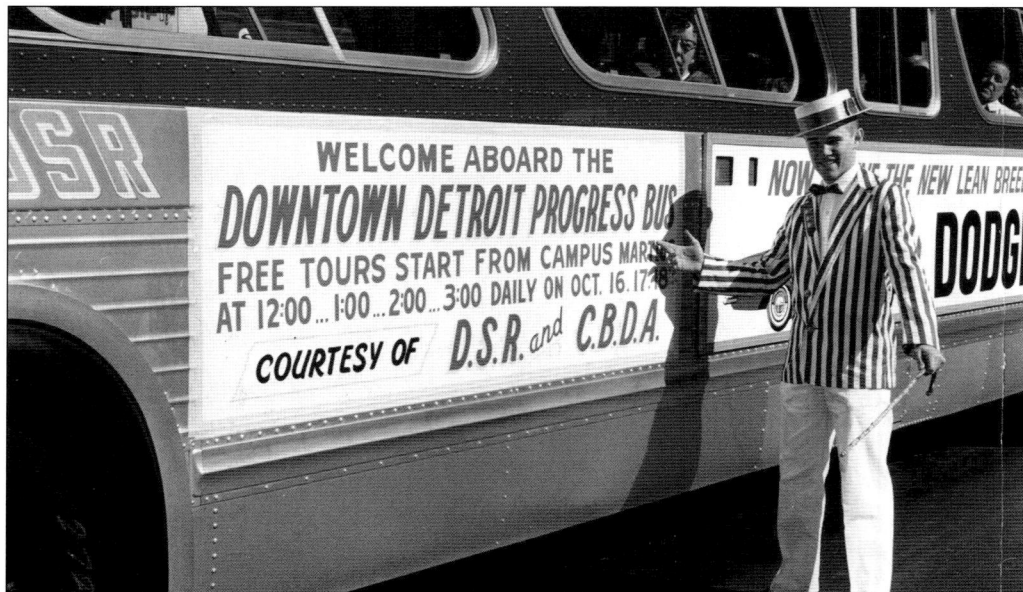

ALL ABOARD FOR A TOUR OF DOWNTOWN'S PROGRESS, 1961. During the autumn, Downtown Detroit Days, the Central Business District Association, and the Department of Street Railways partnered to show off positive new aspects of downtown. The tours were led by Denny Murdock, a Wayne State University student, otherwise known as "Mr. Young Detroit." Miss DDDays was also on hand, distributing prizes to riders. (Courtesy Central Business District Foundation.)

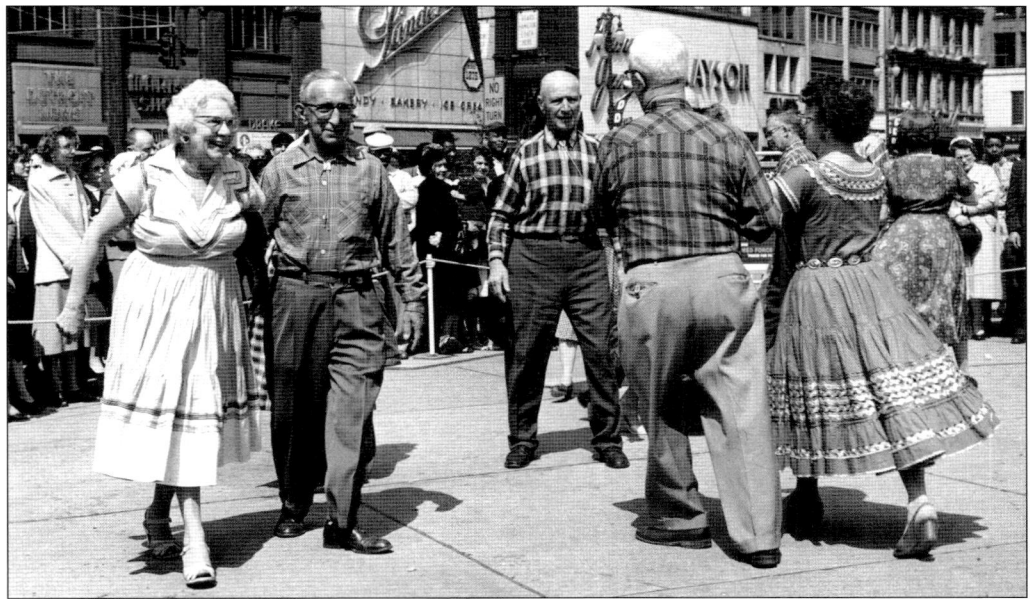

COUNTRY HOEDOWN ON CAMPUS MARTIUS, 1960. The first hoedown to be staged on Woodward Avenue was billed as "the Big Whirl!" More than 1,000 square dancers converged on Campus Martius in swirling skirts and colorful shirts. What formerly was an annual event is today a year-round activity. The Central Business District Association partnered with the Michigan Council of Square and Round Dance Clubs. (Courtesy Central Business District Foundation.)

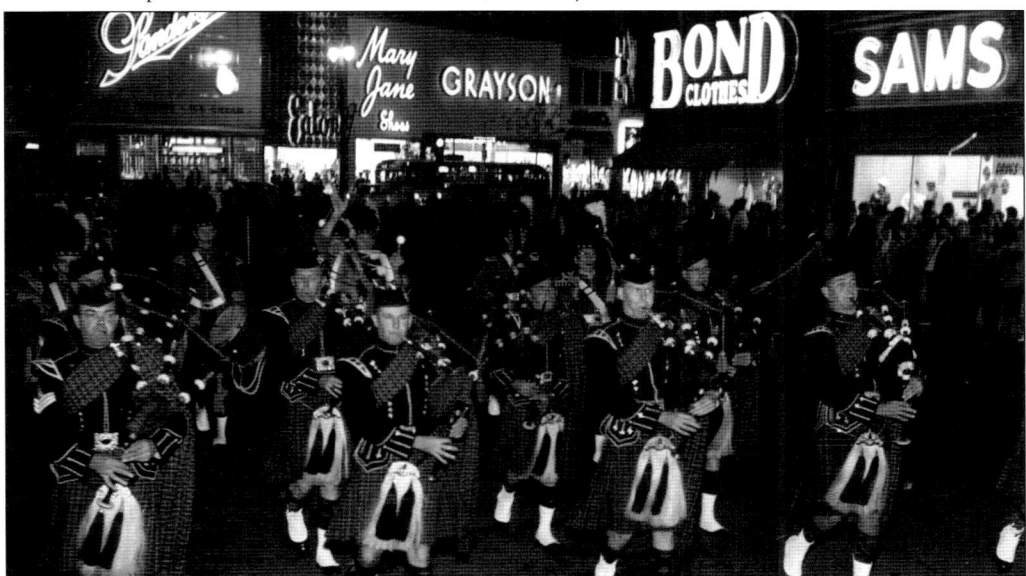

EVENING EVENTS AT CAMPUS MARTIUS, 1961. Evening events produced by the Central Business District Association were very popular in the 1960s. Neon-drenched backgrounds added even more pizzazz to the various activities like the marching of the Chrysler Imperial Highlanders Band, as seen above. Other promotions included the Friday After Dark Tours to ethnic restaurants and outdoor entertainment at the Red Garter Saloon, behind Hudson's. (Courtesy Central Business District Foundation.)

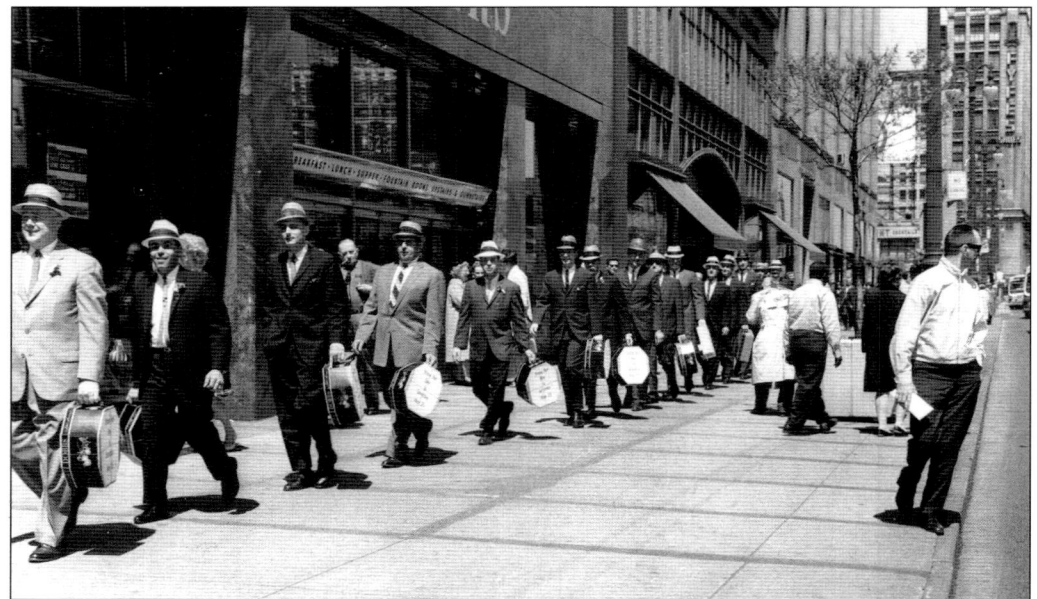

STRAW HAT DAY PARADE DOWN WOODWARD AVENUE, 1963. As a way to boost renewed interest in men's hats, the Central Business District Association instituted an annual Straw Hat Day. Led by a German band, over 50 straw-hatted businessmen from leading downtown retailers paraded down Woodward Avenue. At the city-county building, all were greeted by the mayor and city council. (Courtesy Central Business District Foundation.)

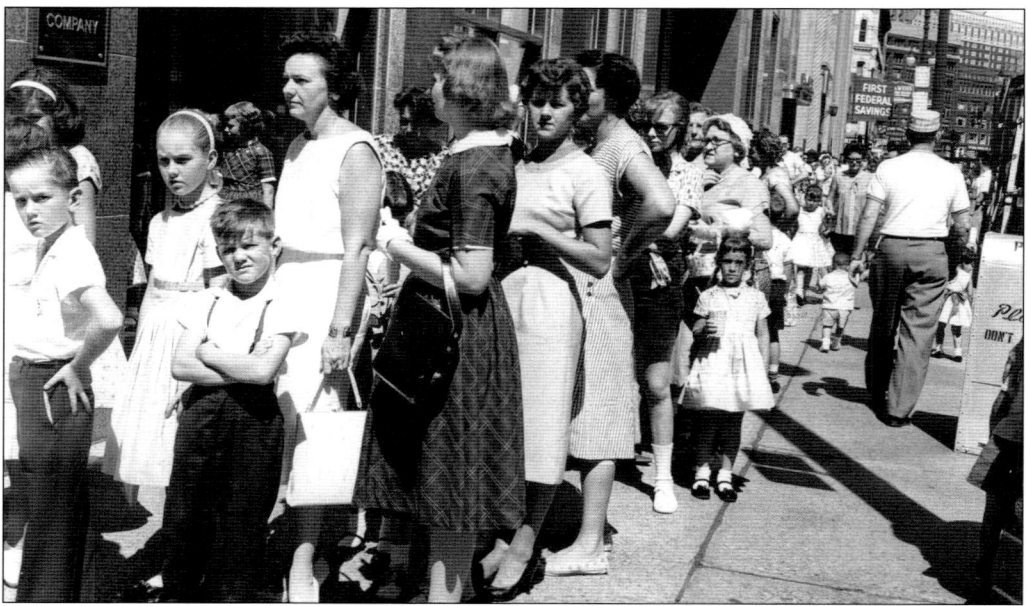

LINED UP FOR CINDERELLA AND PRINCE CHARMING TRYOUTS, 1964. Each summer, the quest was on to find Cinderella, who would reign over Back-to-School Week, and Prince Charming, who had the task of trying the magic glass slipper on the feet of over 7,000 young ladies. The fairy godmother was also on hand to lend support. Tryouts were held at the Dime Building headquarters of Bank of the Commonwealth. (Courtesy Central Business District Foundation.)

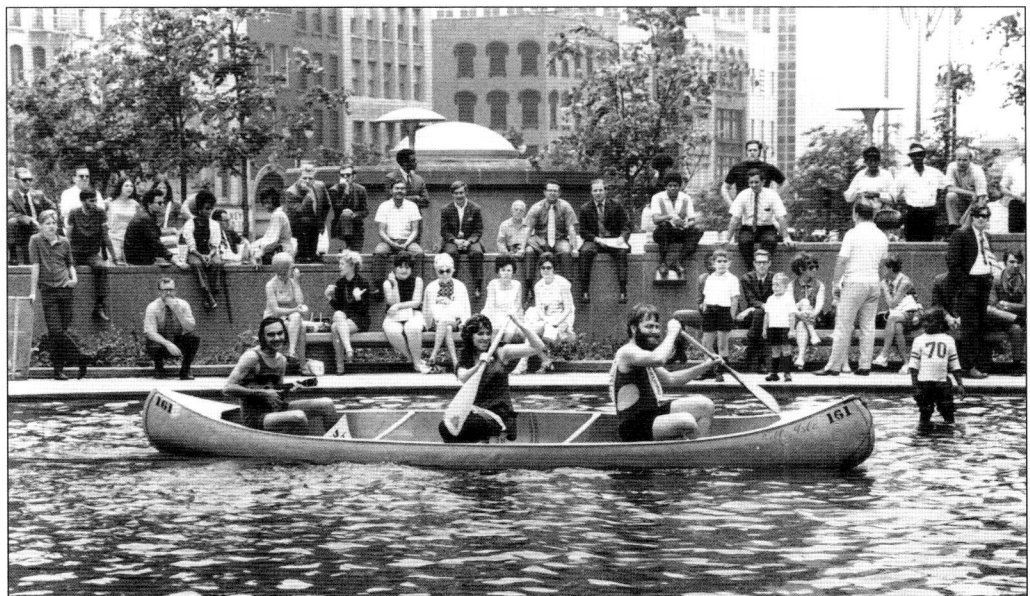

CANOEING IN THE MIDDLE OF THE CITY, 1968. Many of the events that the Central Business District Association and the Detroit Parks and Recreation Department sponsored were simply to have fun, such as canoeing in Kennedy Square. Other programs included the Harmonie Park Art Fair, homemakers' holiday tours of downtown, adventures in Greektown, and bicycle races on Woodward Avenue. (Courtesy Central Business District Foundation.)

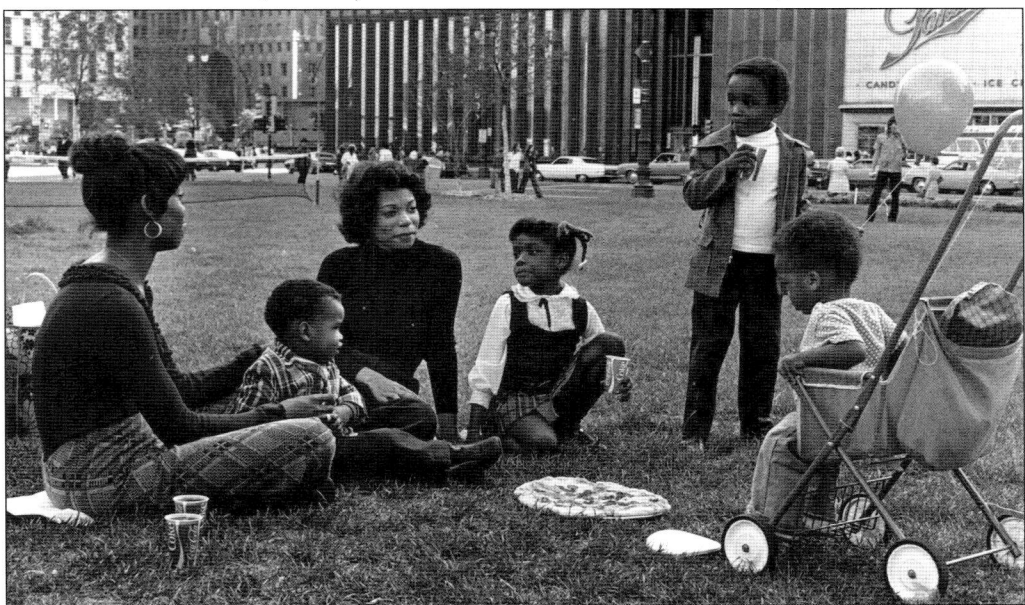

FAMILY FUN ON THE KERN'S BLOCK, 1973. The Central Business District Association made sure that plenty of events, other than feeding the pigeons, kept crowds returning downtown. Once the Junior League assisted with the installation of vinyl canopies, bookings blossomed. Events on the Kern's Block included concerts, hula hoop and Frisbee contests, art shows, fashion shows, carnivals, car shows, and even bingo. (Courtesy Central Business District Foundation.)

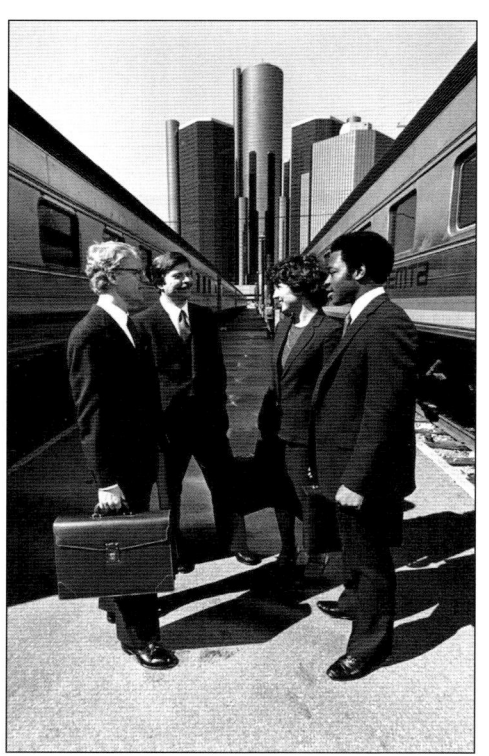

COMMUTER RAIL SERVICE AT FRANKLIN STREET STATION, 1980. The Central Business District Association initiated "shoppers' specials" commuter trains with the Grand Trunk Railway in the 1960s. Peppy hostesses handed out gift certificates on the way downtown. The Southeastern Michigan Transportation Authority later operated the trains, and commuters could board at Pontiac, Bloomfield, Birmingham, Royal Oak, Ferndale, the former Chrysler Center, and New Center. By 1984, the service was deemed too expensive to continue. (Courtesy Central Business District Foundation.)

FLEA MARKET ON LOWER WOODWARD AVENUE, 1969. To stimulate Sunday traffic downtown, the Central Business District Association introduced the Sunday flea market in 1968. Over 125 dealers transformed the three blocks of Woodward Avenue from Jefferson Avenue to Campus Martius into a country fair in the middle of the city. This event was a great companion to the riverfront ethnic festivals. (Courtesy Central Business District Foundation.)

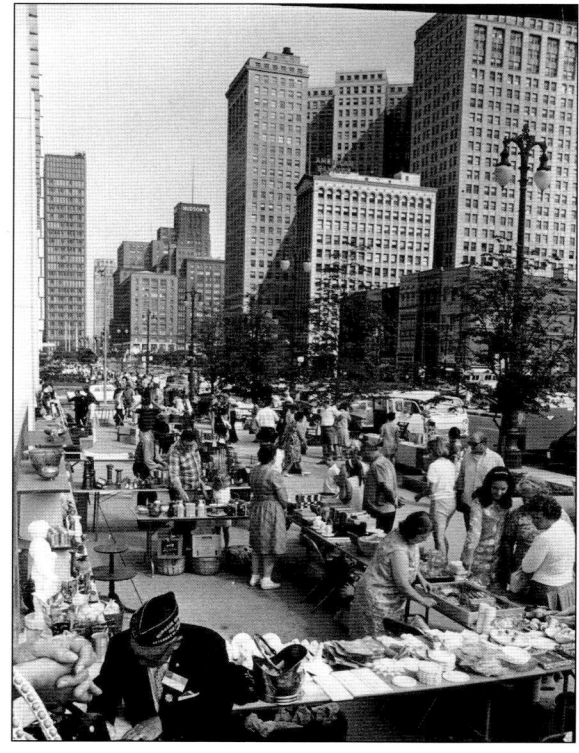

Three

CENTRAL BUSINESS DISTRICT ASSOCIATION HOLIDAY EVENTS

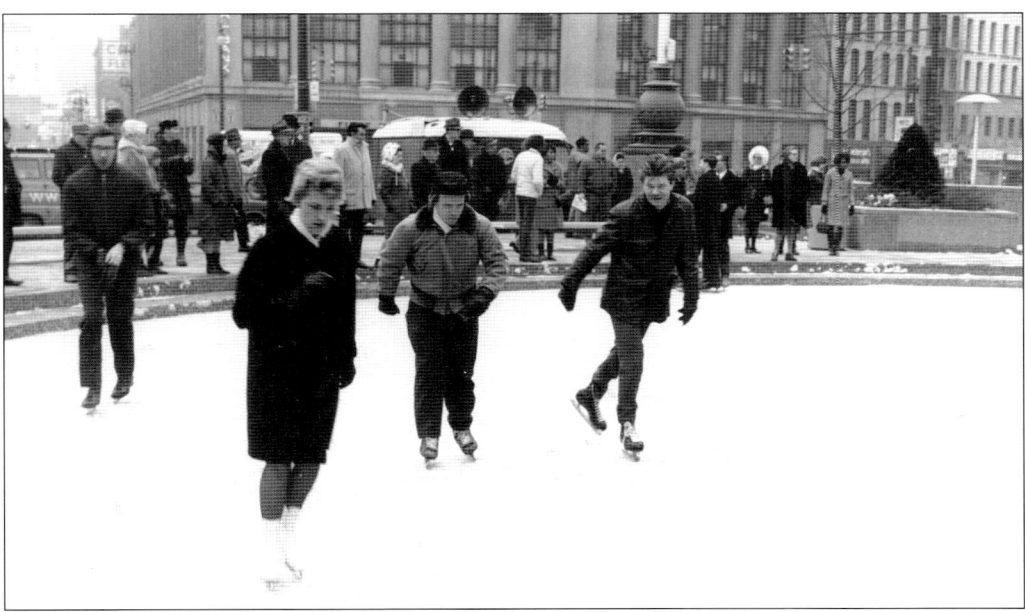

ICE-SKATING ON KENNEDY SQUARE, 1968. The Central Business District Association and the Detroit Parks and Recreation Department hosted downtown's first ice-skating party in 1968 with the opening of the Kennedy Square rink. Downtown office workers and winter sports enthusiasts, including members of the Detroit Skating Club, glided on the ice, surrounded by skyscrapers, with spirited music wafting in the air. (Courtesy Central Business District Foundation.)

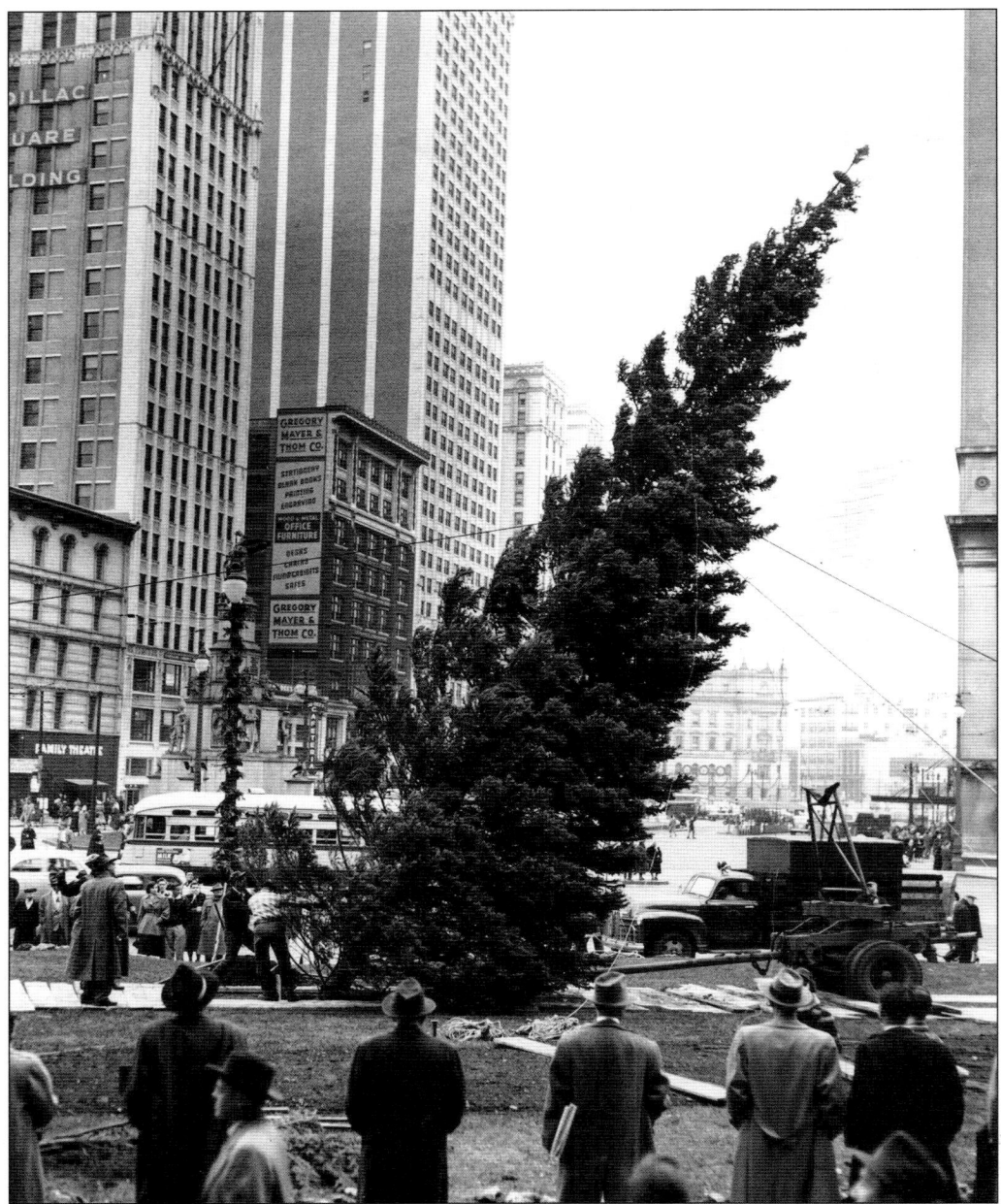

DETROIT'S OFFICIAL HOLIDAY TREE AT OLD CITY HALL, 1950S. Detroit's official tree-lighting ceremony was traditionally lackluster, consisting of a dozen city officials on Christmas Eve with no bystanders. In 1954, the Central Business District Association changed all that and implemented Detroit Aglow. The event was moved to a weeknight and holiday decor and lights were expanded to include major avenues as well as Grand Circus Park. (Courtesy Central Business District Foundation.)

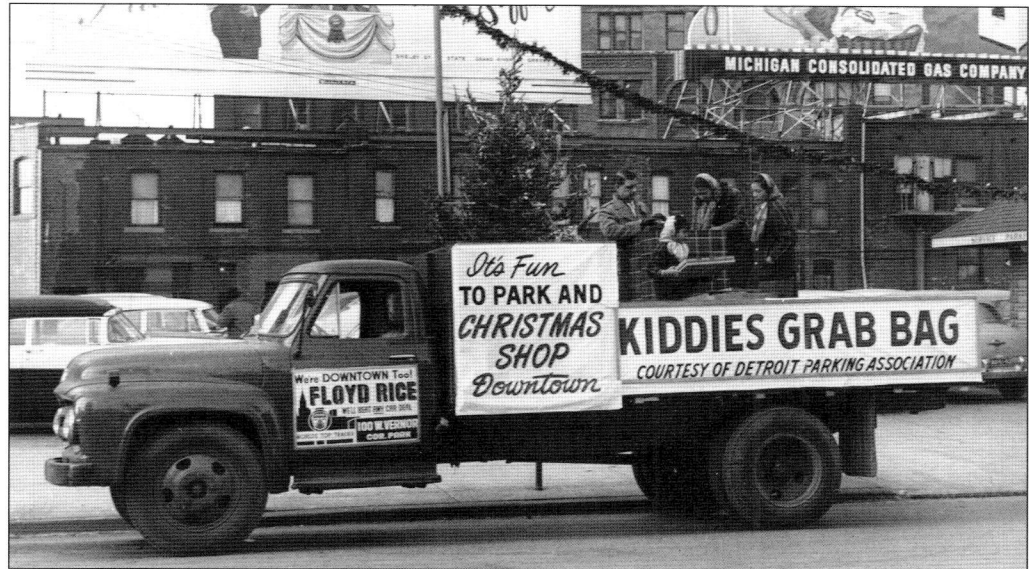

TACKLING THE AGE-OLD ISSUE OF PARKING, 1955. In the 1950s, despite new garages and an increase in the number of surface lots, the public perception was that downtown parking was difficult and expensive. To combat this problem and the growing competition from Northland Center, the Central Business District Association partnered with the Detroit Parking Association to promote the positive attributes of shopping and the ease of parking downtown. (Courtesy Central Business District Foundation.)

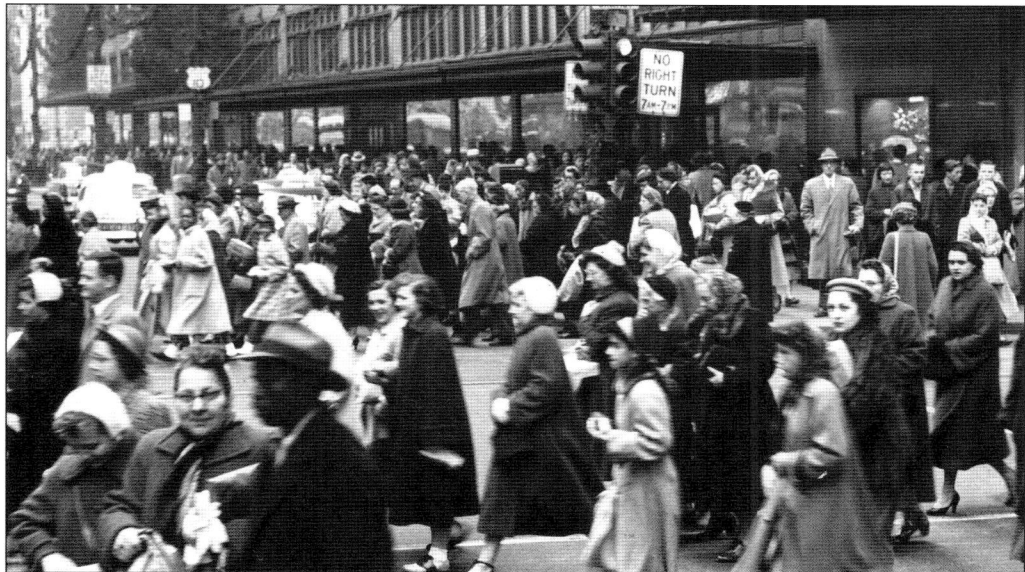

HOLIDAY CRUSH ON WOODWARD AVENUE AT HUDSON'S, 1950S. Despite the offerings of Northland and Eastland Centers, it was difficult for shopping centers to compete with the holiday excitement of downtown—the animated windows, street decor and lighting displays, special events, and, above all, depth of selection drew shoppers back to the familiar downtown setting. Some folks still talk about December 1956, when downtown became gridlocked with a half-million shoppers in automobiles and on foot. (Courtesy Central Business District Foundation.)

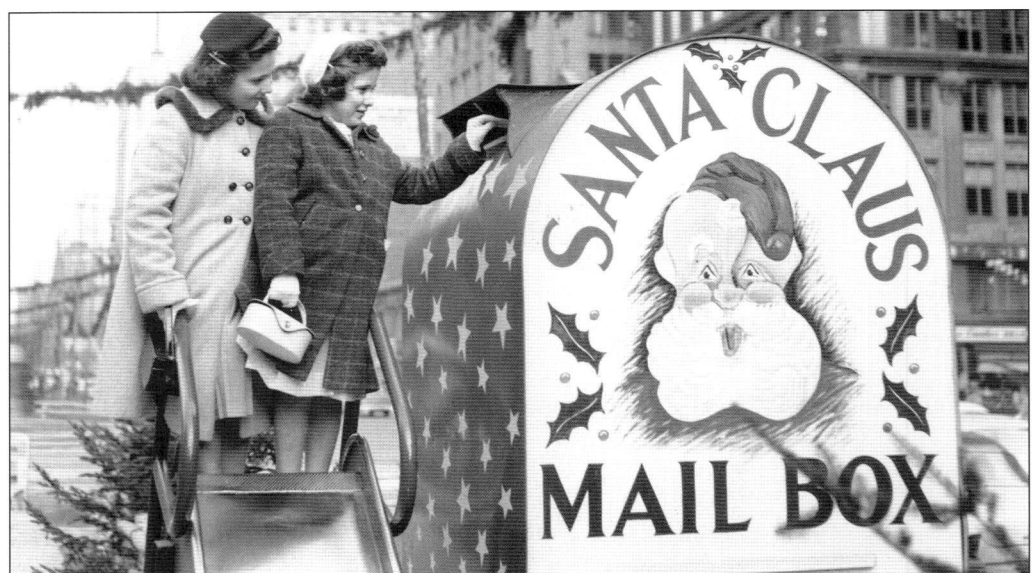

THE WORLD'S LARGEST MAILBOX, WASHINGTON BOULEVARD, 1955. Each holiday season, the Central Business District Association and the Detroit Parks and Recreation Department erected a giant mailbox in front of the Sheraton Cadillac Hotel. The mailbox was equipped with a sliding board so children could speed safely to earth after mailing their letters. The mailbox remained in place until Christmas Eve and the association staff personally answered all letters. (Courtesy Central Business District Foundation.)

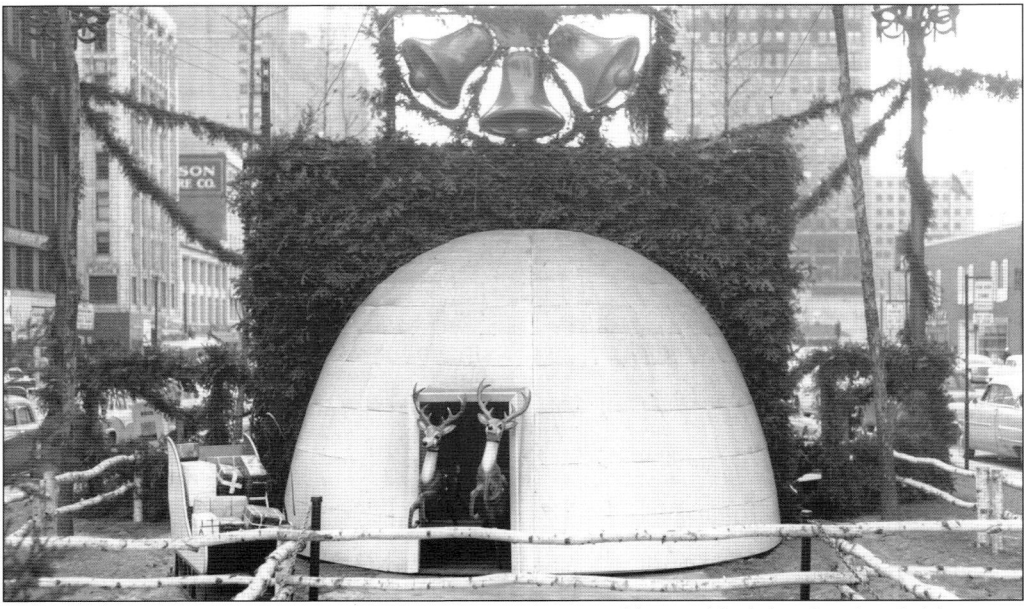

ESKIMO IGLOO ON WASHINGTON BOULEVARD, 1955. Additional holiday fun for children was available at the opposite end of Washington Boulevard, near the Statler Hilton Hotel. The Central Business District Association and the Detroit Parks and Recreation Department erected a giant igloo where carolers gathered each day and children could visit Santa. Holiday garlands and trees also adorned the display. (Courtesy Central Business District Foundation.)

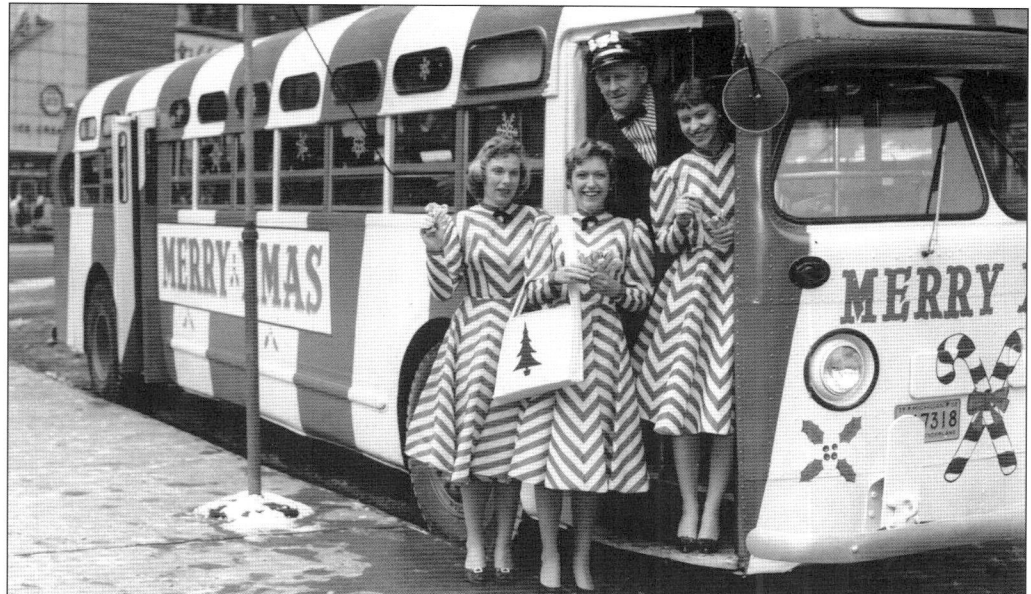

CANDY CANE BUS AT CAMPUS MARTIUS, 1957. The Central Business District Association and the Department of Street Railways collaborated on this fun-filled way to transport downtown shoppers from store to store. Riders were greeted by hostesses wearing candy-striped attire and distributing candy canes and gifts. The interior of the coach was gaily decorated for the holidays, and best of all, the ride was free! (Courtesy Central Business District Foundation.)

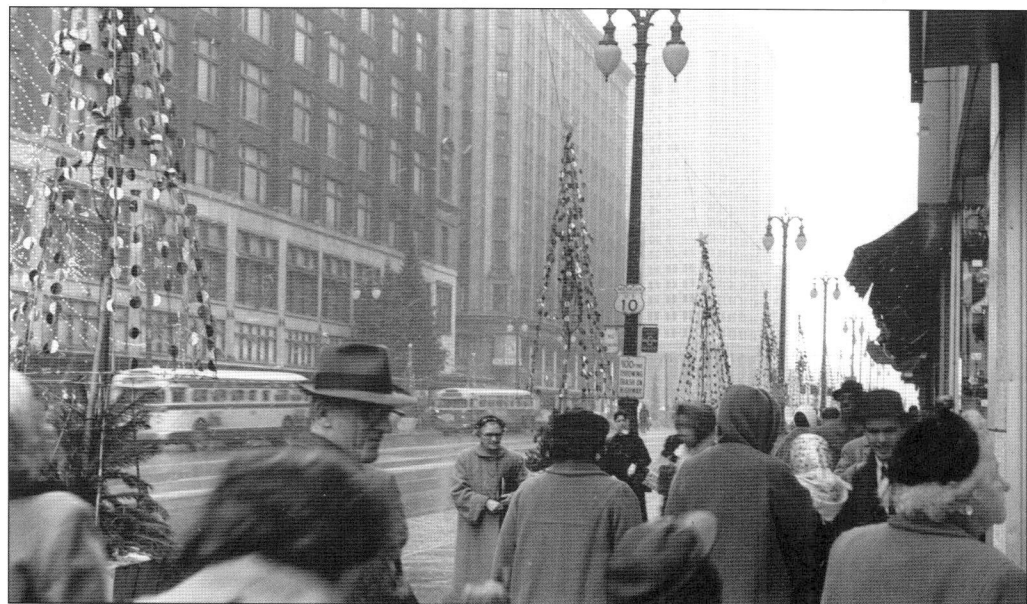

WOODWARD AVENUE, LOOKING TOWARD STATE STREET, 1959. This image depicts busy holiday shoppers on the west side of Woodward Avenue on a cold, slushy day. Hudson's impressive tree of lights is visible on the left, as are the dozens of new trees lining the avenue, courtesy of the Central Business District Association. These were the final days for the Ernst Kern Company, center, which closed on December 23, 1959. (Courtesy Central Business District Foundation.)

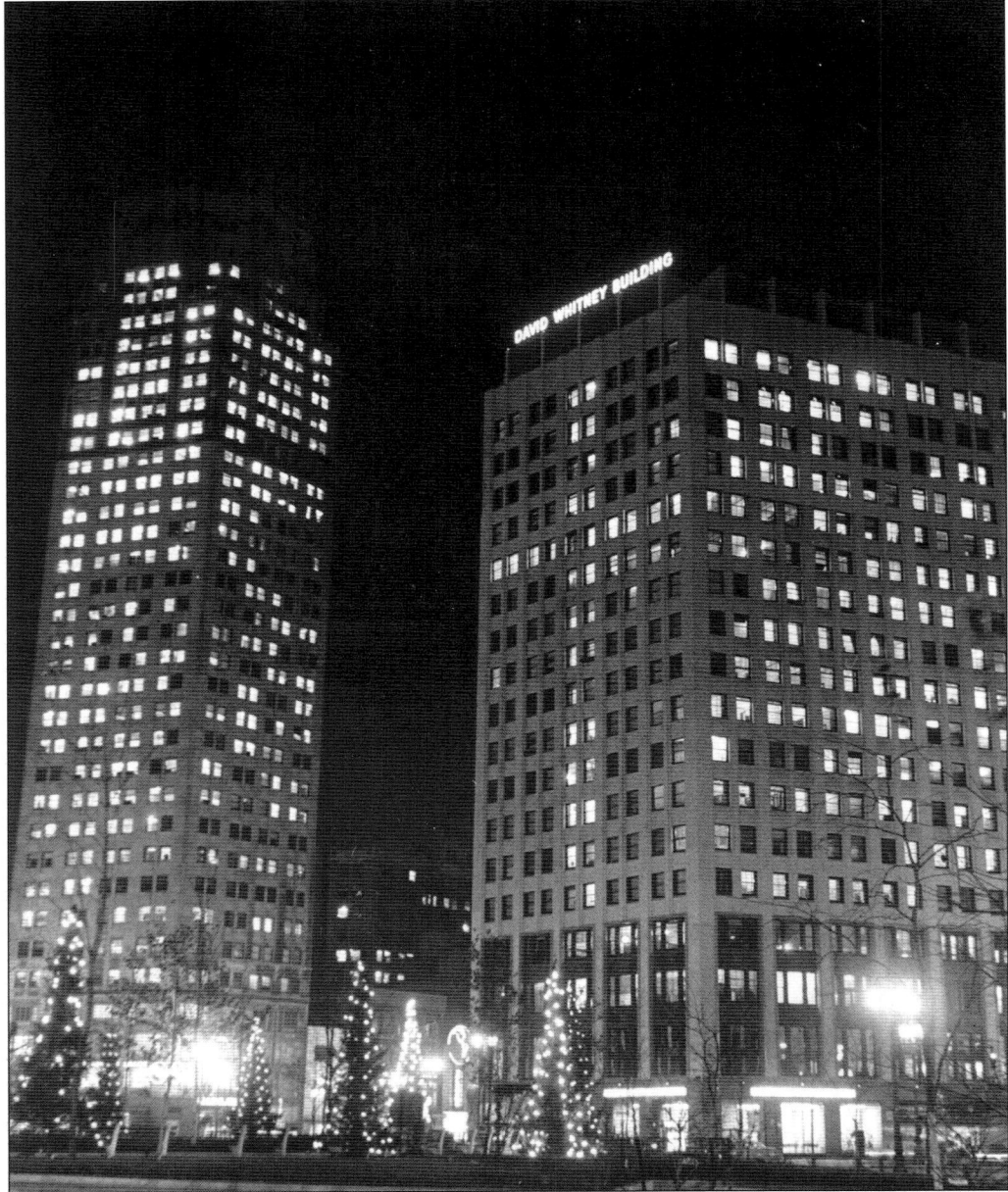

TOWERING OVER GRAND CIRCUS PARK, 1959. The two Davids sparkle in the crisp December air over Grand Circus Park. The 33-story David Broderick Tower looms on the left, with the 18-story David Whitney Building standing majestically on the right. The west side of the park was ringed with 20-foot evergreen trees, adorned with thousands of Italian lights. (Courtesy Central Business District Foundation.)

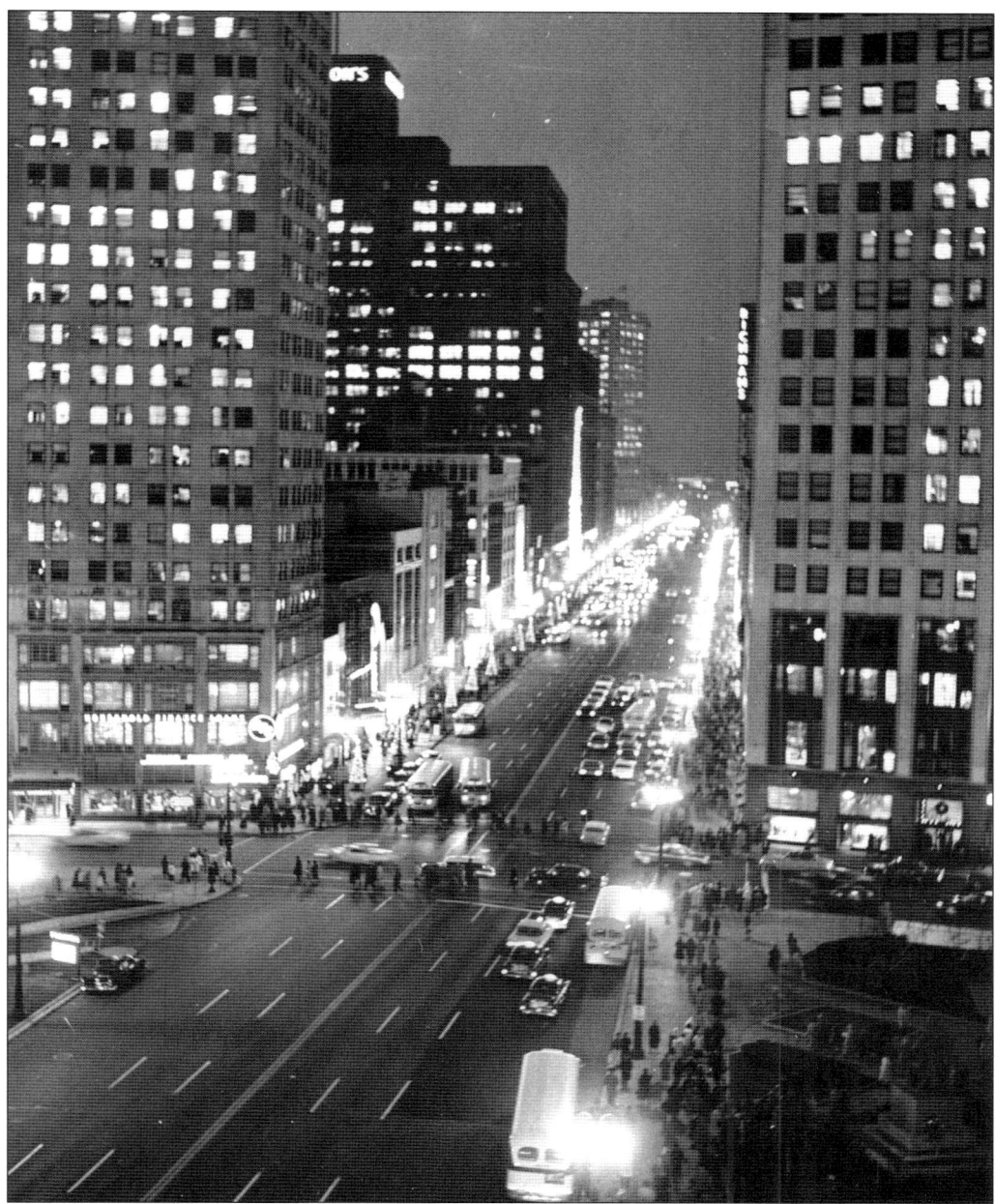

WOODWARD AVENUE HOLIDAY LIGHTS, LOOKING SOUTH, 1959. Detroit's tree-lighting ceremony has been hosted at a number of locales through the years. In the 1950s, Detroit Aglow took place at the old Detroit City Hall and outside Ford Auditorium. In the 1960s, locations included Capitol Park and Kennedy Square. By the 1970s, the event moved to the Blue Cross Service Center and later to Hart Plaza. (Courtesy Central Business District Foundation.)

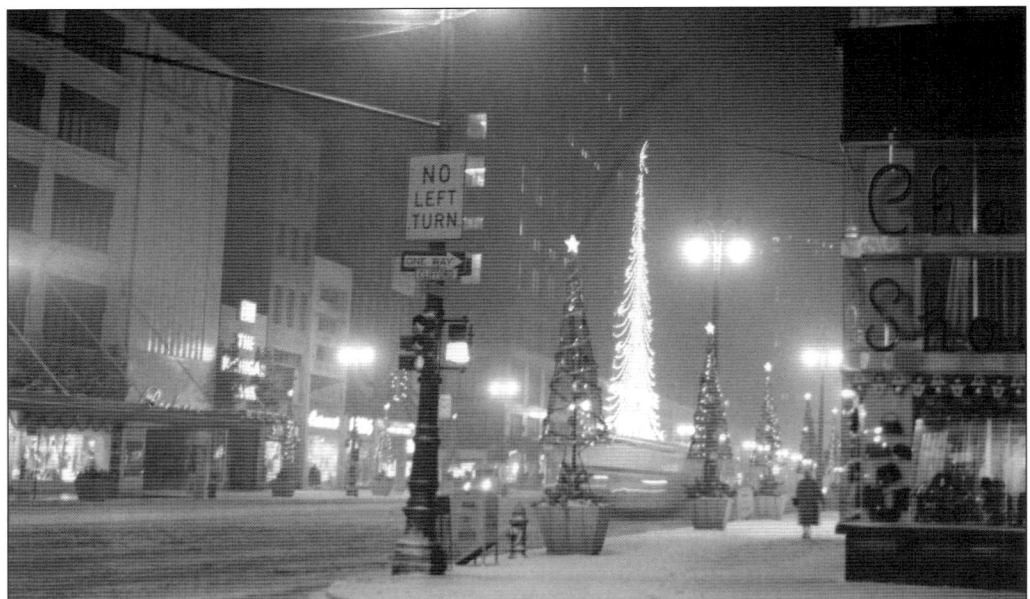

A Blustery Night on Woodward Avenue, 1960. True to tradition at Detroit Aglow, each holiday season the mayor and the Snow Queen touched the "magic" switch that illuminated lights on city streets and in downtown buildings. There were 80 sparkling holiday trees attached to streetlamps and tiny Italian lights laced through the planter box shrubs. (Courtesy Central Business District Foundation.)

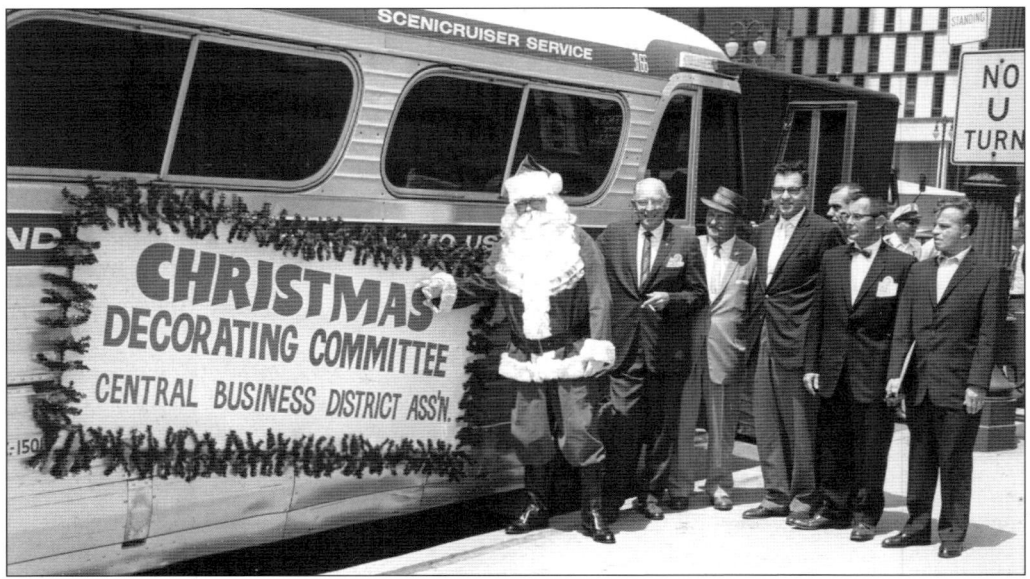

Christmas in July with a Trip to Frankenmuth, 1961. Once the Central Business District Association elevated Detroit's holiday decor to an entirely new level in 1954, the next step was to study what could be done to further enhance downtown during the holiday season. As depicted above, 40 members of the Central Business District Association travel to Bronner's Christmas Wonderland in Frankenmuth to plan major surprises for the upcoming season. (Courtesy Central Business District Foundation.)

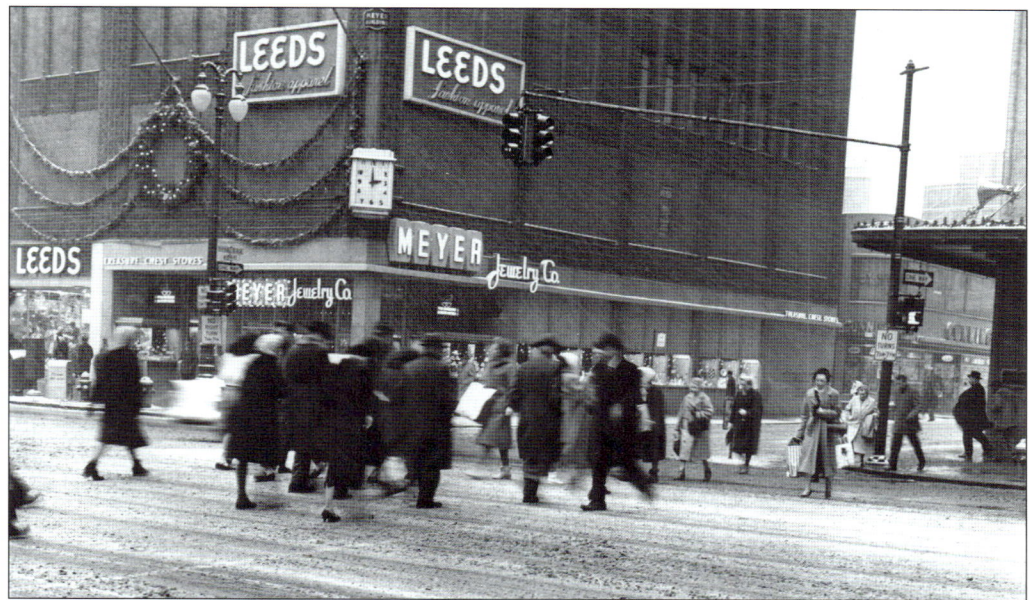

HOLIDAY SHOPPERS AT WOODWARD AND GRAND RIVER AVENUES, 1961. Detroit Aglow, besides featuring local personalities, regularly brought in nationally known guests, including Jim Backus, Fran Allison, Julie Harris, and Soupy Sales. The ceremony was broadcast over WXYZ Television. Cunningham's Drugs can be seen in the background, as well as a portion of Hudson's marquee on the right. (Courtesy Central Business District Foundation.)

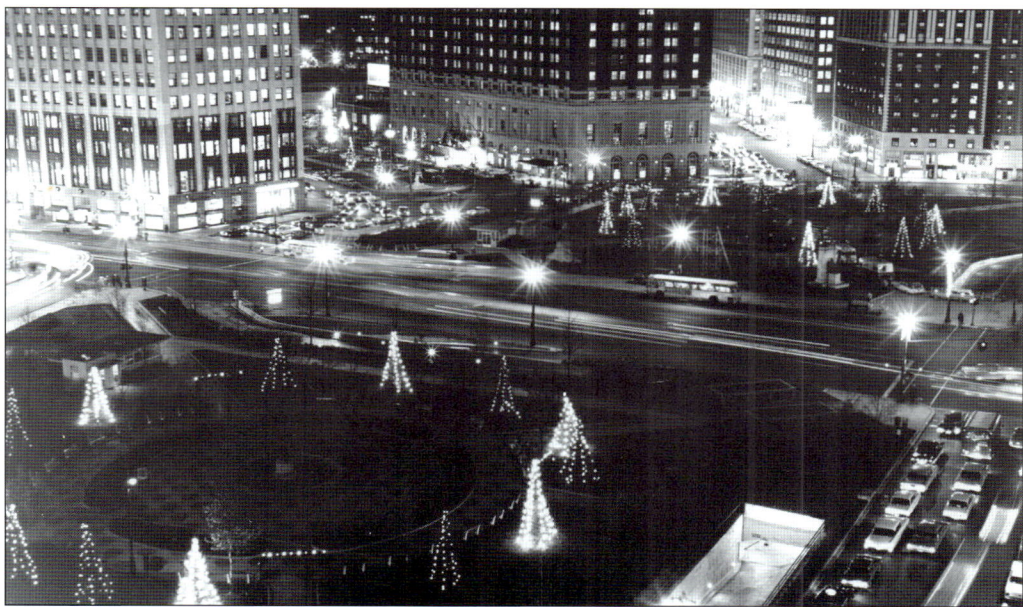

DETROIT AGLOW AT GRAND CIRCUS PARK, 1961. The Central Business District Association was able to convince building owners to leave their interior lights burning for the Detroit Aglow ceremony. This view captures the 20-foot lit trees in Grand Circus Park and the bright lights of the David Whitney Building (left), Statler Hilton Hotel (center), Tuller Hotel (right), and the former United Artists Building. (Courtesy Central Business District Foundation.)

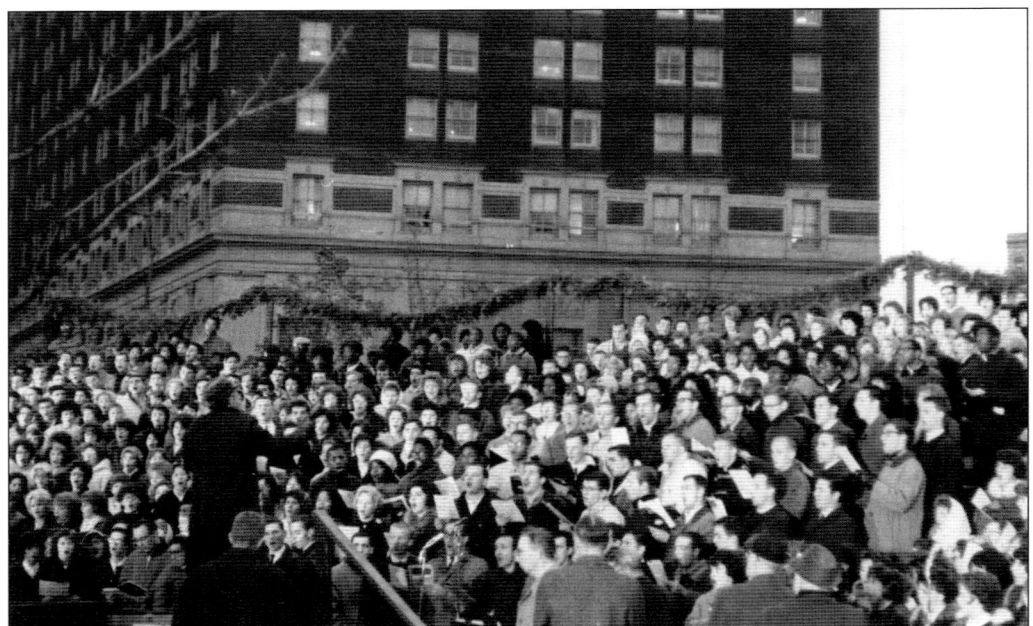

MUSIC IN THE AIR AT GRAND CIRCUS PARK, 1962. As the holiday lights were turned on for Detroit Aglow each year, a 1,200-voice choir comprised of students from 20 Detroit and suburban schools sang the "Hallelujah Chorus." The Boy Scouts served as honor guards. The Statler Hilton Hotel is in the background. (Courtesy Central Business District Foundation.)

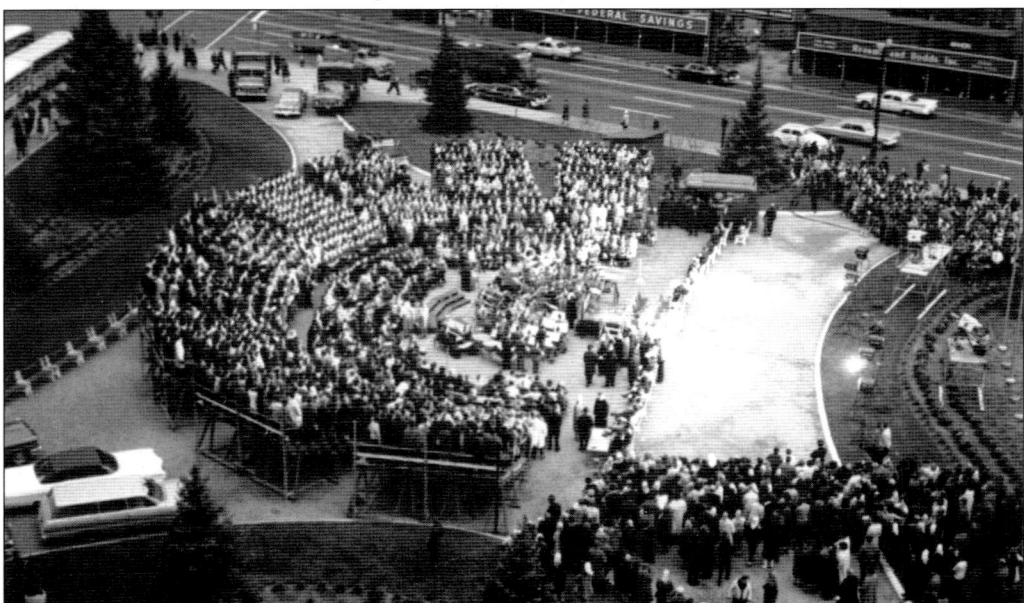

DETROIT AGLOW AT KENNEDY SQUARE, 1963. In 1961, the Detroit Parks and Recreation Department opened Santa Claus Land on the site of the old Detroit City Hall. It was referred to in the media as "the world's most valuable playground." Besides Santa and Rudolph, the playground included a walk-in dollhouse, animals, a toy soldier sentry, a jack-in-the-box, a large snowman, and a sleigh pulled by live reindeer. (Courtesy Central Business District Foundation.)

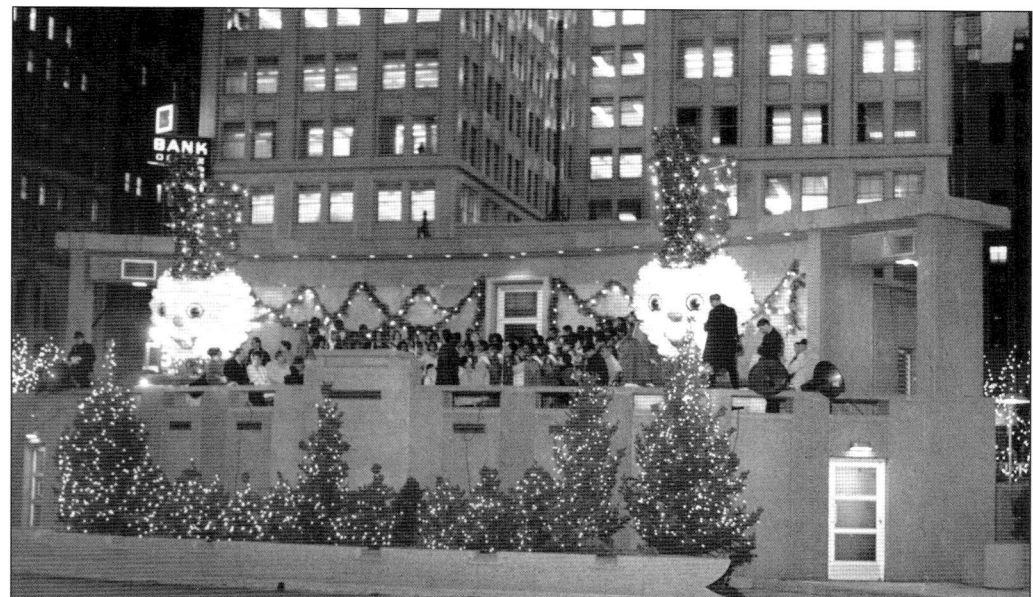

HOLIDAY HAPPENINGS ON KENNEDY SQUARE, 1967. In the 1960s, Kennedy Square was decorated for the holiday season with trees, garlands, poinsettias, and thousands of twinkling lights. Following the annual Detroit Aglow lighting ceremony, it was time to sing carols, ice-skate, and enjoy delicious hot chocolate or head over to Hudson's for its "holiday burger" or "reindeer scramble" in the Riverview Room. (Courtesy Central Business District Foundation.)

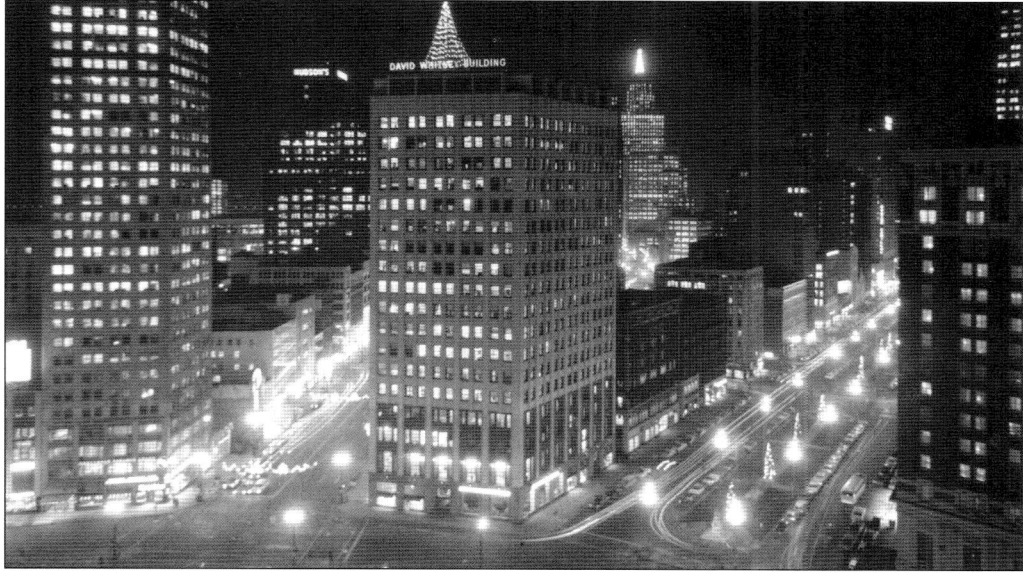

SPECTACULAR DOWNTOWN HOLIDAY LIGHTING, 1964. After much prodding, the Central Business District Association convinced management at the Penobscot Building (then the tallest building downtown at 47 stories) to erect a tree of lights atop the structure. The tree was 90 feet tall and featured 60 strands of lights, 10,000 feet of wire, and 2,400 bulbs. The image above shows the David Broderick Tower (left), Hudson's, the David Whitney Building (center), and the Penobscot Building (right). (Courtesy Central Business District Foundation.)

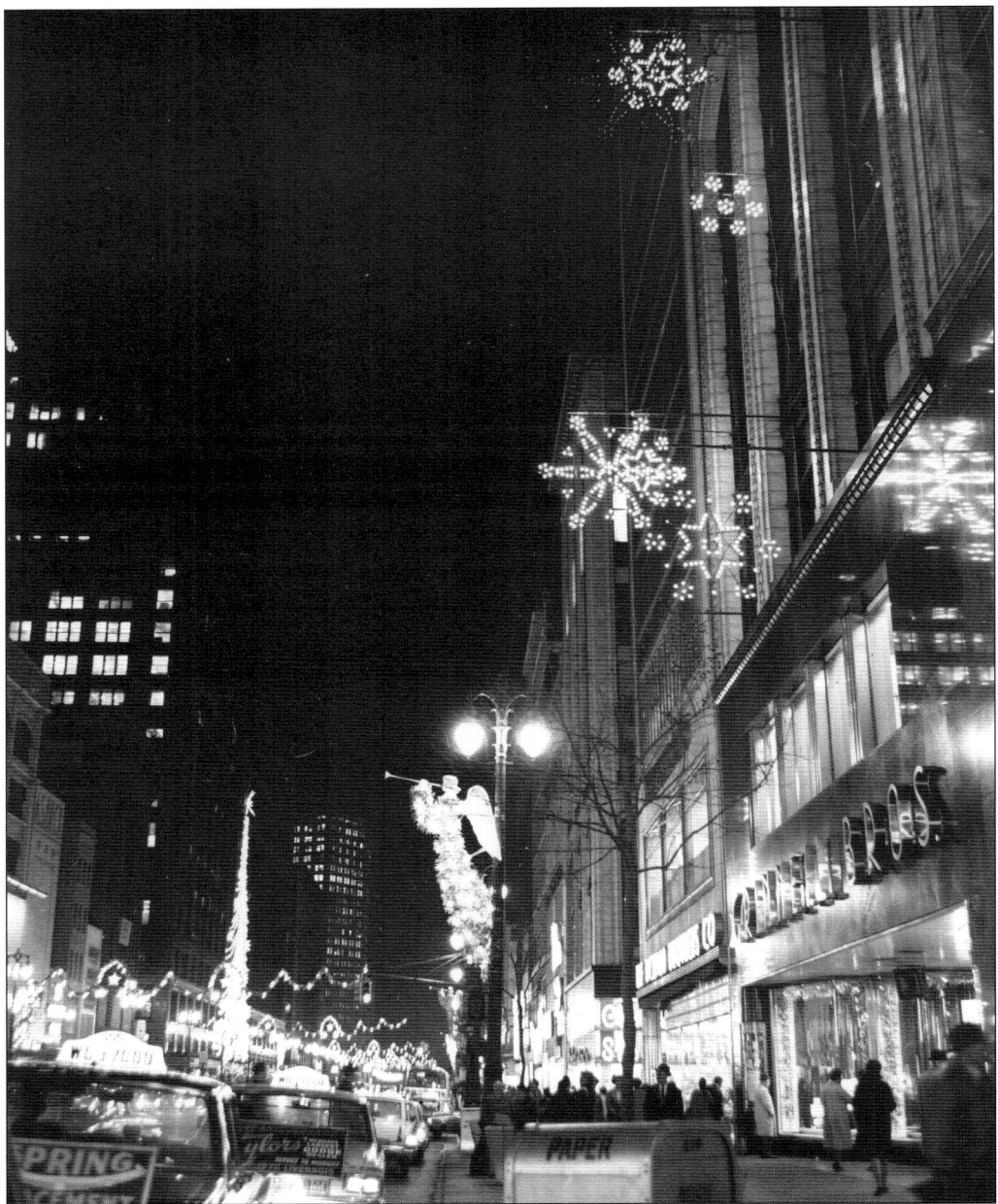

WOODWARD AVENUE, SOUTH OF GRAND CIRCUS PARK, 1963. Along with holiday trees and lights, Woodward Avenue was adorned with 15-foot angels on lampposts. Giant lit snowflakes were a highlight at Grinnell Brothers music store (right), and Hudson's nine-story tree of lights can be seen on the middle left. Illuminated garlands were draped above Woodward Avenue from East Jefferson Avenue to Grand Circus Park. (Courtesy Central Business District Foundation.)

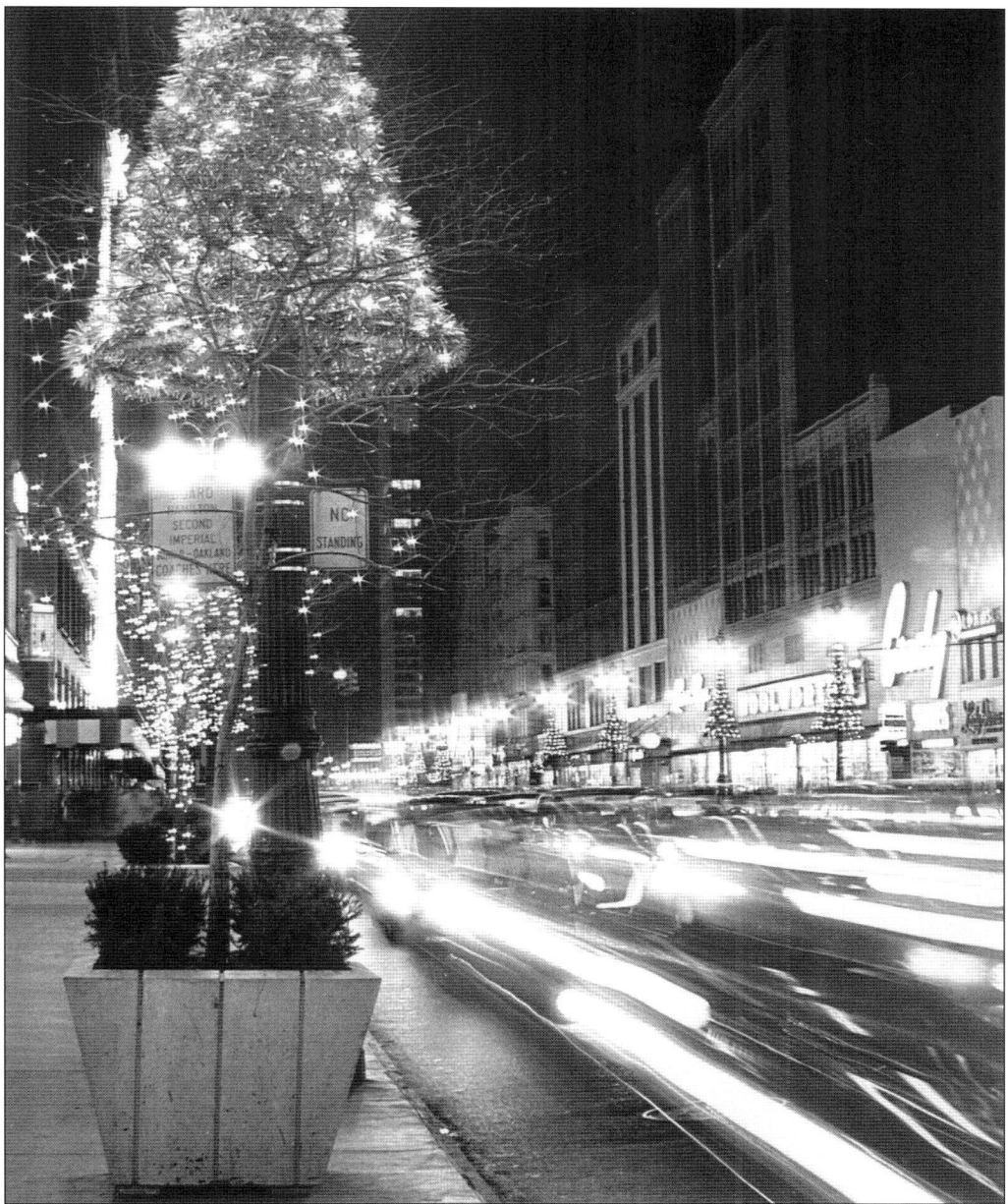

WEST SIDE OF WOODWARD AVENUE, 1965. This time-lapse view during the holidays captures the urban vibrancy of Woodward Avenue. The west side of the neon-coated street features (from right to left) Lady Orva Hosiery, Crosby Shoes, Woolworth's, Lerner Shops, and Kresge's. Hudson's marquee can be seen on the left. Farther south, Crowley's marquee featured large evergreens and a tall lit cross. (Courtesy Central Business District Foundation.)

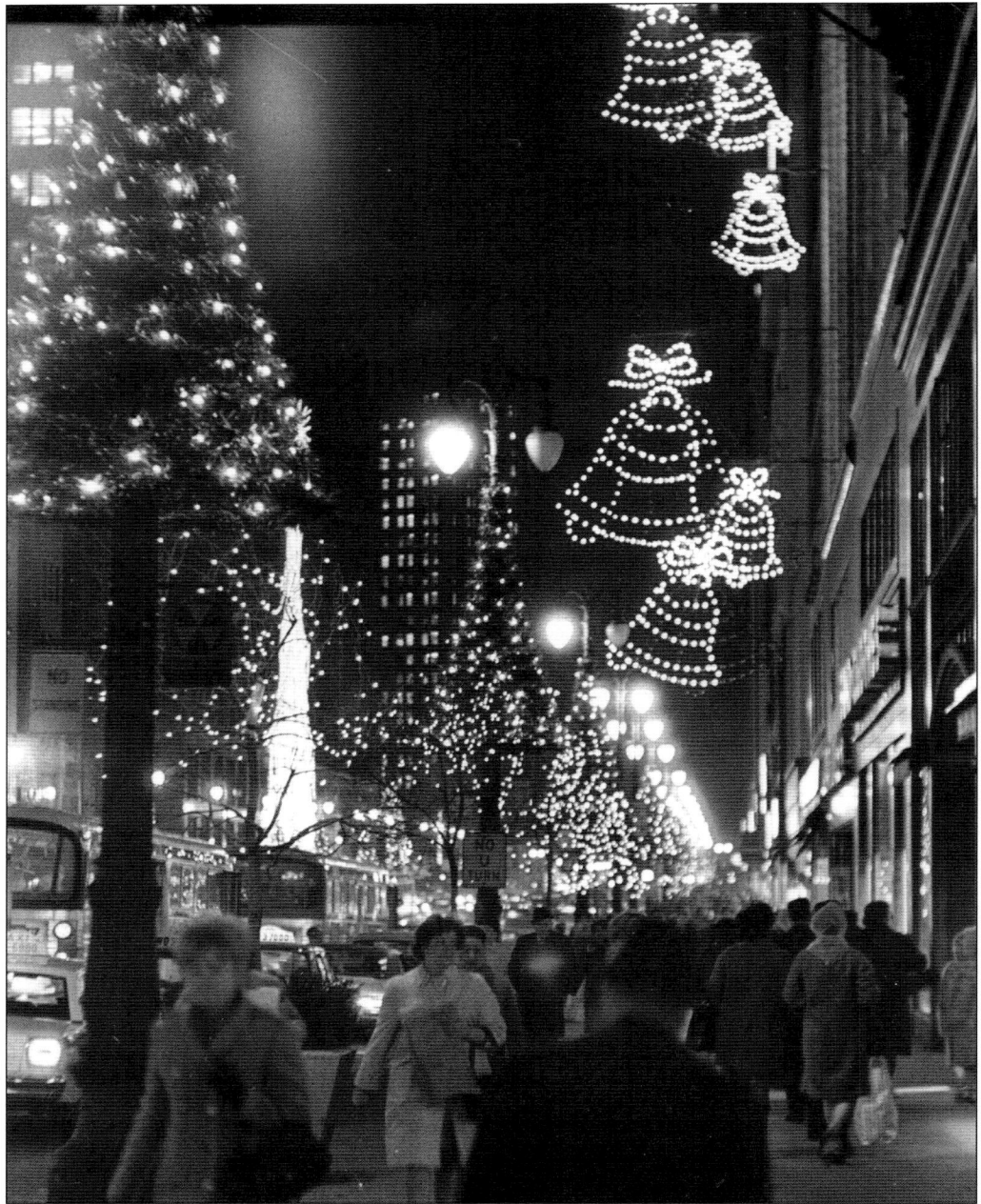

EVENING SHOPPING ON WOODWARD AVENUE, 1966. Grinnell Brothers' animated bells rang out their silent seasonal wishes to match the Christmas carols that were broadcast onto the street. New in 1966 were lit castles that were installed on lampposts in Grand Circus Park. Wednesday evening was a popular night to shop downtown, enjoy a meal, or catch a film at any one of the dozen first-run movie theaters. (Courtesy Central Business District Foundation.)

Four
The J. L. Hudson Company

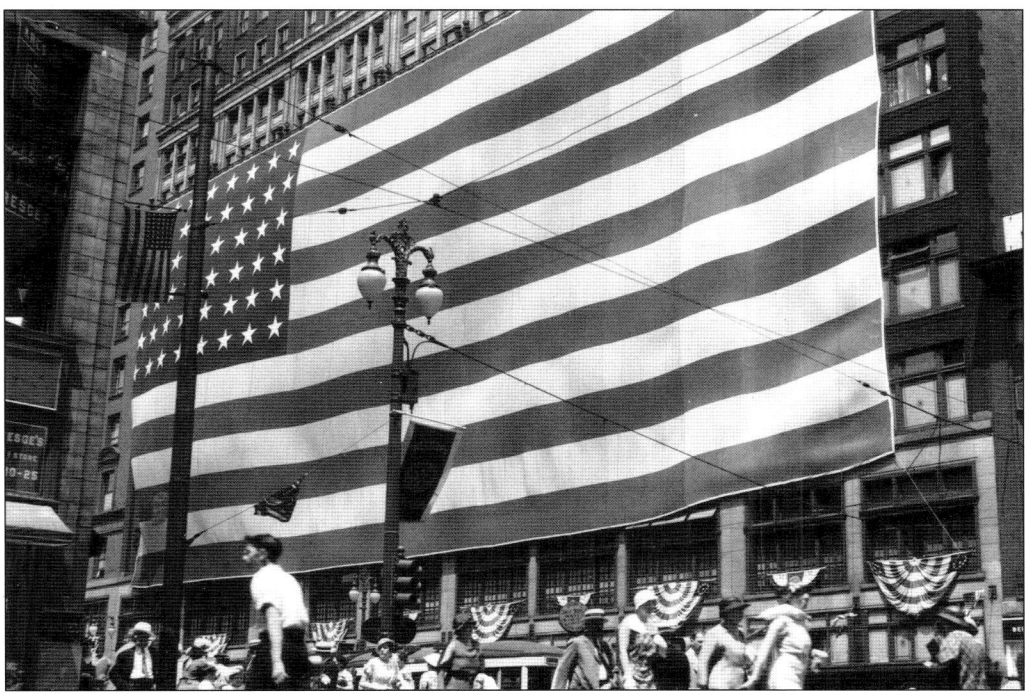

Old Glory Majestically Displayed at Hudson's, 1950s. Almost 20,000 bystanders, including local civic and government officials, cheered as the world's largest flag was unfurled on the Woodward Avenue facade of the J. L. Hudson Company for its final public display on Flag Day 1976. The Detroit Symphony Orchestra played patriotic music, and the fun later continued on the Kern's Block with birthday cakes from each of the 50 states. (Courtesy Central Business District Foundation.)

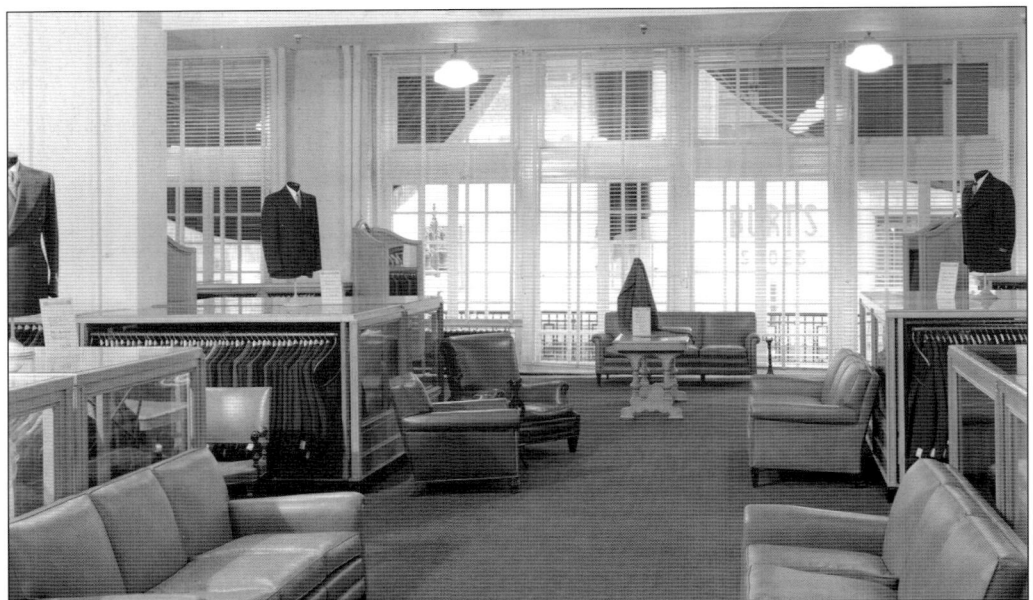

HUDSON'S SECOND-FLOOR MEN'S SUITS, 1928. This is a view of the men's suit department looking west toward Woodward Avenue. Note the large windows and plenty of seats for guests to relax. Men's clothing departments on the second floor included a university shop, a casual shop, and a custom shop. Men's shoes and a sports shop were also nearby. (Courtesy Manning Brothers Historical Collection.)

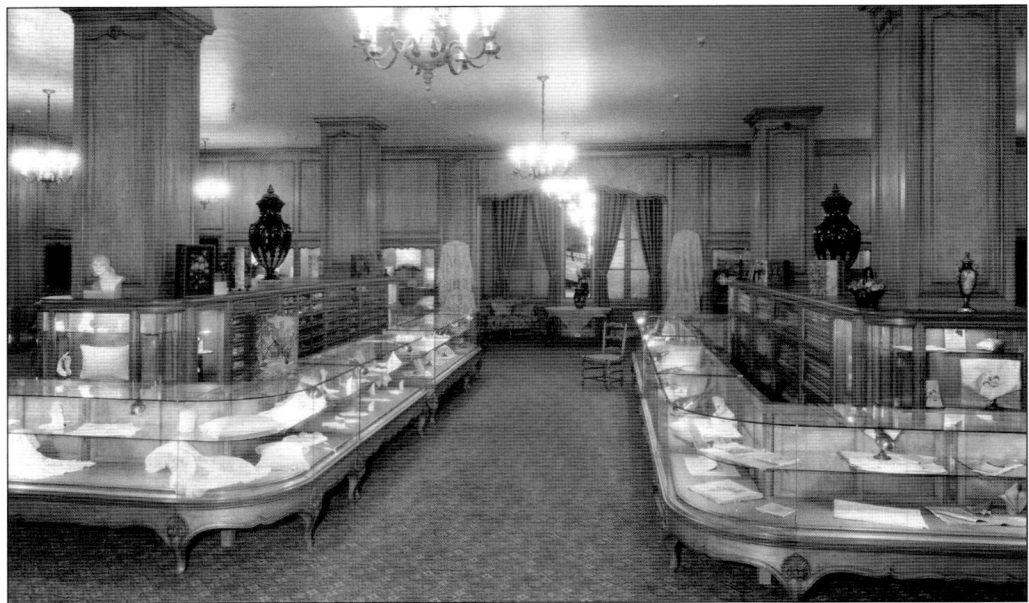

THE BENTLIF SHOP FOR FINE HANDMADE GOODS, 1935. This shop-within-a-shop on the third floor was acquired by Hudson's when it purchased the neighboring Newcomb Endicott department store in 1927. The shop consisted of two large rooms, paneled in cypress, with arched doorways and elegant showcases. This created a unique atmosphere for selling handmade tapestries, pillows, robes, and lace accessories. (Courtesy Manning Brothers Historical Collection.)

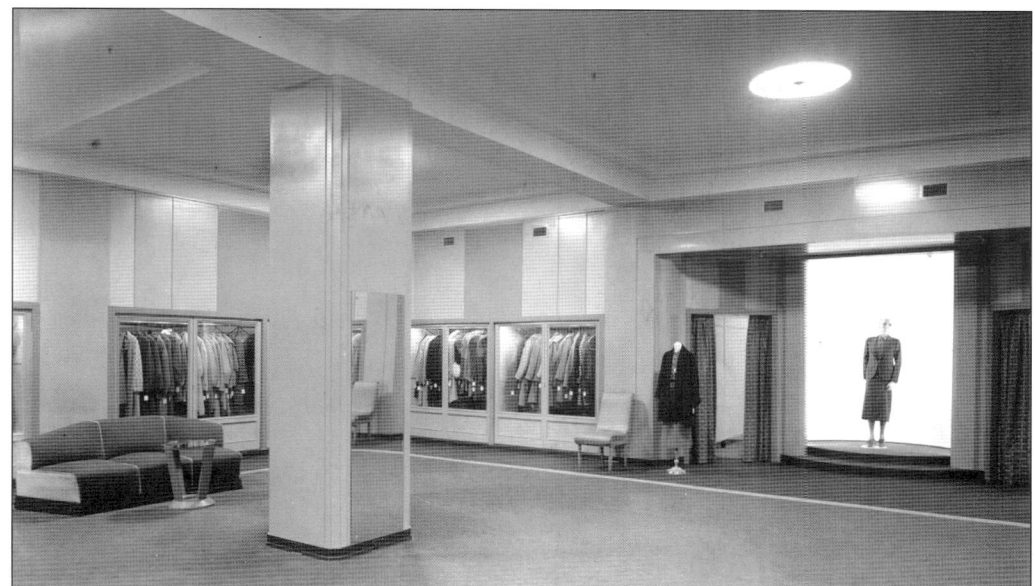

HUDSON'S SIXTH-FLOOR COAT AND SUIT DEPARTMENT, 1936. The leading fashion designers of the United States and Europe were well represented at Hudson's. There were 20 apparel departments on the fifth and sixth floors offering suits, coats, dresses, sportswear, and furs. There were 400 private fitting rooms available for customers on these floors. The seventh floor boasted four shoe departments and three millinery salons. (Courtesy Manning Brothers Historical Collection.)

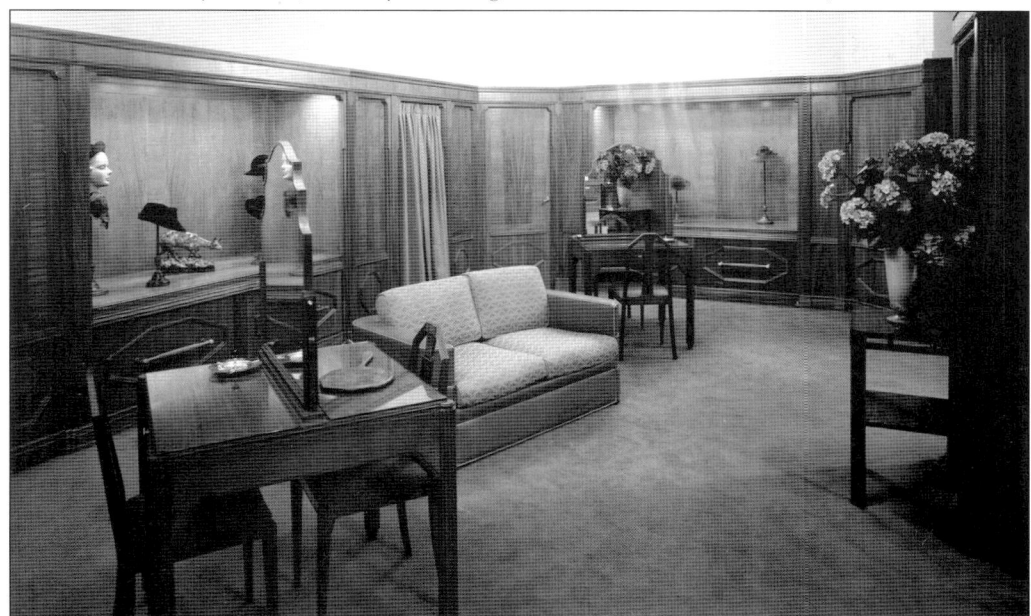

MILLINERY SALONS AT HUDSON'S, 1936. The millinery department (hats and head dressing) at Hudson's filled the entire Grand River Avenue side of the seventh floor. The area was divided into nine distinct rooms that included the Dobbs, the French, the Debutante, the Bridal, the Popular, and the Dache Rooms. In the 1930s and 1940s, a staff of 75 associates was employed in this department. (Courtesy Manning Brothers Historical Collection.)

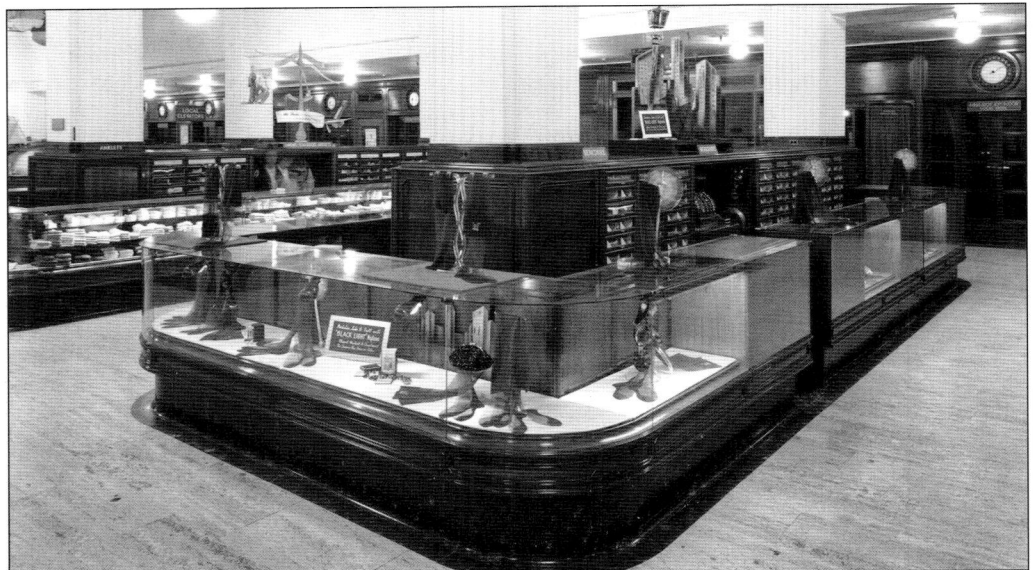

BERKSHIRE HOSIERY COUNTER, HUDSON'S MAIN FLOOR, 1930. As women filled their wardrobes with an array of styles, colors, and textures, they demanded to see everything that was available. Thus, it was inevitable that self-selection would lend itself better to this merchandise rather than displaying it in showcases and behind counters. Manufacturers followed by packaging merchandise individually and modifying fixtures. (Courtesy Manning Brothers Historical Collection.)

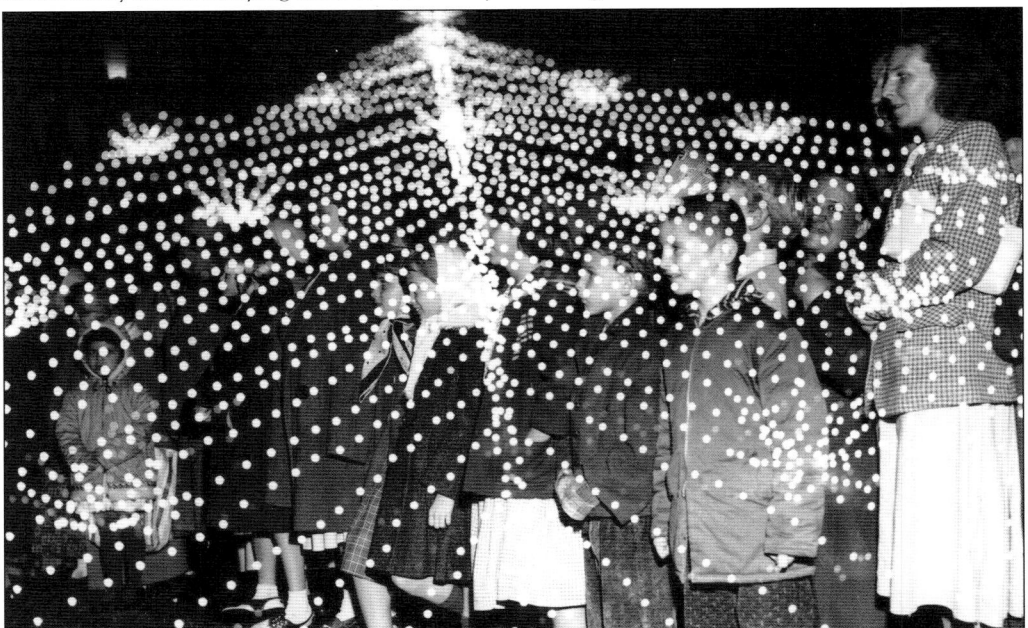

CHILDREN ENJOY THE DEBUT OF HUDSON'S HOLIDAY WINDOWS, 1958. Each holiday season, Detroit children anxiously awaited the thematic animated windows to be unveiled at Hudson's downtown. The windows were conceived, designed, and executed by the visual merchandising department at Hudson's and built by George Silvestri of New York, the world's foremost manufacturer of animated figures. (Courtesy Central Business District Foundation.)

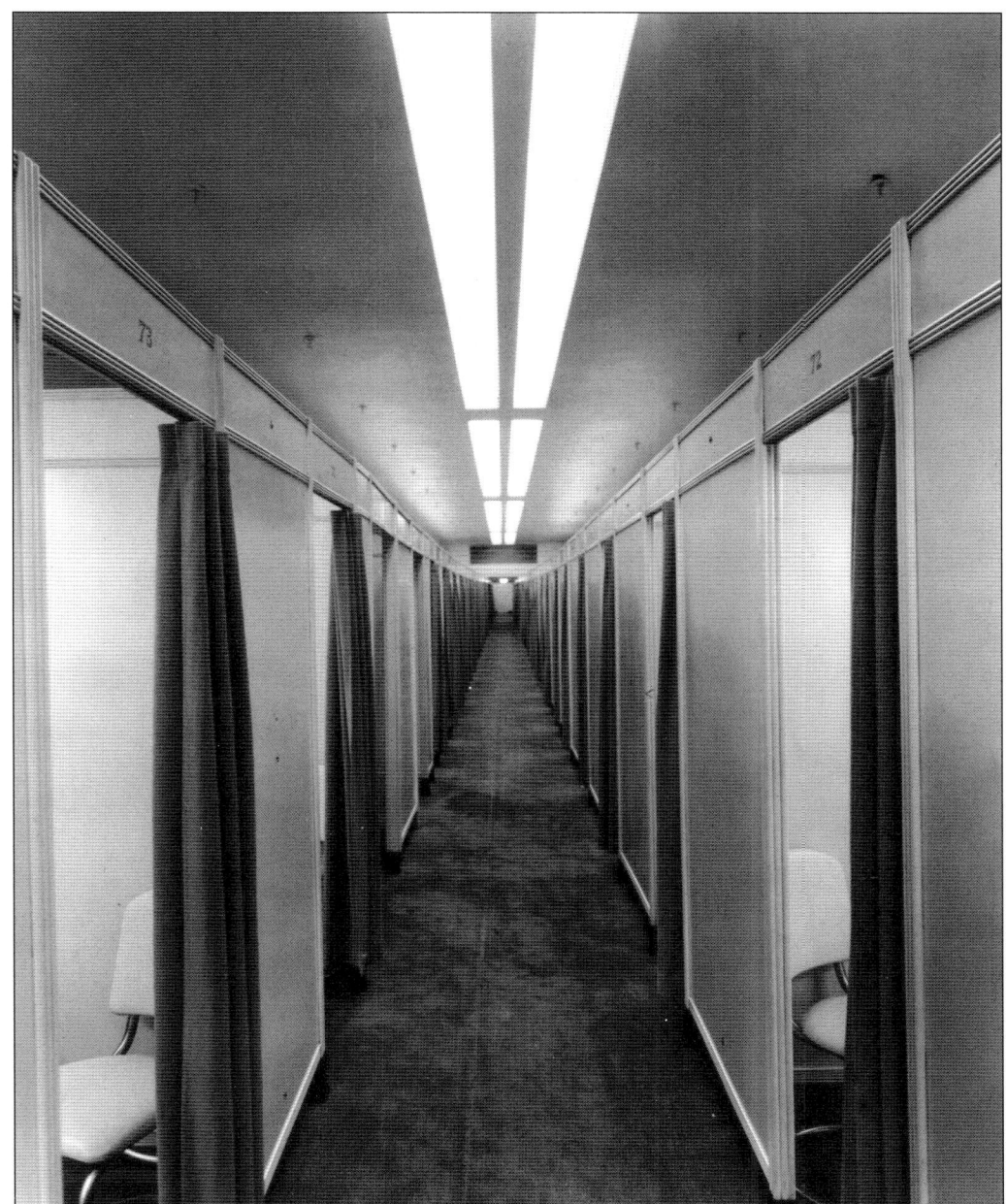

FITTING ROOMS AS FAR AS THE EYE COULD SEE, 1940. Hudson's in downtown Detroit contained more private fitting rooms than any other retailer in North America. Including the basement store, there were 705 fitting rooms. The department store handled 20,000 alterations a year. The alterations staff was comprised of 33 operators, 2 pressers, 4 fitters, 2 tailors, and 10 stock sewers. (Courtesy Manning Brothers Historical Collection.)

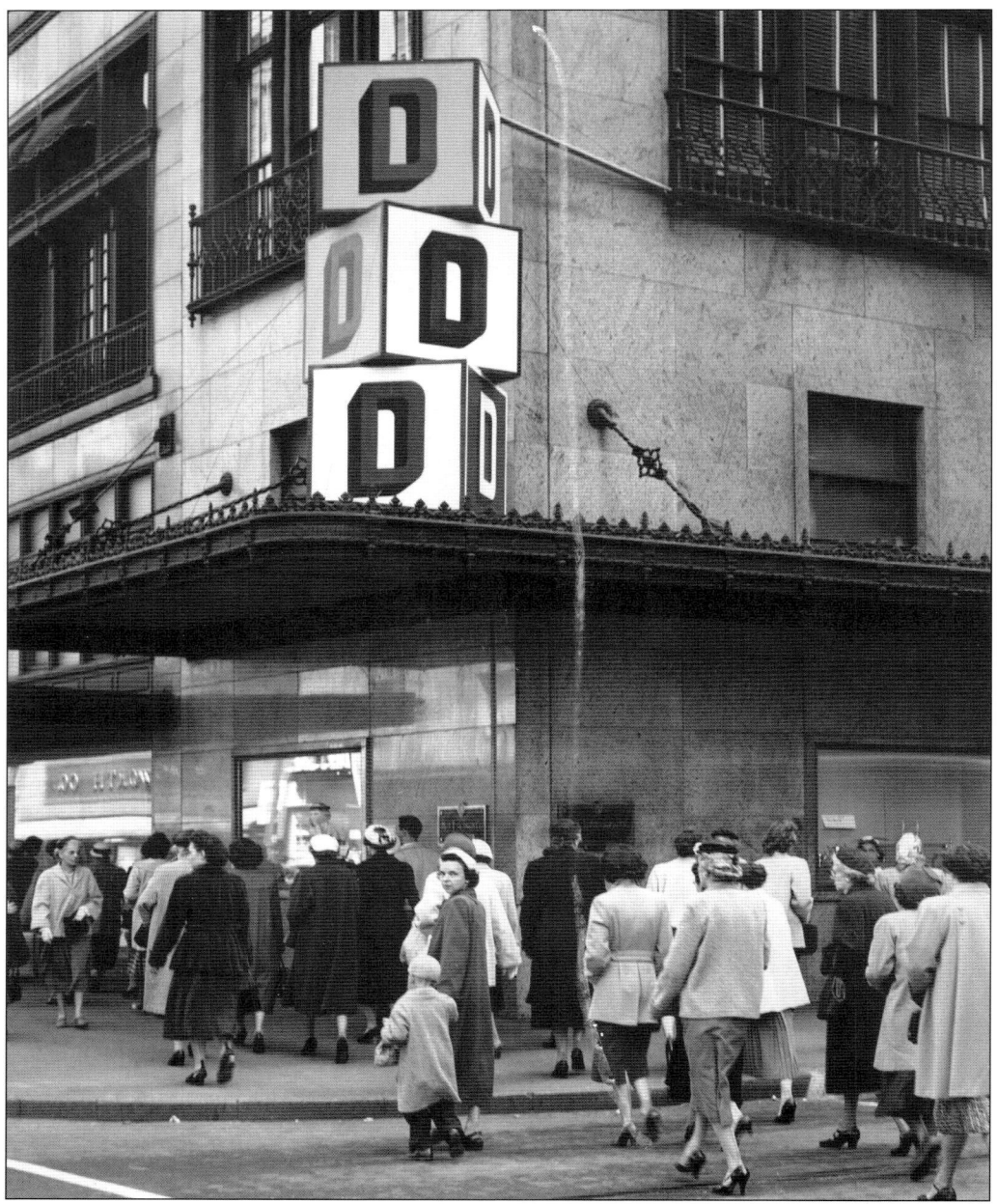

DOWNTOWN DETROIT DAYS AT HUDSON'S, 1965. Next to Christmas, Downtown Detroit Days appeared to be shoppers' favorite holiday. Hudson's executives certainly loved this promotion, as it perennially provided them with million-dollar-sales days. In 1974, Hudson's decided to open the downtown store for the first time on Sundays and featured special events, restaurant specials, parking specials, and even a special television lounge for football fans. (Courtesy Central Business District Foundation.)

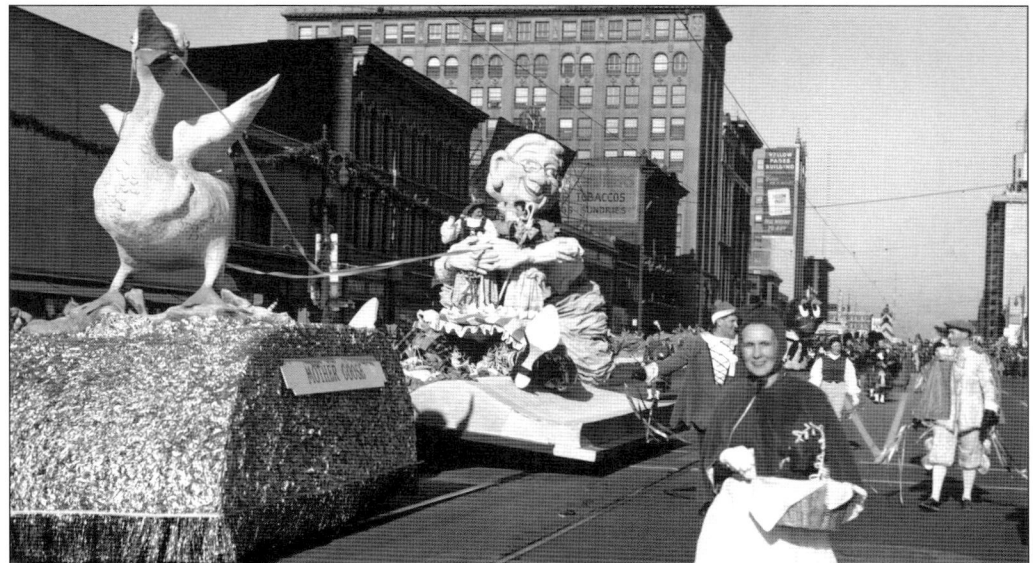

HUDSON'S THANKSGIVING DAY PARADE, 1954. Hudson's holiday parade for children marched down Woodward Avenue every year beginning in 1924. The exception was 1941–1942 due to a shortage of materials during World War II. (The store donated the rubber from toy animal balloons to the war effort.) Typically 250 Hudson's associates prepared the floats at the Fort Street warehouse, and 2,000 additional employees assisted with the parade. (Courtesy Central Business District Foundation.)

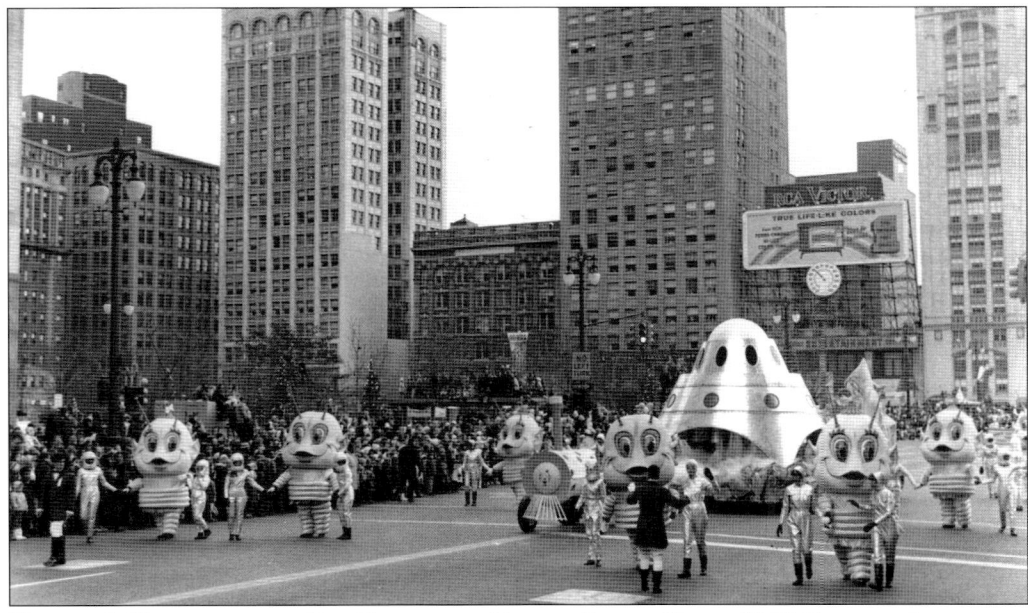

HUDSON'S THANKSGIVING DAY PARADE AT GRAND CIRCUS PARK, 1967. Because of a runaway horse team during a parade in the early years, manpower was used for many years with as many as 24 individuals pulling a single float. Sometimes cold weather caused the metal-rimmed wheels on floats to freeze to the street surface. This led to mechanization, and by the 1960s, the floats were pulled by powerful tractors. (Courtesy Central Business District Foundation.)

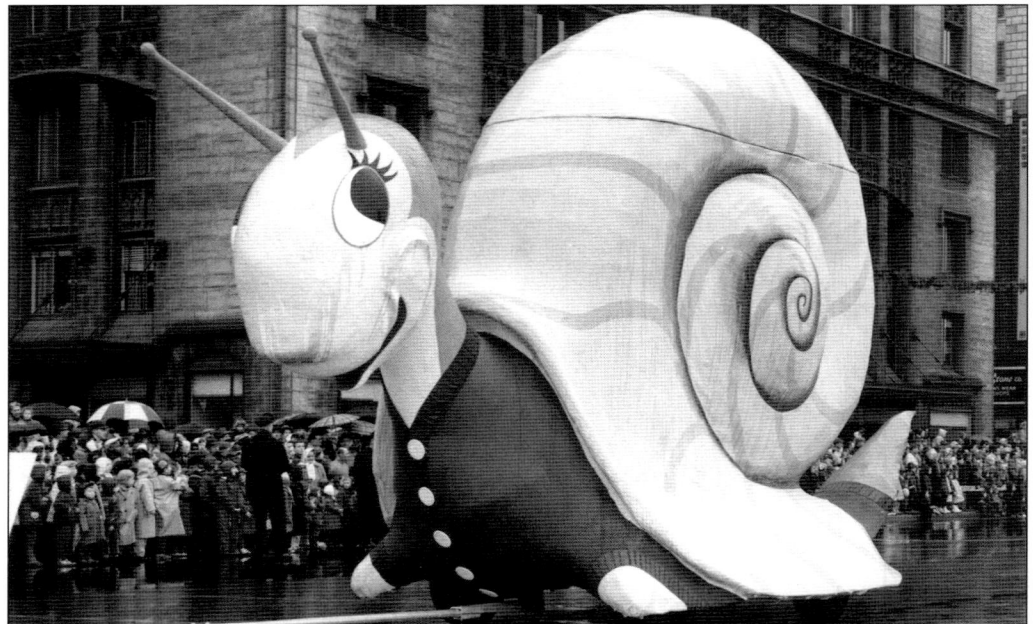

COLORFUL FLOAT ON WOODWARD AVENUE AT ADAMS STREET, 1974. Each year, Hudson's parade floats were either completely renovated or reconstructed as a new float for the next parade. By tradition, one of the floats was designed by schoolchildren from Detroit elementary schools. Children were invited to submit designs to a panel of judges at Hudson's, and the winning design or idea was constructed for the parade. (Courtesy Central Business District Foundation.)

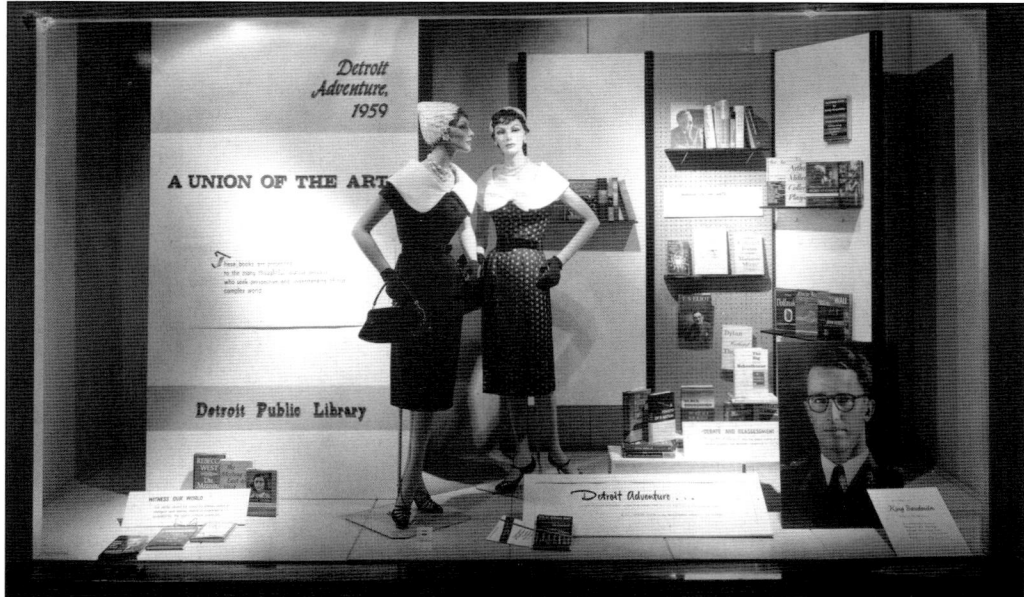

PUBLIC SERVICE DISPLAY WINDOW AT HUDSON'S, 1959. Display windows as well as interior displays were important selling aids. Hudson's maintained a staff of 50 visual merchandising associates. A display-manufacturing facility was housed on the 15th floor where large displays and spectacles were designed, created, and assembled. (Courtesy Central Business District Foundation.)

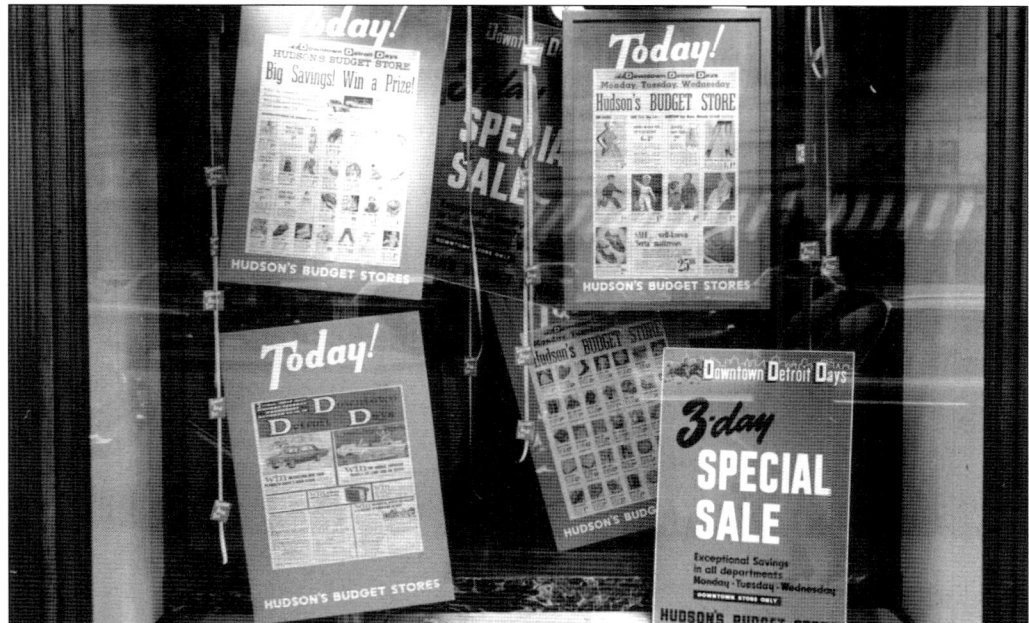

BASEMENT STORE PROMOTES DOWNTOWN DETROIT DAYS, 1963. In 1925, the basement store at Hudson's doubled its size to 75,000 square feet and, at the time, was the only basement store with an escalator, designed to carry 50,000 shoppers a day. Each basement department purchased and sold its own merchandise. (Courtesy Central Business District Foundation.)

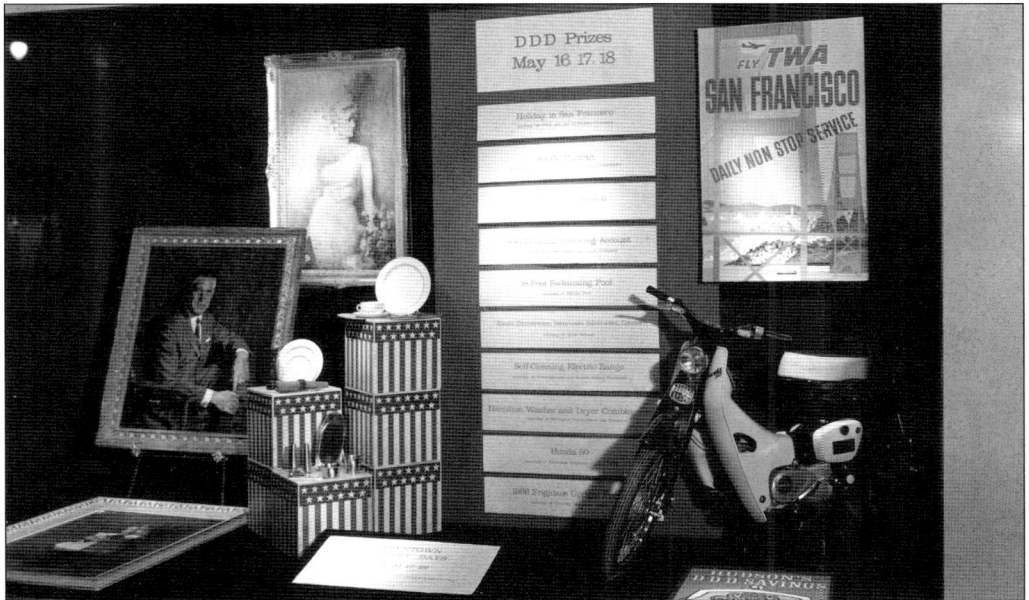

WINDOW DISPLAY PROMOTING DOWNTOWN DETROIT DAYS, 1966. The prize giveaways for this promotion were astounding for the time, usually $20,000 worth. One could register to win everything from a California trip to a motor scooter. Hudson's also maintained a complete line of tire and automobile accessories (with free installation) on the 12th floor and at the park-and-shop garage at Monroe and Randolph Streets. (Courtesy Central Business District Foundation.)

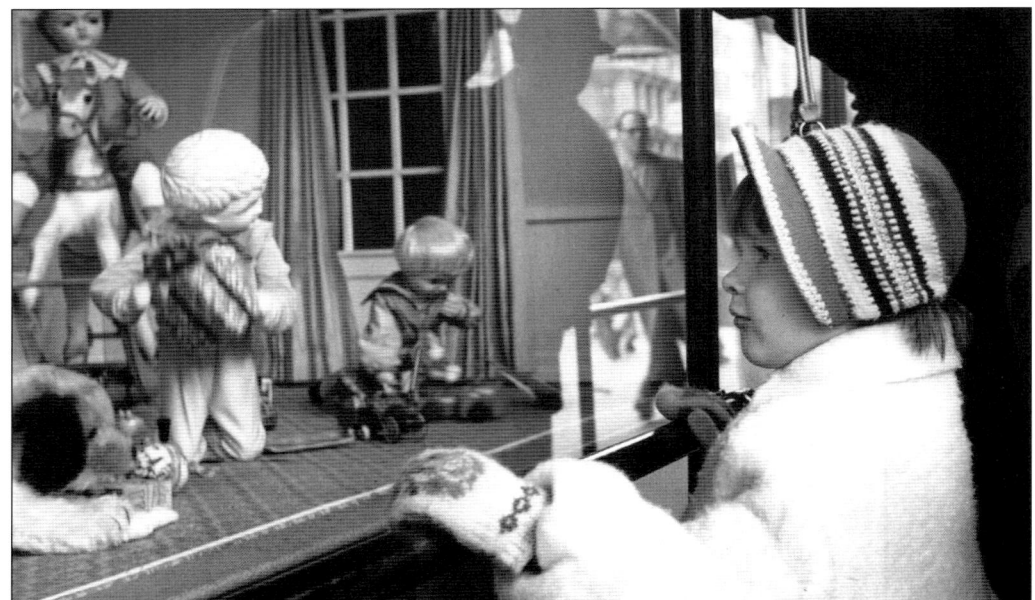

HOLIDAY ENCHANTMENT AT 1206 WOODWARD AVENUE, 1960S. Up on the 20th floor, the Hudson's carillon rang out favorites like "Silver Bells" for harried shoppers to enjoy down at street level. During the holiday season, the telephones at Hudson's never stopped ringing. A staff of 40 telephone operators at the downtown store typically handled 35,000 calls a day. (Courtesy Central Business District Foundation.)

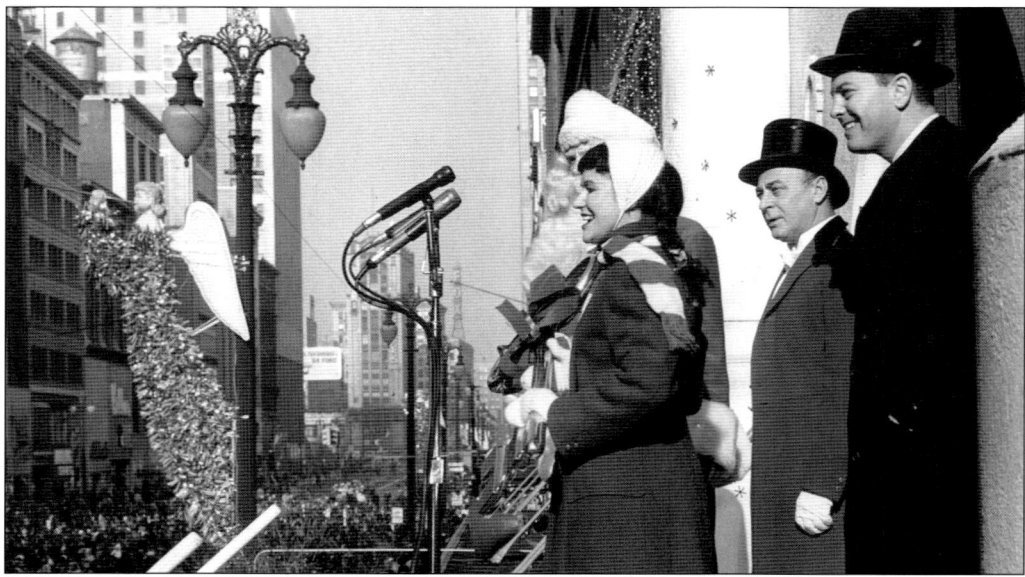

SANTA AND CHRISTMAS CAROL ON HUDSON'S MARQUEE, 1963. Little did the public realize how much the combined efforts of many Hudson's associates it took to make the parade a success. Assistance for parade day was needed from store carpenters, floor service, deliverymen, warehouse men, and porters. The carpentry crew set up Santa's platform on the marquee, and floor service worked to get the warehouse and store back in shape for business. (Courtesy Central Business District Foundation.)

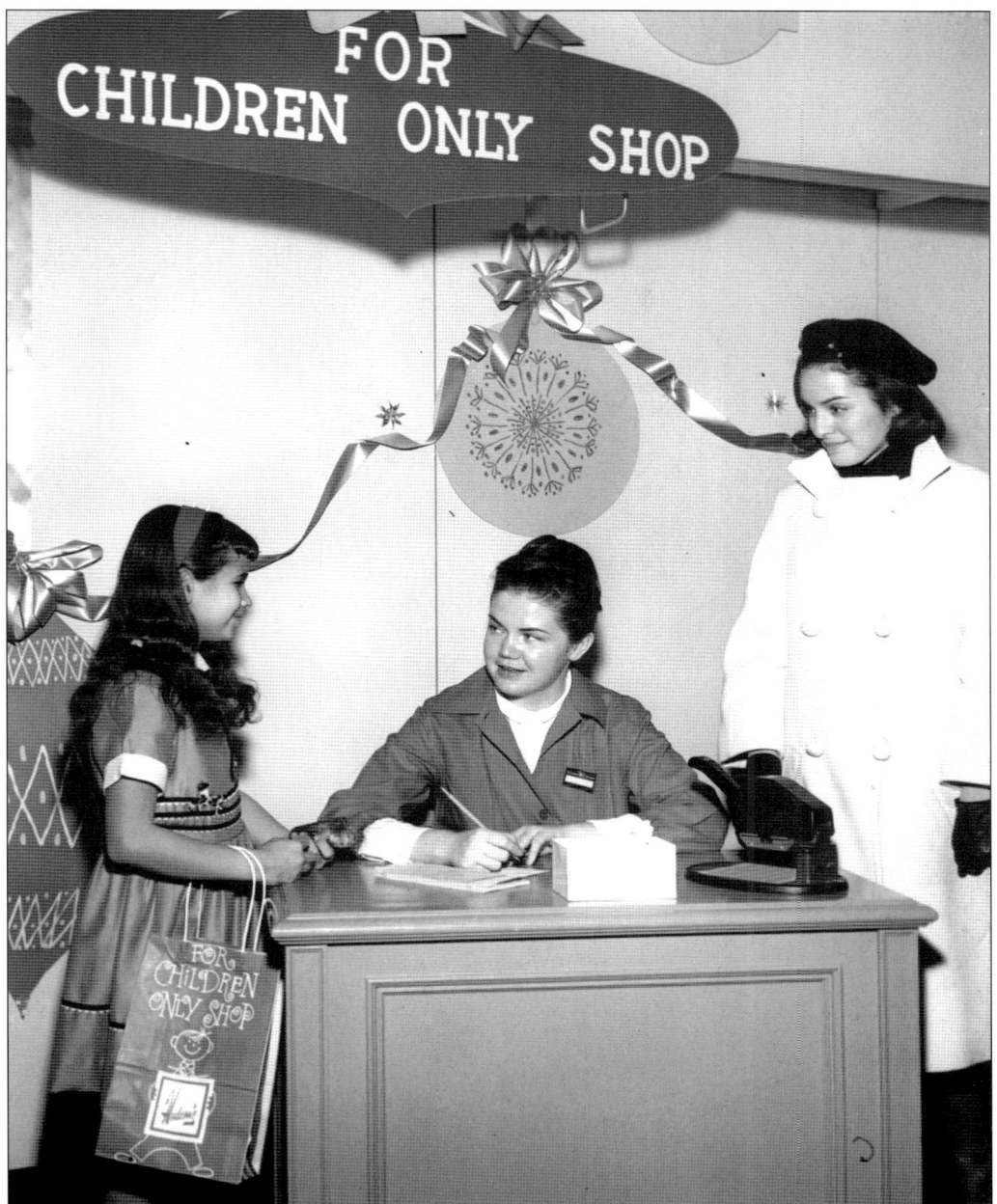

HUDSON'S FOR CHILDREN ONLY SHOP, 1964. This exclusive shopping area was located on the fourth floor of the downtown store. Above, Hudson's employee Pat Deeny assists Rita Alsaro (left) with her gift list as Snow Queen Mari Jo Rogers observes. Merchandise was selected especially for young customers and their budgets. Even the display fixtures were scaled for children. The 35 trained counselors assisted 5,000 children who shopped here each holiday season while mom and dad waited nearby. (Courtesy Central Business District Foundation.)

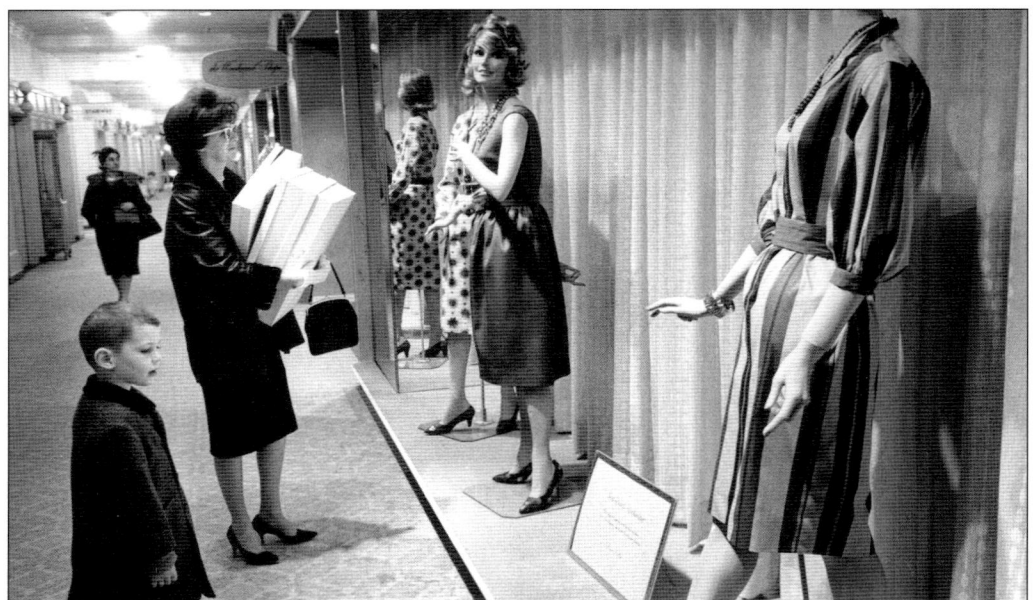

ADMIRING FASHION DISPLAYS IN THE WOODWARD SHOPS, 1960S. With the opening of the exclusive Woodward Shops on the seventh floor in 1948, Hudson's "owned" the better designer business in Michigan. Madelyn Coe was Hudson's fashion director for over 40 years and was known as Detroit's "first lady of fashion." Coe helped popularize the little black dress in the 1950s and the chemise in the 1960s. (Courtesy Central Business District Foundation.)

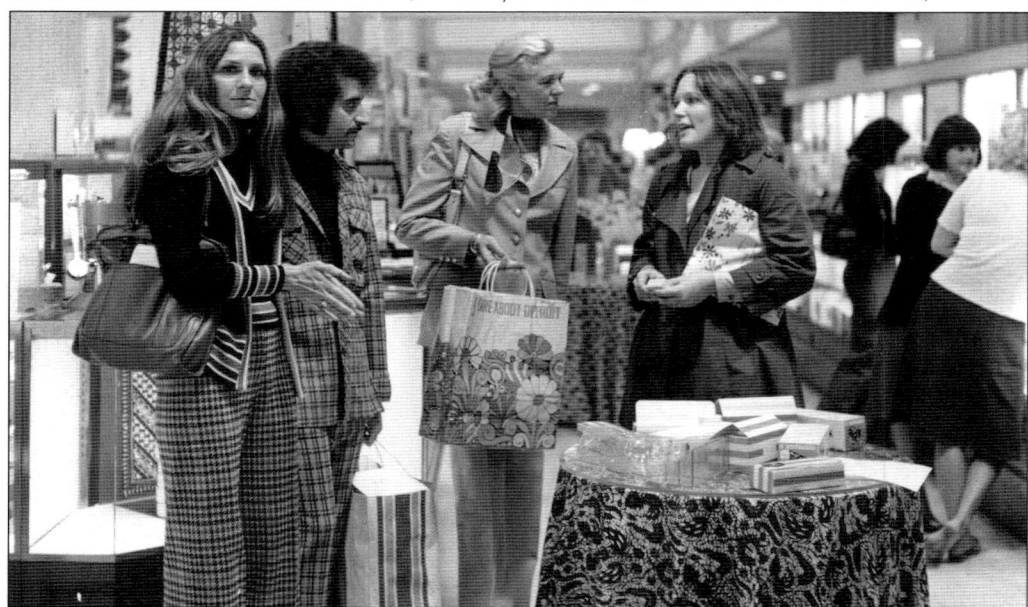

SALAD DAYS PROMOTION AT HUDSON'S, 1975. Each spring, Hudson's created a storewide promotion to capture the essence of summer living in the Great Lakes. One of the most popular tie-ins was the farmer's market and stage beneath the Gratiot Avenue and Farmer Street marquees. Here one could find fresh flowers, sausages, cheeses, fresh fruits and vegetables, breads, and ice cream while enjoying music. (Courtesy Central Business District Foundation.)

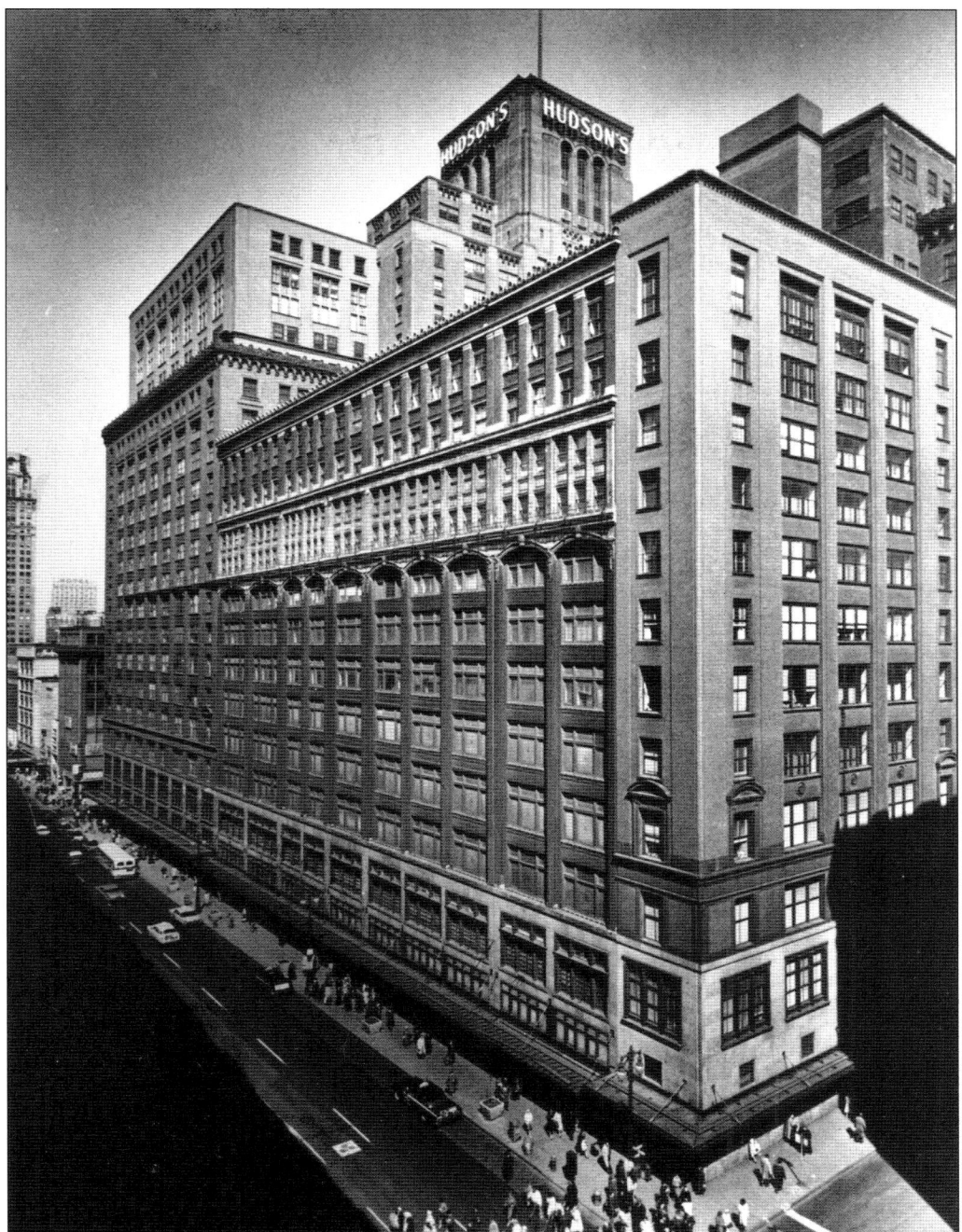

DOWNTOWN HUDSON'S AS DETROITERS REMEMBER IT, 1950S. This city-within-a-city produced some amazing statistics through the years. Even in the late 1960s, there were 18 million transactions a year, which averaged out to over 344,000 a week or 58,000 a day. The store additionally handled 60,000 pieces of mail a day for telephone and mail orders. One could shop in 420 departments, and the store distributed 590,000 shopping bags a year. (Courtesy Central Business District Foundation.)

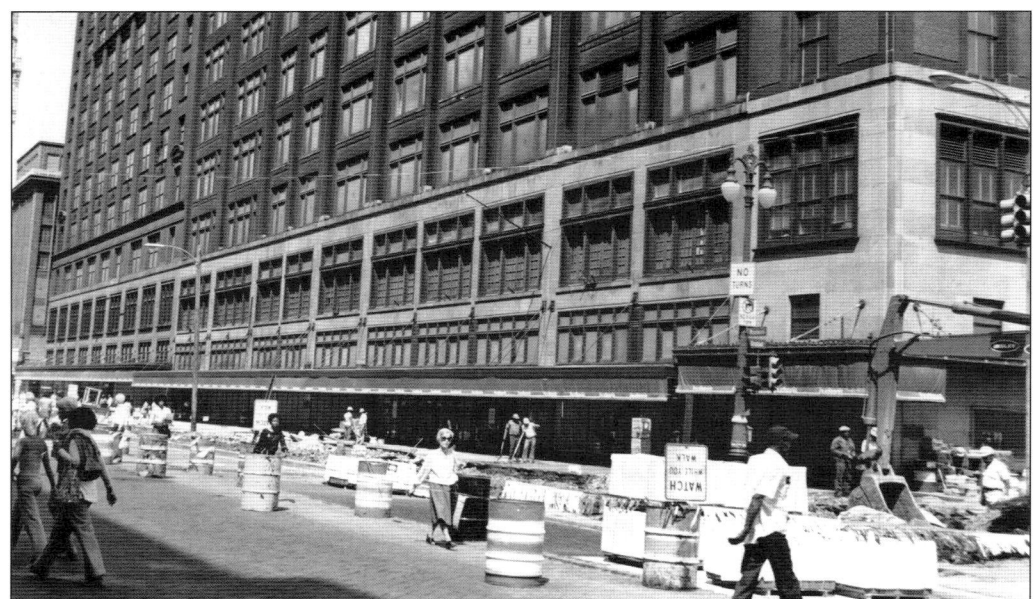

THE "MALLING" OF WOODWARD AVENUE, 1976. The two-year construction of the Woodward Mall was undertaken to generate traffic at Hudson's downtown. A popular addition was valet parking at the Farmer Street entrance. The store also provided additional space for special clearance centers on the fashion floors and the home furnishings departments. (Courtesy Central Business District Foundation.)

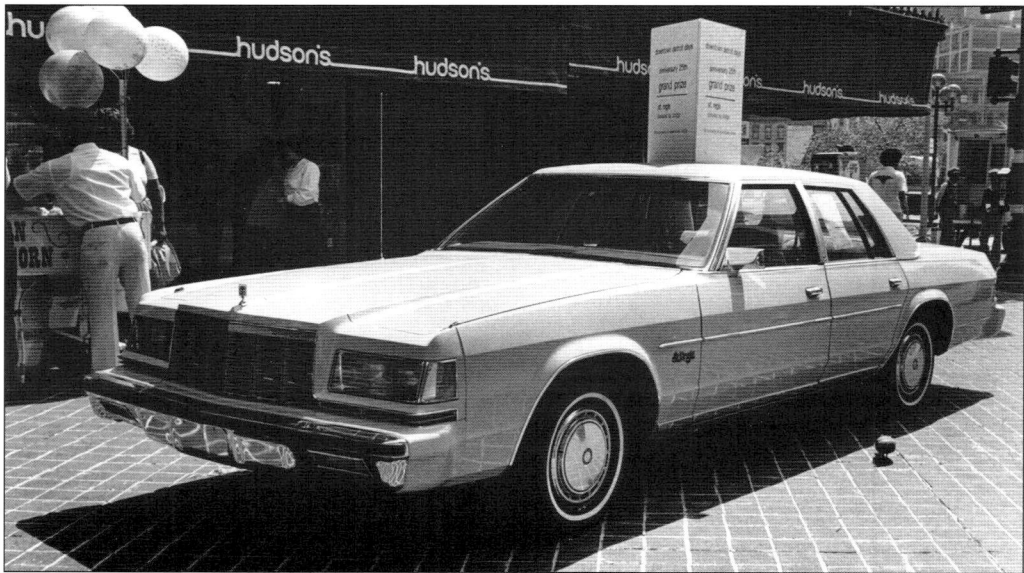

AUTOMOBILE GIVEAWAY FOR DOWNTOWN DETROIT DAYS, 1979. As far back as 1972, there were rumors that Hudson's would be closing all floors above the fifth floor in the downtown store. To combat that negativity, the company spent hundreds of thousands of dollars relocating departments, including the Woodward Shops, and renovating other floors. A new electronic telephone system was also installed for the telephone order department. (Courtesy Central Business District Foundation.)

COMPETING WITH THE DISCOUNTERS, 1973. To combat growing competition from discounters, Hudson's renamed and remerchandised the basement store. The new Rainbow store placed a greater emphasis on brands, coordinated themes, more open spaces, and imaginative displays. The upstairs store opted for more Hudson-brand goods and lower markups on selected items and opened youthful shops-within-a-shop. (Courtesy Central Business District Foundation.)

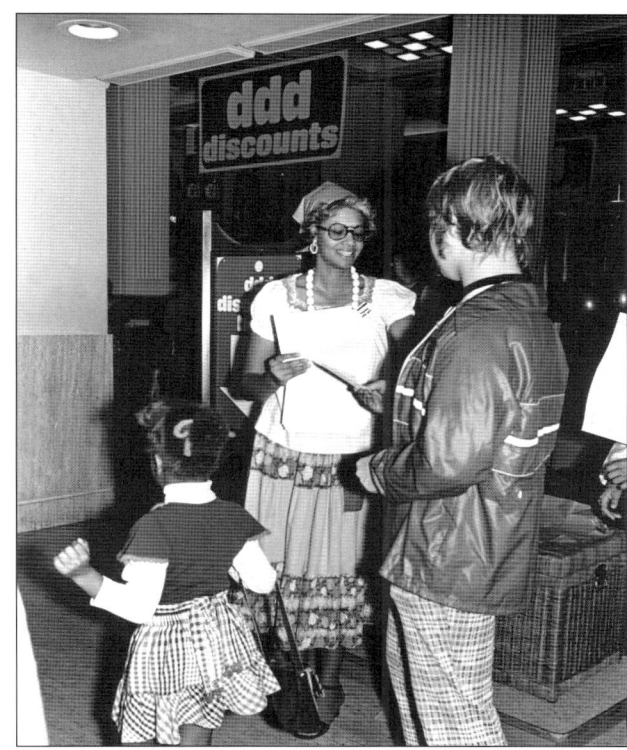

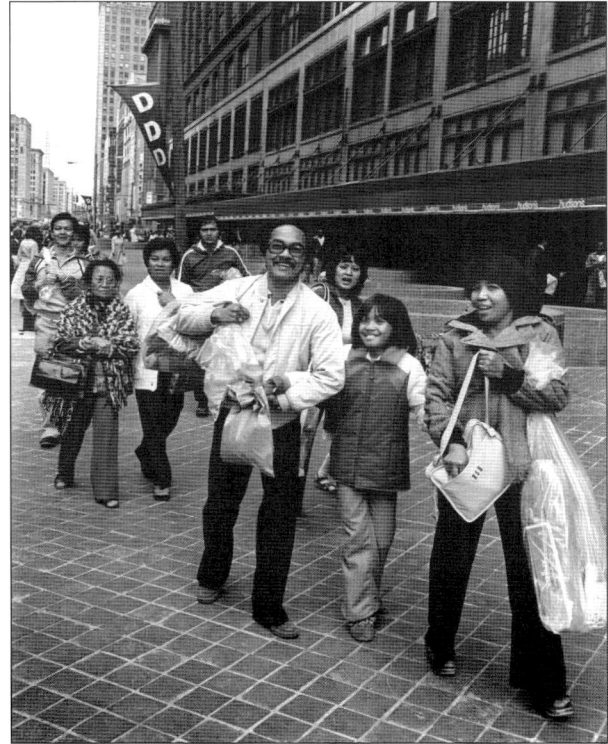

HUDSON'S FINAL PARTICIPATION IN DOWNTOWN DETROIT DAYS, 1982. Thousands flocked to the hallowed floors where soon only memories would remain for events such as the Motor City Sale, Discovery Days, the Sunkissed and Picnic promotions, and Hurry Spring! (Courtesy Central Business District Foundation.)

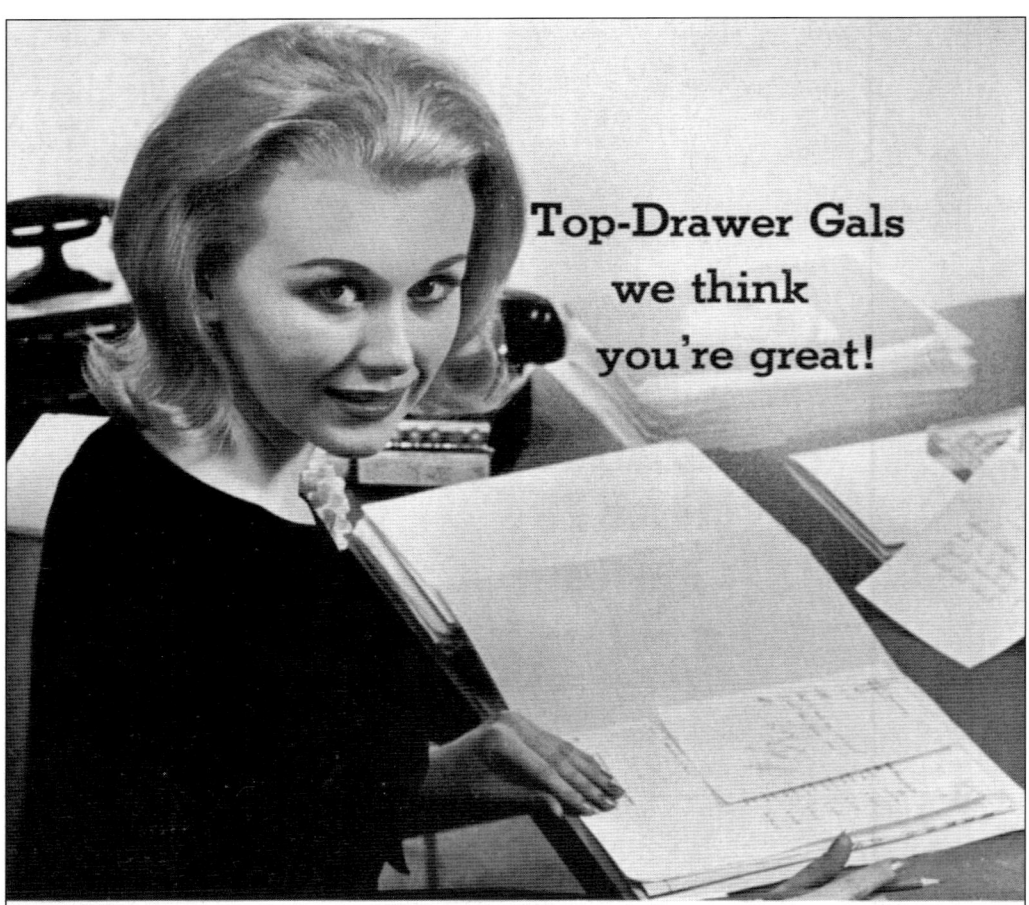

SALUTE TO WOMEN WHO WORK WEEK, 1965. Beginning in 1955, the Central Business District Association sponsored the Salute to Women Who Work Week, a unique (for the time period) event. Ten top working women in metropolitan Detroit were selected from nominations sent to a panel of judges. Over 2,000 working women attended the banquet as guests of their respective companies. Hudson's staged a fashion show each year featuring a famous New York designer. (Courtesy Central Business District Foundation.)

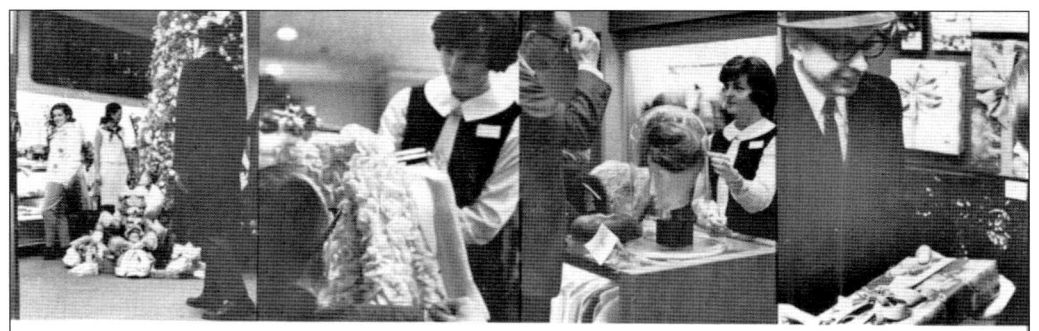

Send him to Hudson's For Men Only Shop for gifts you'll love

He'll be delighted—so will you—with the results of his gift-shopping in this unique shop. Scores of wonderfully feminine gifts have been pre-selected and conveniently located in this quiet, secluded corner. No women allowed except for the saleswomen who are gift experts, and secretaries who may shop for the boss before noon. The size chart is for *you* to fill out, for *him* to carry. Downtown, 6th.

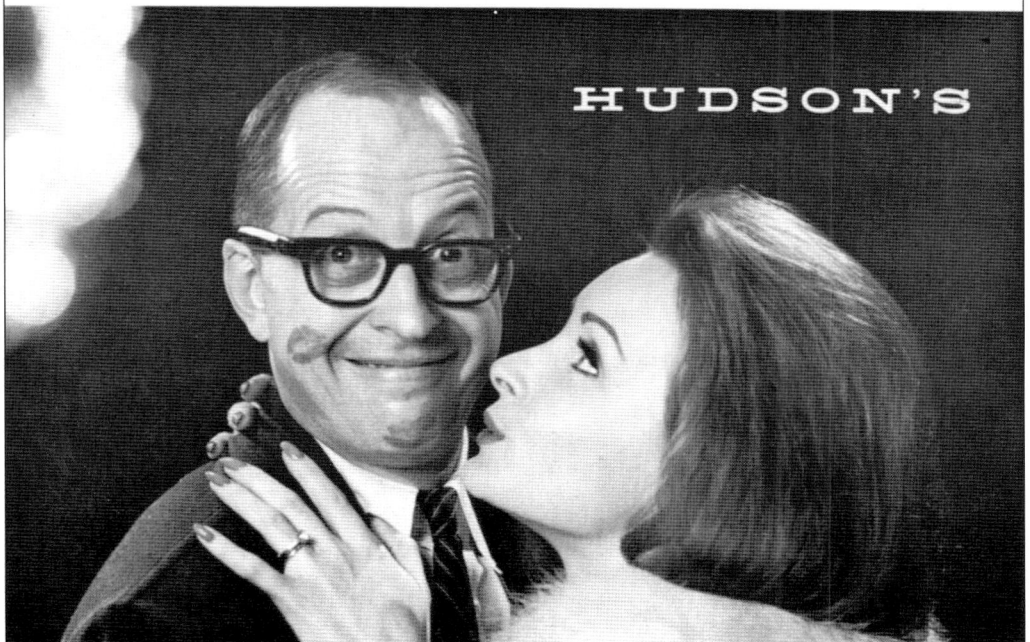

FOR HIS EYES ONLY, 1965. Each holiday season, one of the most popular spots in the downtown Hudson's was the For Men Only Shop and relaxation center. This area was stocked with merchandise from 65 departments and staffed by 21 specially trained associates. Male customers received advice on colors and sizes, could select specialty gift wraps, and were even treated to live models. (Courtesy Central Business District Foundation.)

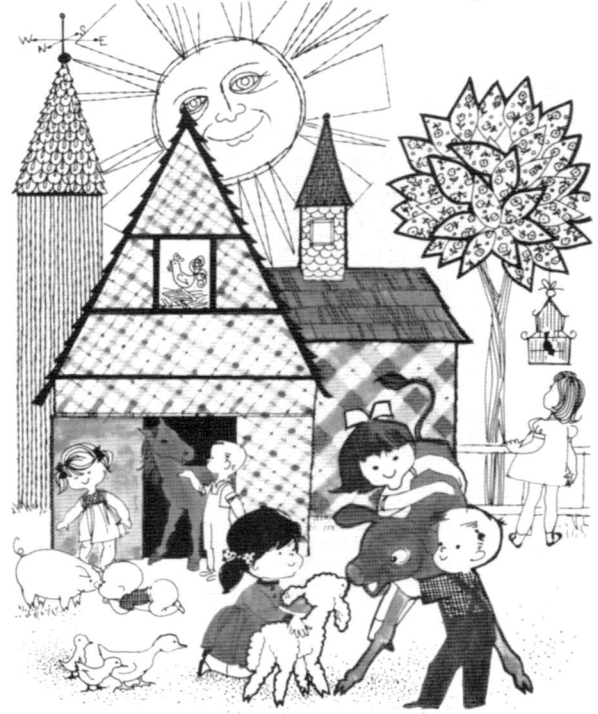

EASTER TRADITION IN THE 12TH-FLOOR AUDITORIUM, 1964. Another highly anticipated family event began in 1955 with Peter Rabbit's Barnyard. This Easter extravaganza featured burros, lambs, pigs, rabbits, chickens, ducks, a calf, and even a skunk. Feeding cribs and troughs were built, and extra refrigerators were installed to keep additional milk for baby pigs. Two perfume machines filled with deodorizer were installed in the ceiling. (Courtesy Central Business District Foundation.)

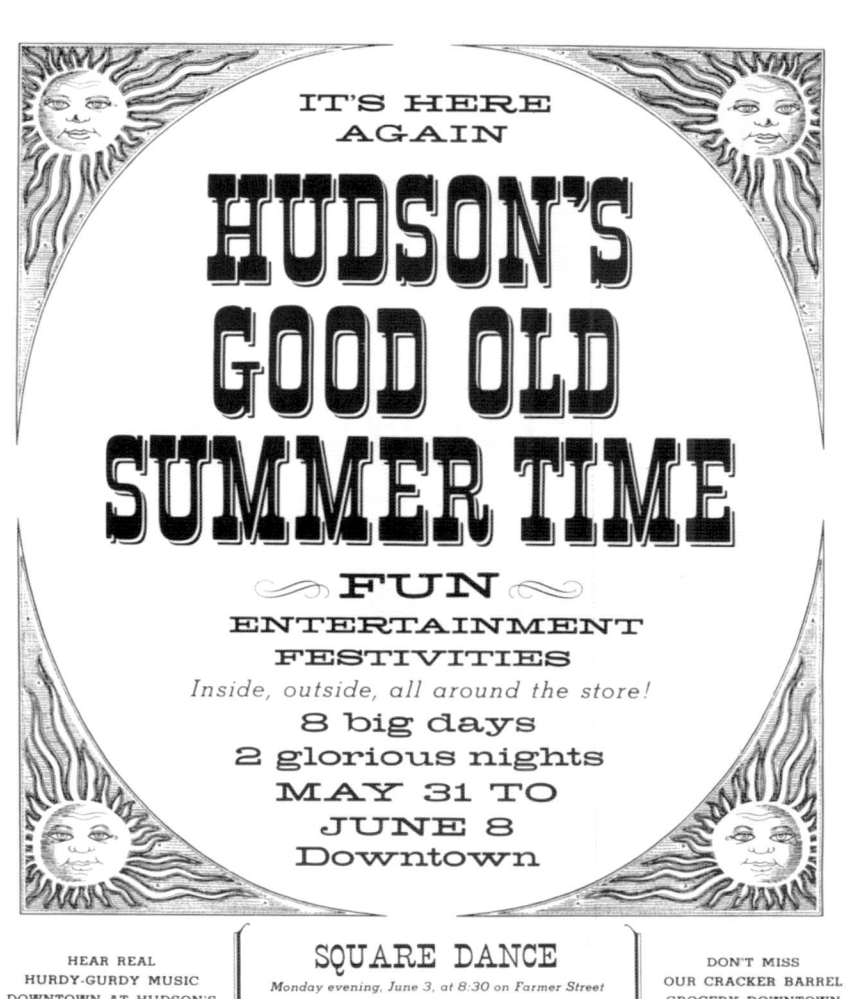

SUMMERTIME FUN AT DOWNTOWN HUDSON'S, 1963. First implemented in 1962, the Good Old Summer Time promotion proved to be the most talked about event of that year. A weeklong celebration of events and food recaptured the summer fun of yesteryear. New events were added each year, including lit displays on the Woodward Avenue marquee. (Courtesy Central Business District Foundation.)

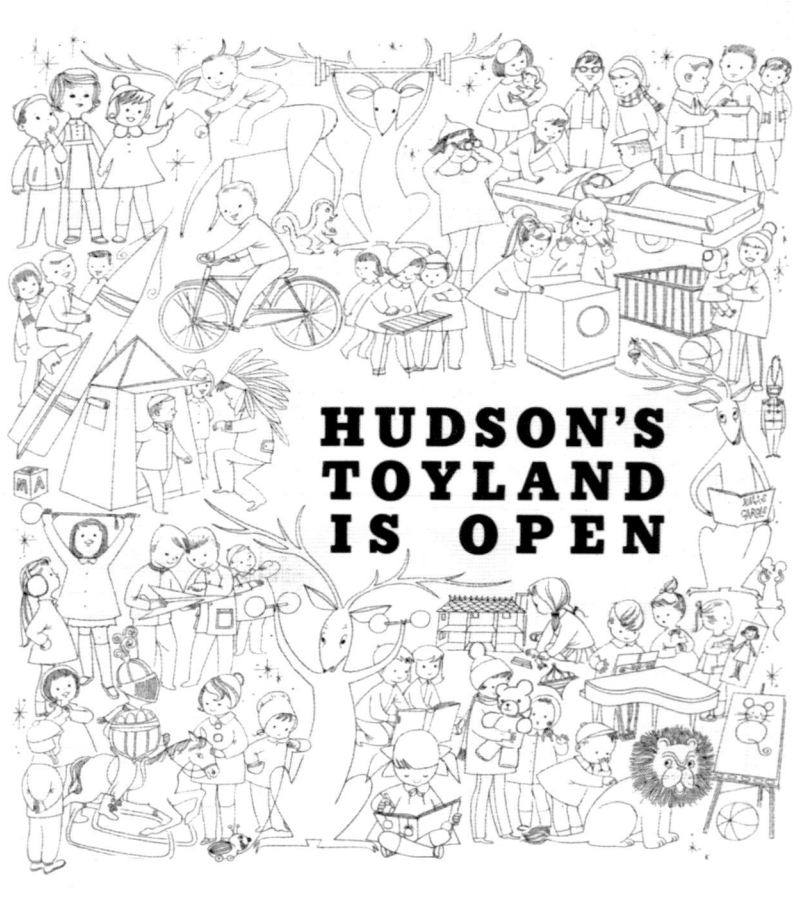

Hudson's Magical World of Toys, 1962. Children from throughout Michigan and Ontario eagerly awaited the opening of Toyland each year. Many adults also secretly looked forward to this day because it brought back happy memories of their childhoods. The department featured one of the largest model railroad displays in the country. Thousands of families crowded express elevators daily to reach the wondrous 12th floor. (Courtesy Central Business District Foundation.)

Five
Crowley Milner and Company

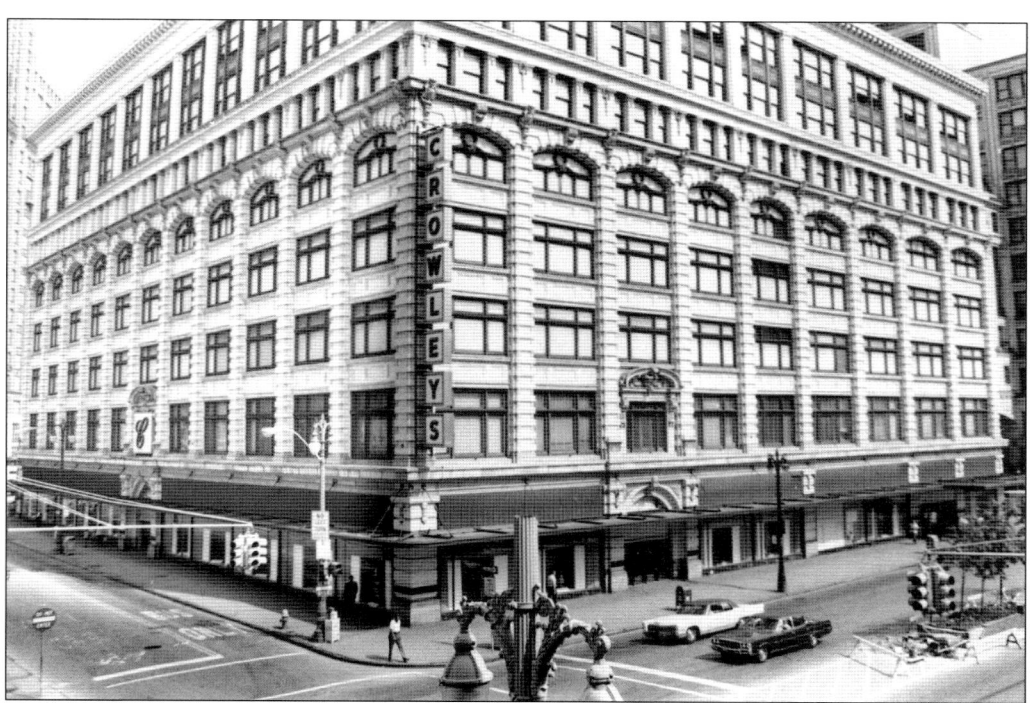

Crowley's, Monroe and Farmer Streets, 1960s. Crowley Milner and Company was founded in 1909 when brothers Joseph, William, and Daniel Crowley and William Milner joined forces to purchase the Partridge and Blackwell (P&B) department store. P&B, which began in the nearby Majestic Building, opened a block-long six-story emporium, facing Farmer Street, in 1907. Economic problems of the time almost forced P&B into bankruptcy. (Courtesy Detroit Historical Museum.)

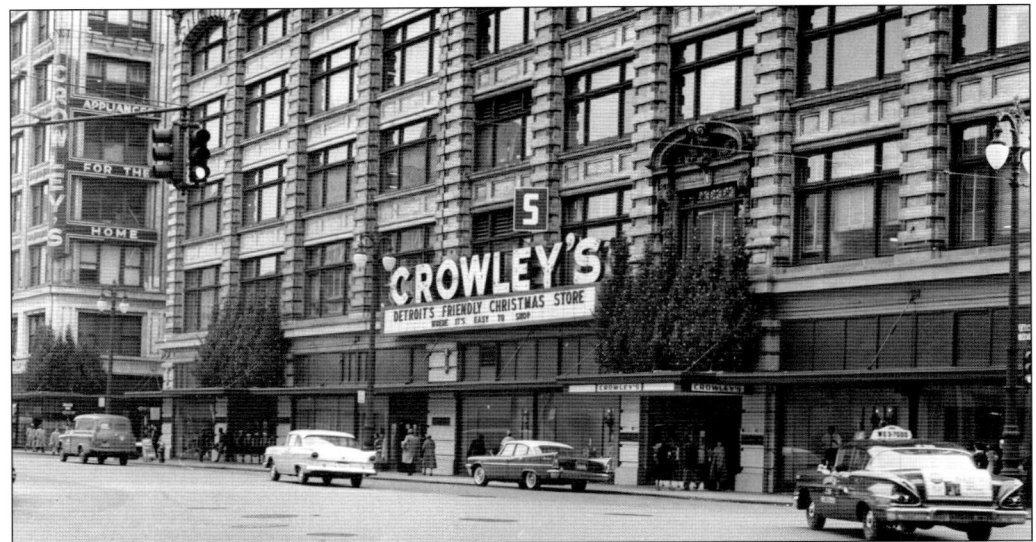

HOLIDAY VIEW OF CROWLEY'S, GRATIOT AVENUE AND LIBRARY STREET, 1958. Crowley's built an addition in 1915–1916, extending the store back to Library Street and adding two more stories. In 1919, two more floors were added to the original building facing Farmer Street. In 1920, the former Goldberg store on Library Street was acquired and became Crowley's east building, connected to the main store via a tunnel. The final expansion occurred in 1925–1926, consisting of an 11-floor warehouse with a five-story bridge to the main store. (Courtesy Central Business District Foundation.)

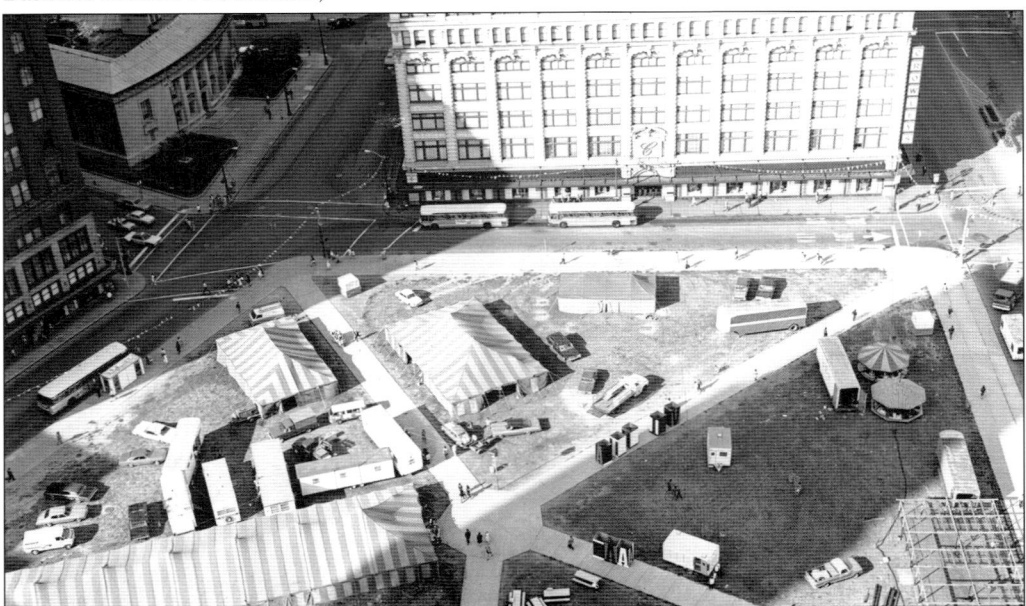

CROWLEY'S AND THE ADJACENT KERN'S BLOCK, 1971. Crowley's various buildings were designed under the direction of Fred Smith, founder of Smith, Hinchman and Grylls Architects. These structures were constructed of white glazed terra-cotta with carved limestone trim over a shell of steel girders and reinforced concrete. Crowley's was an excellent example of the Chicago school of design with Beaux-Arts detailing. (Courtesy Central Business District Foundation.)

Promotional Postcard from Crowley's Pharmacy, 1950s. Detroit's favorite television comedian, Soupy Sales, was a spokesperson for Bexel Vitamin Syrup for children. Crowley's mailed these postcards to draw customers to its pharmacy, located on the mezzanine. Bexel's tagline was "In school you'll do well, if you will take Bexel, orange flavored and nutritious, Jimminy Crickets, it's delicious!!" (Courtesy Michael Hauser.)

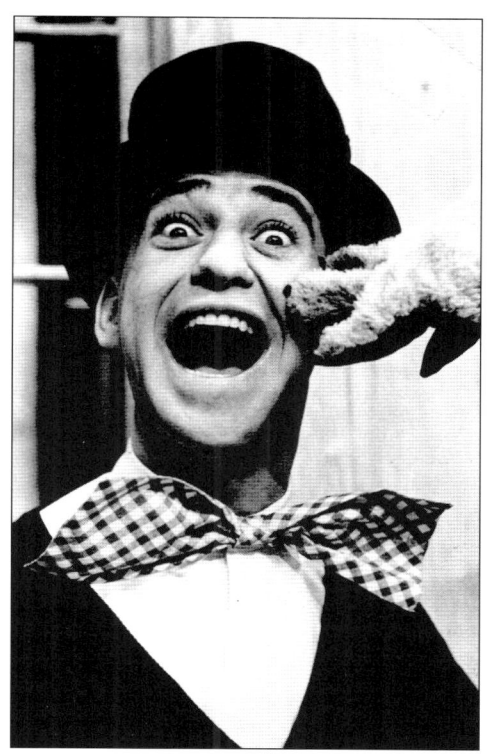

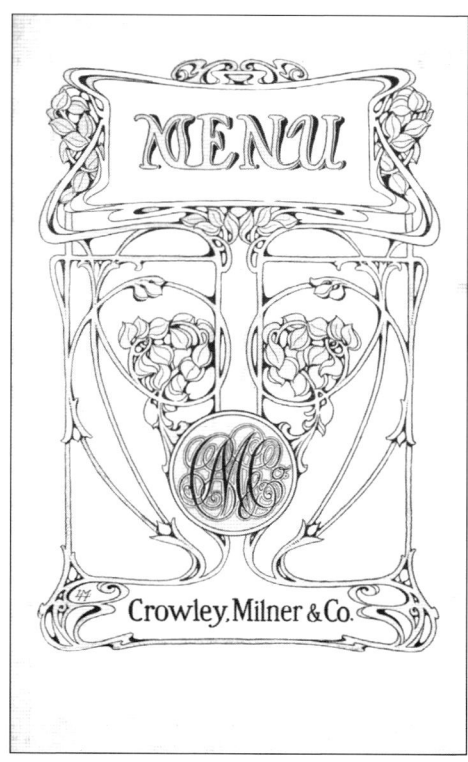

Menu from Crowley's Mezzanine Dining Room, 1910. Food service was synonymous with Crowley's. In the early days, lunch was served from 11:00 a.m. to 2:00 p.m., afternoon tea took place from 2:30 p.m. to 5:30 p.m., and formal dinner was served on Saturday evenings from 5:30 p.m. to 8:00 p.m. Musical accompaniment from well-known operas was played on pianos from Grinnell Brothers music store. A cafeteria, soda fountain, and snack bar were located on the basement level, as was one of city's finest grocers. (Courtesy Michael Hauser.)

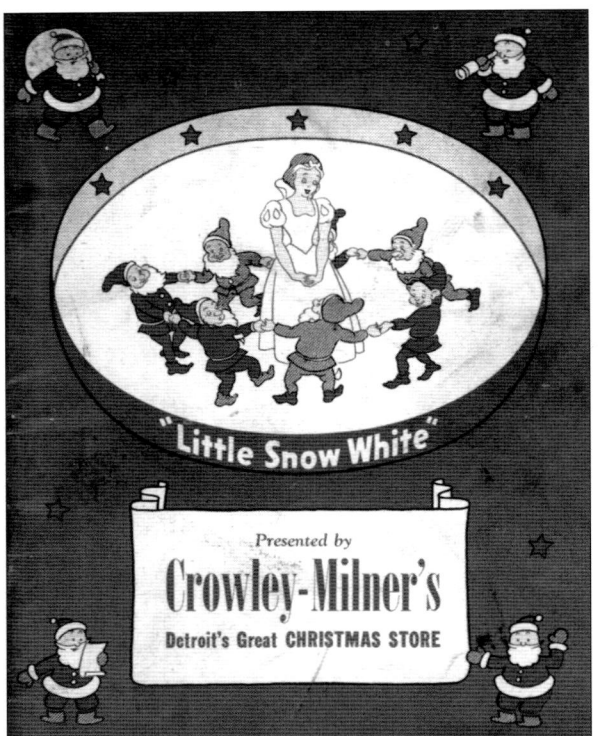

SNOW WHITE HOLIDAY PROMOTION, 1937. Crowley's was known for elaborate holiday animated displays in its toy land, or Fairyland, as it was promoted. Themes through the years included Snow White, a magic enchanted forest, and Mickey Mouse. In the 1930s and 1940s, puppet shows and two-reel films enhanced the experience for families in the store auditorium, followed by a visit with Santa. (Courtesy Michael Hauser.)

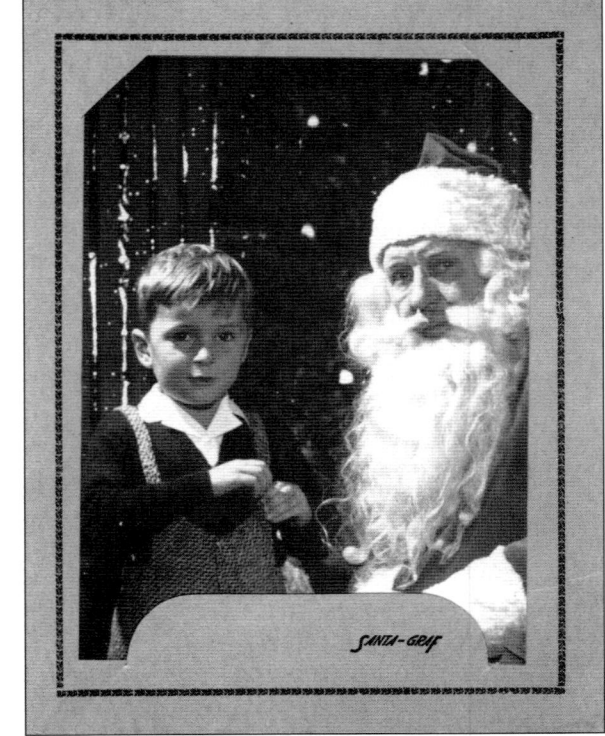

SANTA-GRAF PICTURES AT CROWLEY'S, 1950S. Crowley's was one of the first stores to offer souvenir photographs of a child posing with Santa. The Lunch with Santa program began in 1951, and many Detroiters still cherish their "I just had lunch with Santa at Crowley's" mugs. During the 1950s and 1960s, the Crowley's auditorium was transformed into a holiday festival, featuring carnival rides, a children's snack bar, and surprise packages from Santa. (Courtesy Michael Hauser.)

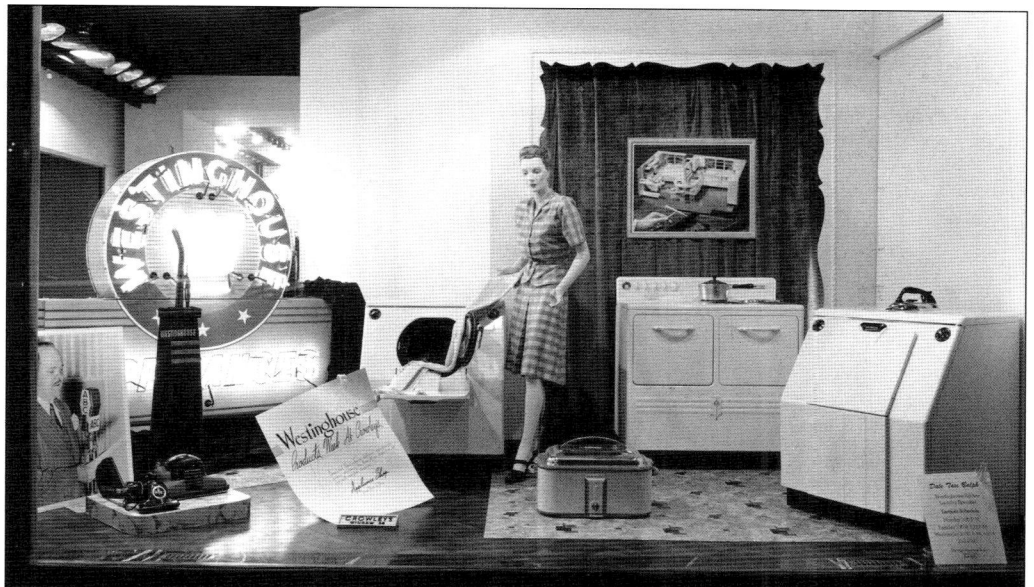

WINDOW DISPLAY PROMOTING WESTINGHOUSE PRODUCTS, 1940S. Twice a year in the 1920s and 1930s, Crowley's staged its famous two-week-long Mill End sale. The store was adorned with yellow and black banners, with bargains announced from the balcony. Over 700 extra sales associates were hired for these sales, as near-cost prices brought tremendous crowds to the store. In 1928, over 275,000 customers visited Crowley's in a single day! (Courtesy Detroit Historical Museum.)

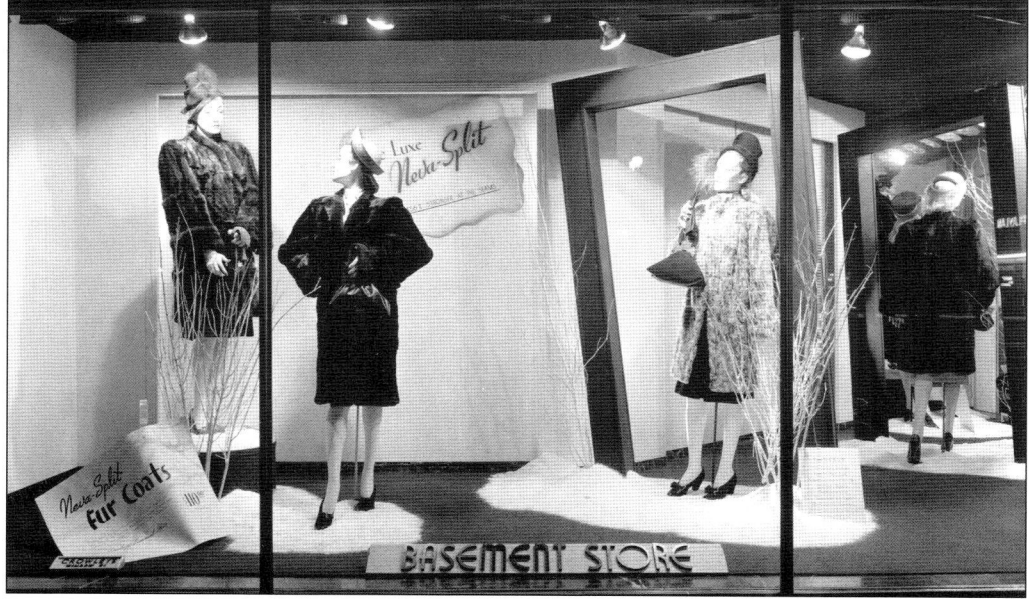

WINDOW DISPLAY FOR CROWLEY'S BASEMENT STORE, 1950S. The Crowley's basement store debuted in 1925. During the Depression, this store-within-a-store became an important contributor to the bottom line. Sales plummeted from $40 million in 1928 to $10 million by 1933. During those lean years, Crowley's endeared itself to schoolteachers and city workers by accepting scrip issued by bankrupt cities in lieu of cash. (Courtesy Detroit Historical Museum.)

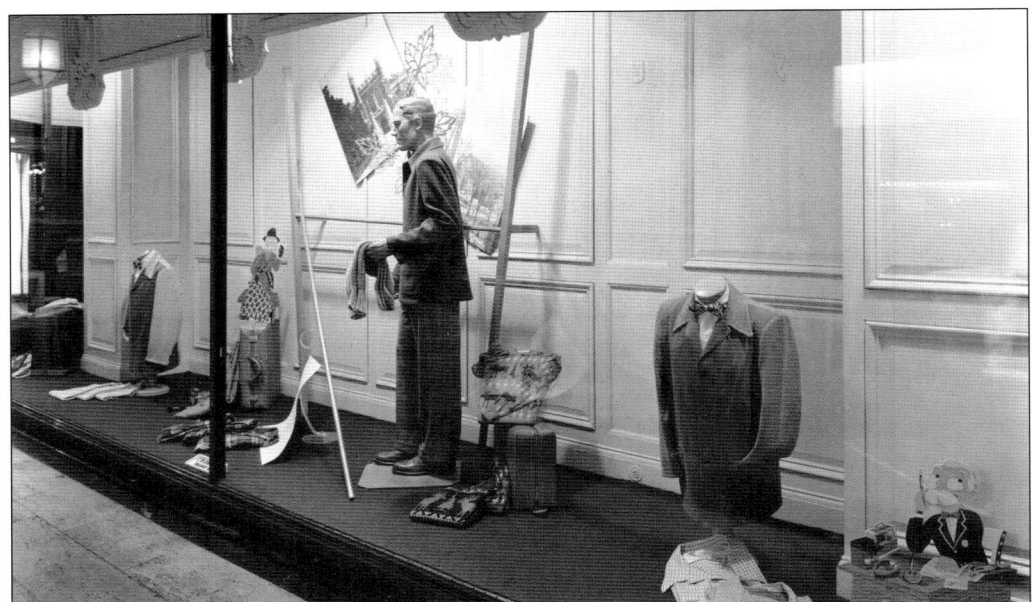

MEN'S DEPARTMENT DISPLAY, 1946. Besides elaborate interior displays, Crowley's prided itself on its seven blocks of exterior display windows on Monroe Street, Gratiot Avenue, and Farmer and Library Streets. Sales associates were knowledgeable regarding the merchandise in each numbered window should a customer have specific questions. The store also staged Saturday fashion shows in the mezzanine restaurant. (Courtesy Detroit Historical Museum.)

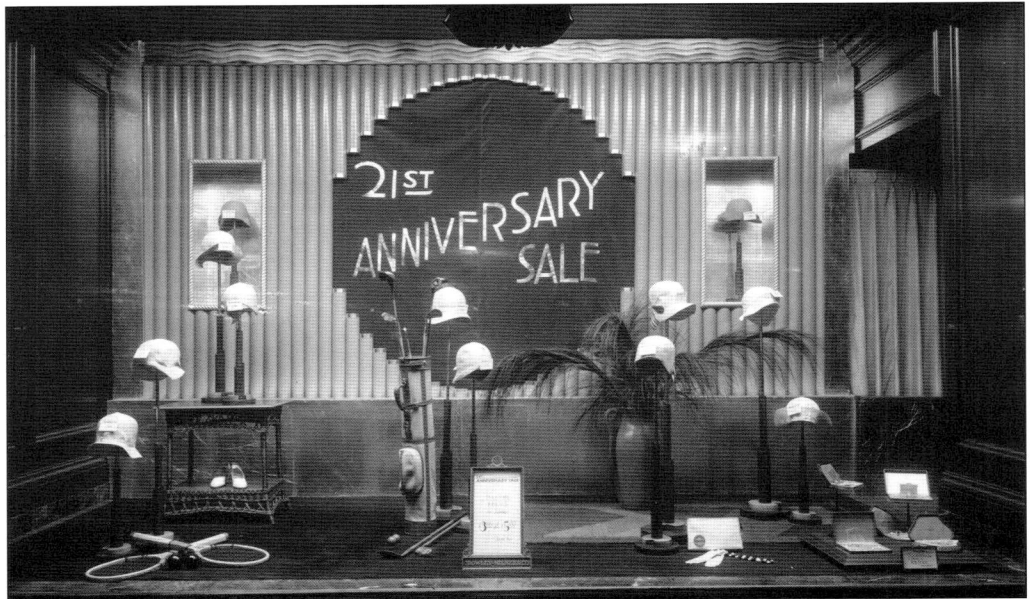

DISPLAY WINDOW CELEBRATING CROWLEY'S 21ST ANNIVERSARY, 1930. Crowley's incorporated Motor City history in many of its window displays through the years. Exhibits included a parlor suite with a pipe organ, the store's original 1909 switchboard, Clara Ford's wedding gown, and Gov. Lewis Cass's desk. Vintage automobiles were on display throughout the store. For many decades, Crowley's was known as "the friendly store." (Courtesy Detroit Historical Museum.)

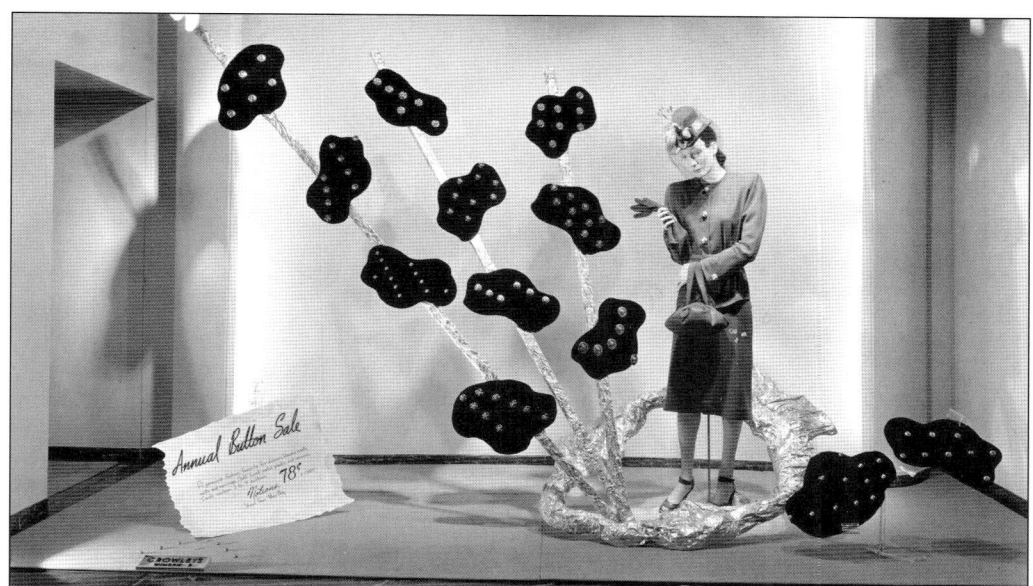

CROWLEY'S DISPLAY WINDOW PROMOTING BUTTONS, 1940S. By 1946, the downtown Crowley's store covered almost 800,000 square feet with 17.5 acres of floor space and 1,450 sales associates. The store achieved two Detroit firsts with escalator installations. In 1903, an escalator was installed in the center of the main floor. It was deemed impractical and later removed. In 1928, Crowley's memorable wooden escalators debuted, providing service up to the sixth floor and remaining in service until the store closed in 1977. (Courtesy Detroit Historical Museum.)

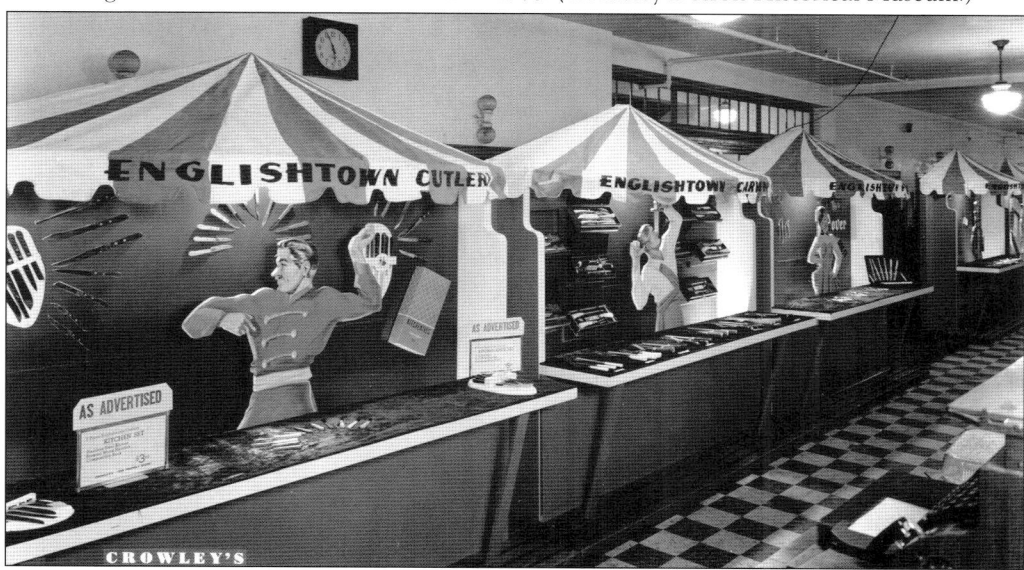

ENGLISHTOWN CUTLERY DISPLAY AT CROWLEY'S, 1940S. In the 1950s, Crowley's attempted to lure young families to the store by opening a large children's play center on the sixth floor of the east building. Children between 3 and 10 years of age could be left in a nursery school atmosphere with projects, overseen by trained teachers, while mom and dad shopped. By 1960, the upper floors of the east building continued to be utilized for nonselling functions, while the lower floors were leased to the Veterans Administration for offices. (Courtesy Detroit Historical Museum.)

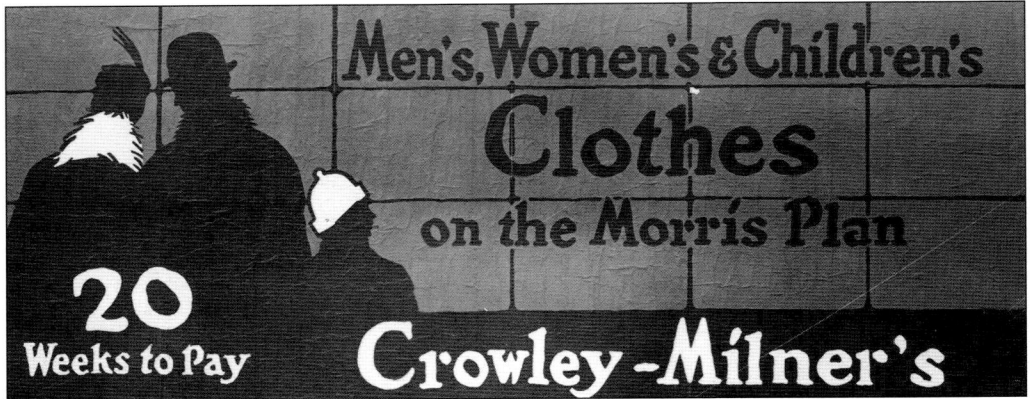

BILLBOARD FOR MORRIS PLAN AT CROWLEY'S, 1920. Crowley's was the first retailer to initiate time-payment sales on all general merchandise, with the sales financed through the Morris Plan Bank. Other Crowley firsts include being the first retailer to change from horse-drawn delivery wagons to gasoline-powered vehicles and implementing the first charge-a-plate system and cycle-billing program in Detroit. (Courtesy Detroit Historical Museum.)

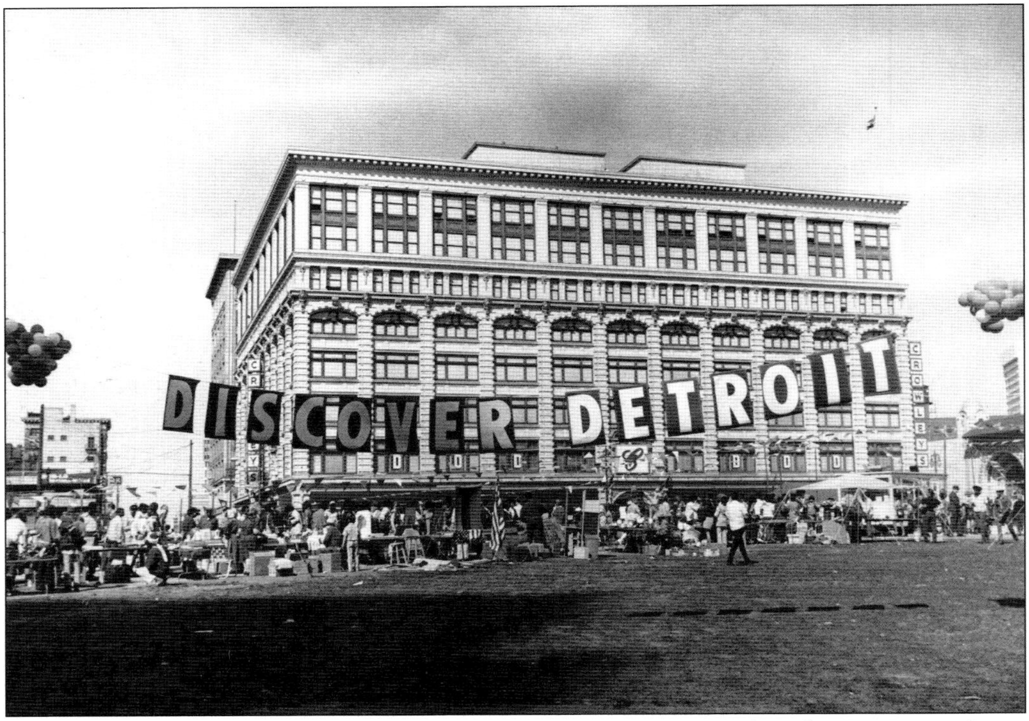

CROWLEY'S AS VIEWED FROM THE KERN'S BLOCK, 1971. To stimulate deteriorating sales in the 1960s and 1970s, Crowley's initiated unique auditorium events, such as its rummage sale and shoe consolidation sales. Sunday shopping hours were added in 1973. These measures were to no avail, as sales slid to $9 million in 1976—lower than the Depression era. The downtown store was doomed, and the doors closed on July 2, 1977. After 68 years, the telephones would no longer ring at WOodward 22400. (Courtesy Central Business District Foundation.)

Six

THE ERNST KERN COMPANY

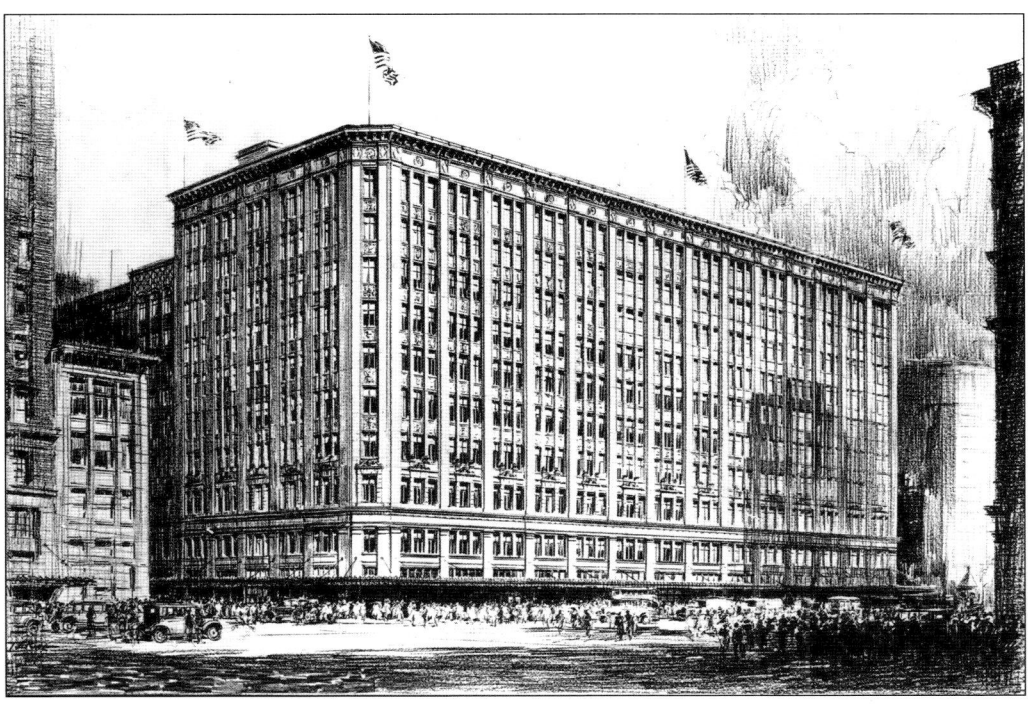

LITHOGRAPH OF ERNST KERN COMPANY, 1030 WOODWARD AVENUE, 1929. The Ernst Kern Company was one of Detroit's leading department stores for 76 years. Three generations of Kern family members operated the firm until 1957, when the company was sold. In its prime, Kern's employed 500 associates. In 1962, three years after the store closed, city officials announced the razing of Kern's, citing interest from Macy's and Marshall Field's to build new edifices on this block. (Courtesy Detroit Historical Museum.)

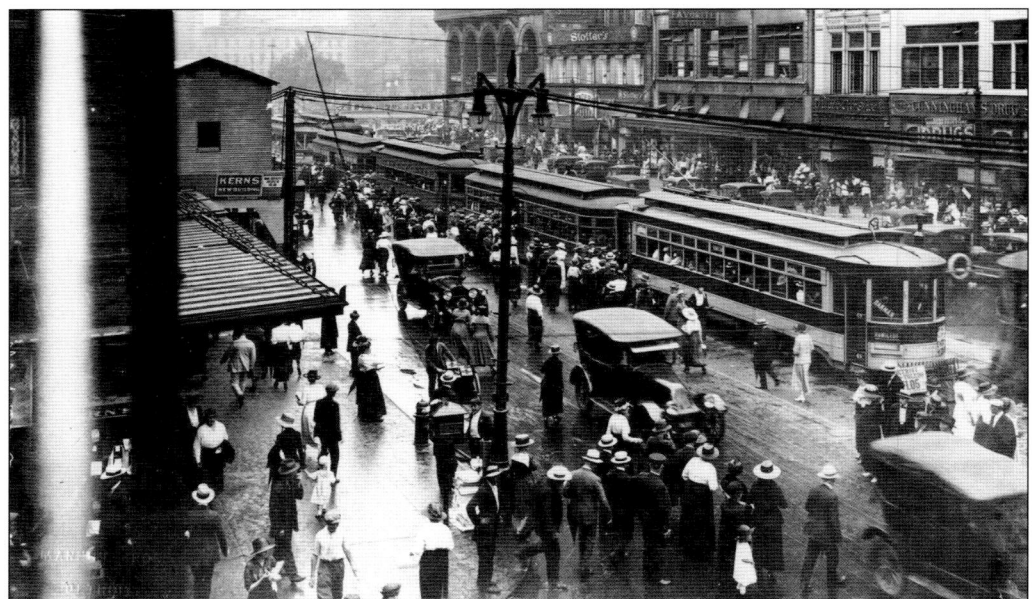

KERN'S EXPANSION ON WOODWARD AVENUE, 1919. Kern's was founded in 1883 by Ernst Kern Sr. and his wife Marie Held Kern and was located at St. Antoine and East Lafayette Streets. Kern was a German immigrant who specialized in imported fabrics, laces, and ribbons. Note the retailers on the west side of Woodward Avenue: Sanders, Stoller's Women's Wear, Heyn's Bazaar, Walk-Over Shoes, and Cunningham's Drugs. (Courtesy Manning Brothers Historical Collection.)

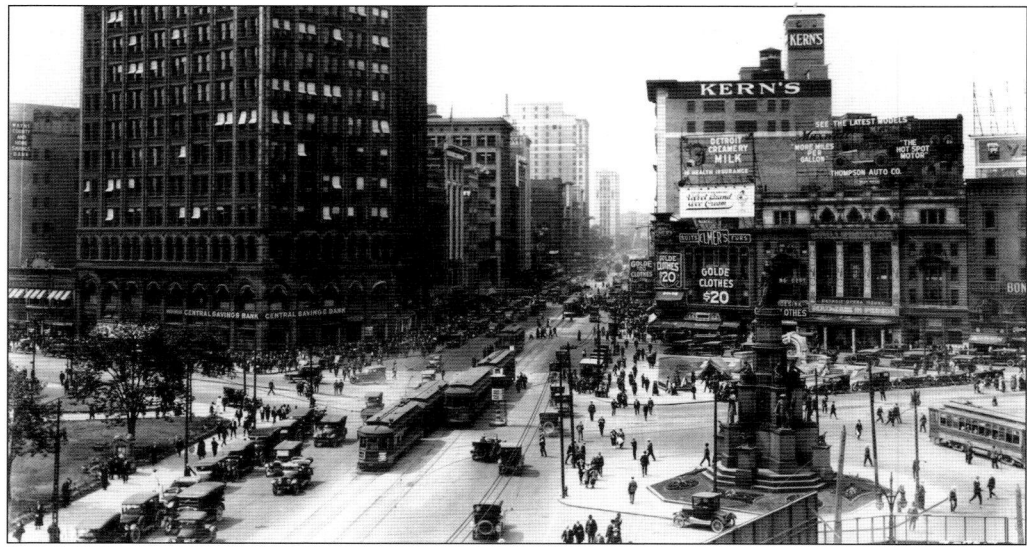

A VIEW OF KERN'S FROM CAMPUS MARTIUS, 1920. In 1886, The first Kern's store on St. Antoine Street was destroyed by fire, and the retailer moved to Randolph and Monroe Streets. In 1897, the firm acquired a five-story structure at Woodward and Gratiot Avenues. Sons Ernst and Richard took over company reins following the death of their father in 1901. Growth occurred again in 1919 with the acquisition of the nine-story Weber Building. A 10-story addition was completed in 1923 with a bridge joining the two structures. The original 5-story structure was demolished in 1928 for another 10-story addition. (Courtesy Manning Brothers Historical Collection.)

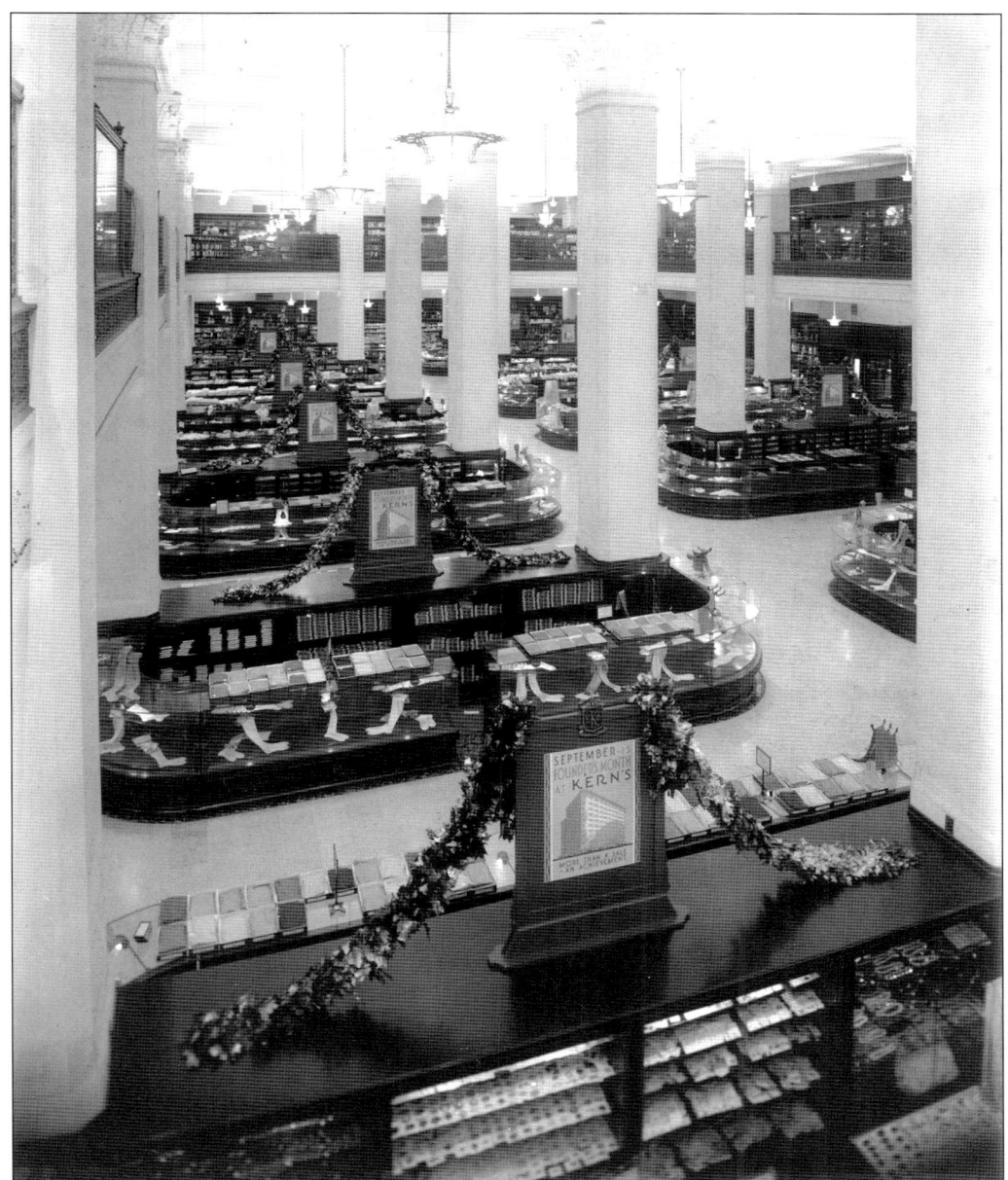

VIEW OF KERN'S MAIN FLOOR, 1929. Kern's spacious main floor had a rich art deco look. The marble floors were accentuated with a 30-foot-high ornamental ceiling, decorative cast-iron railings, and rich mahogany counters. New additions to the store included an auditorium, a roof garden, an employee gymnasium, a dining room, an elevator bank featuring 21 cars, and new street entrances directly to the basement store. In 1937, Kern's leased three floors of the new adjoining Bond's Clothing Store. (Courtesy Detroit Historical Museum.)

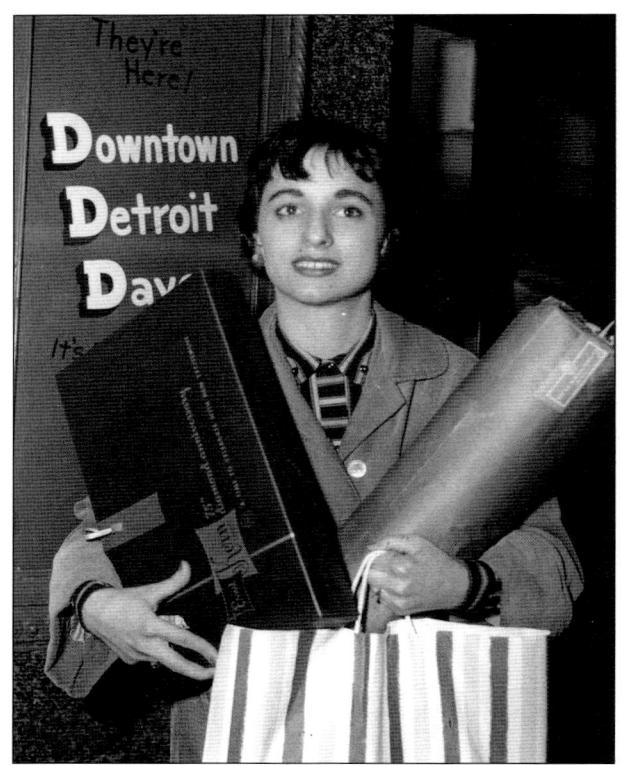

A Happy Kern's Shopper during Downtown Detroit Days, 1957. In the mid-1930s, the third generation of Kern family members managed the firm. Otto Kern's son, Ernst F. Kern, joined the store as general manager, and Richard C. Kern became vice president of sales promotion. After the passing of the elder Ernst Kern in 1948, Otto became president. (Courtesy Central Business District Foundation.)

Final Holiday Season at Kern's, 1959. Kern's pioneered mail-order services to out-of-state customers who seldom made the trek to Detroit. Having an easy-to-remember telephone number also helped: WOodward 57000. The store also featured a Brentano's Book Shop and in earlier years a lending library. Kern's was also famous for its Basement Dollar Days. (Courtesy Central Business District Foundation.)

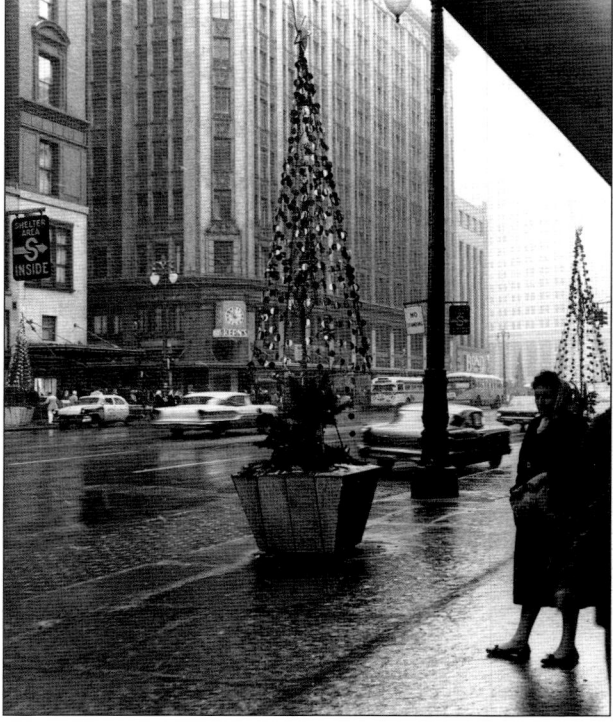

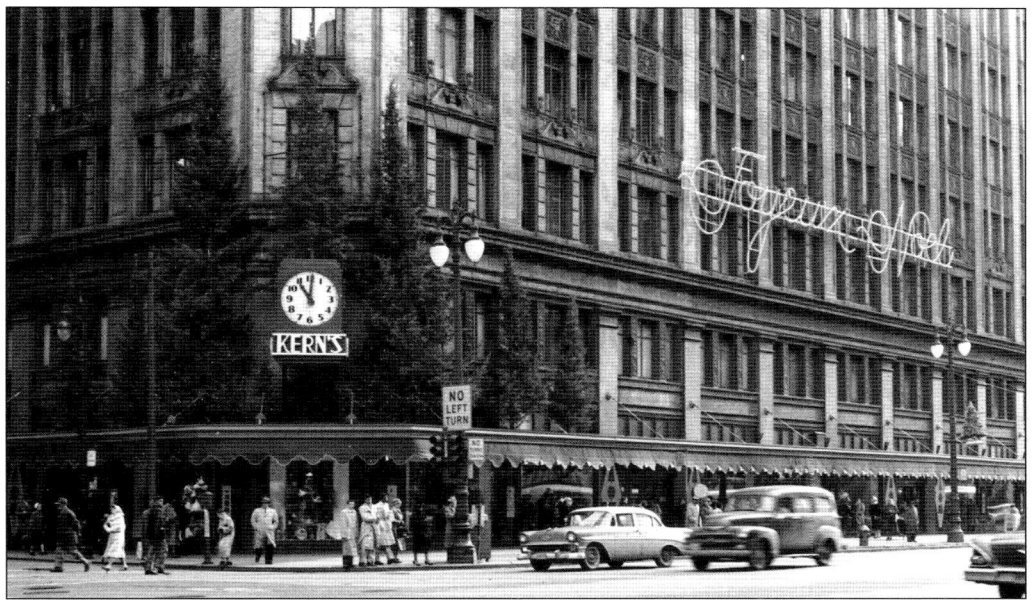

EXTERIOR VIEW OF KERN'S HOLIDAY DECOR, 1958. Kern's won the Central Business District Association's award for best interior and exterior holiday displays in 1958. "Joyeaux Noel" was the theme that year with elaborate exterior lighting, large evergreen trees on the marquee, colorful awnings, and imaginative holiday window displays. (Courtesy Central Business District Foundation.)

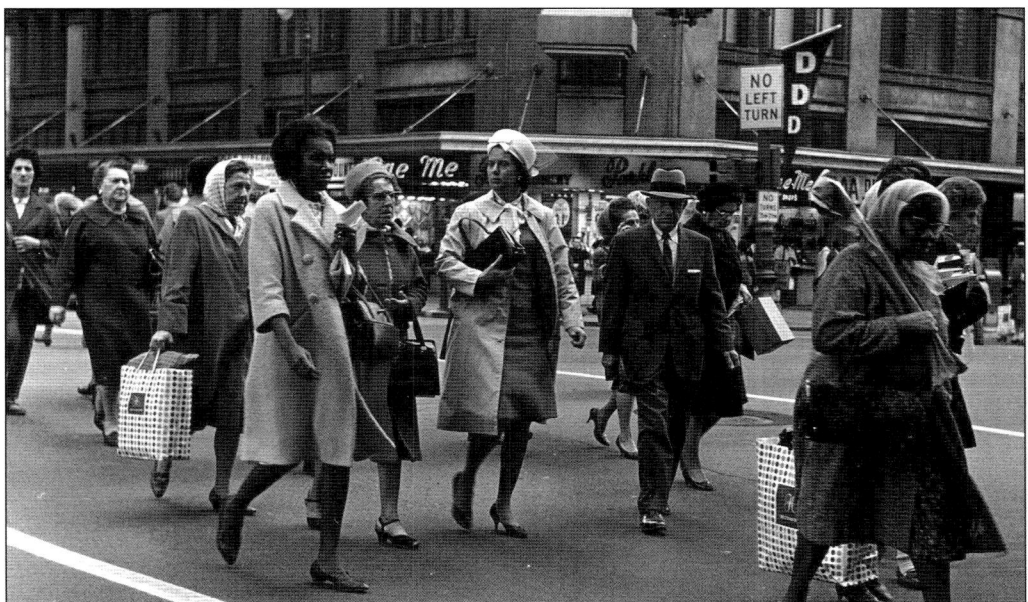

TEMPORARY RETAIL ON KERN'S MAIN FLOOR, 1965. The holiday season of 1960, one year following the closing of Kern's, provided shoppers with several new retailers. Parklane Hosiery and Rae Me Jewelry and Handbags opened their doors. Part of the difficulty of renting space in the building after Kern's closed was that the store sat on six parcels of land, owned by 19 different interests, representing 50 owners. (Courtesy Central Business District Foundation.)

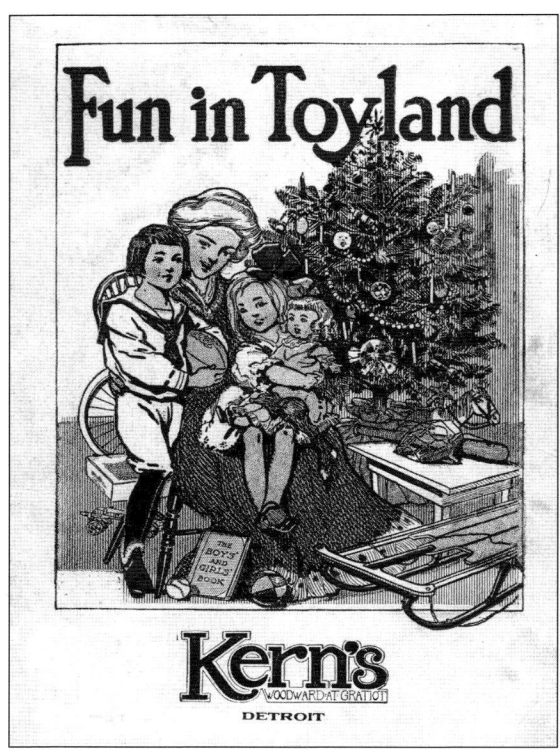

KERN'S FOURTH-FLOOR TOYLAND, 1920s. Kern's had a memorable acronym for spurring holiday sales in its toy department: "K stands for Kern's and Kris Kringle too! E stands for everyone, big folks and small. R is for reindeer. They pull Santa's sleigh from the North Pole to Kern's. N is for note—short for a letter: to write Kris is wise, to see him is better! S stands for Santa, whose home is at Kern's." (Courtesy Michael Hauser.)

KERN'S HOLIDAY CATALOG, 1958. Little did the public realize that this would be Kern's final holiday season. Shoppers flocked to Michigan's busiest corner, and street vendors still sold apples and roasted chestnuts at the front door of Kern's. Another Kern's tradition was carried on as well: 400 orphans were selected each year and treated to a special visit to the store's toyland that included a visit with Santa and a stocking filled with candy and toys. (Courtesy Michael Hauser.)

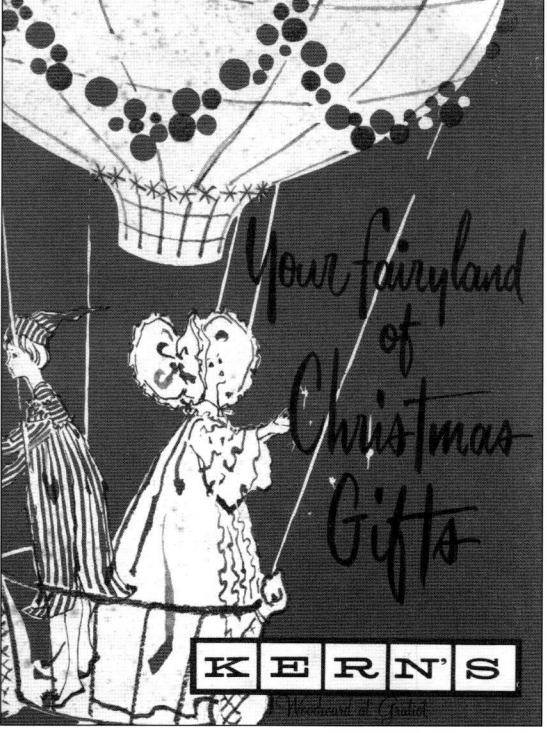

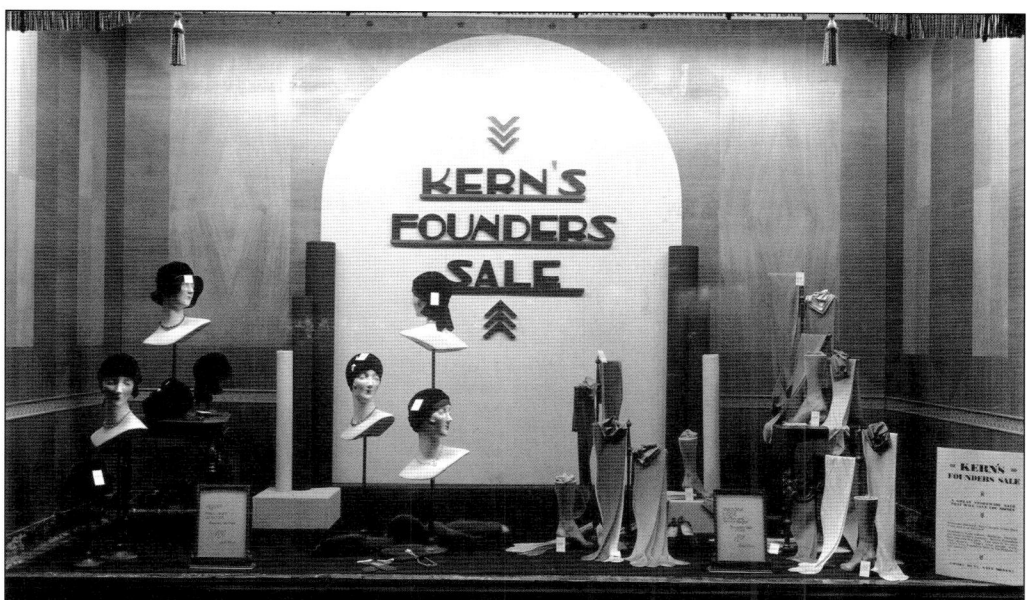

KERN'S FOUNDERS SALE WINDOW DISPLAY, 1920s. The Founders Sale was Kern's largest storewide sale conducted each September. The crowds became so immense for this extravaganza in the late 1930s that Chevrolet offered courtesy automobiles to shuttle shoppers home with their purchases. Signage and newspaper advertisements proclaimed the event was more than a sale, it was an achievement! (Courtesy Detroit Historical Museum.)

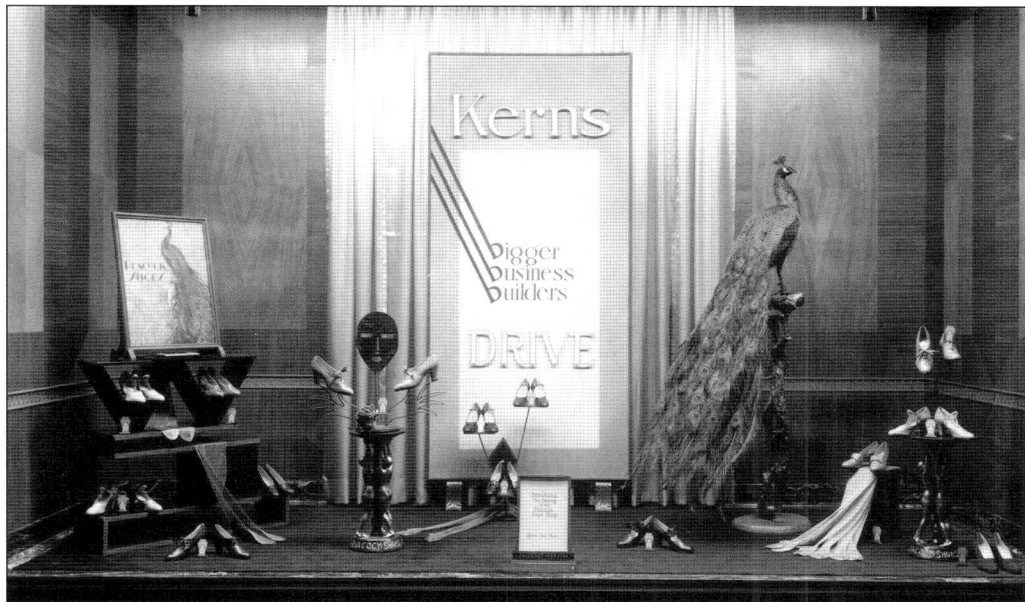

DISPLAY WINDOW PROMOTING KERN'S SALES DRIVE, 1920s. Display windows effectively acted as silent salespersons for the great amount of foot traffic on Woodward Avenue. The window above promotes the opening of the Peacock Shoe Salon on Kern's fashion floor. Kern's also created advisory boards comprised of high school and college students. These young folks provided merchandising advice to store buyers. (Courtesy Detroit Historical Museum.)

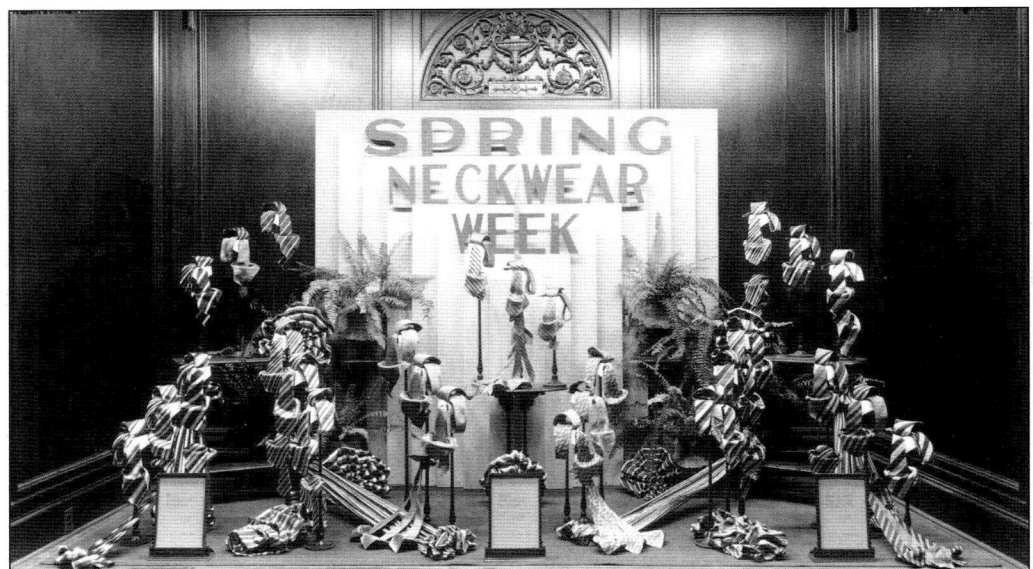

A CREATIVE WINDOW DISPLAY FOR MEN'S NECKWEAR, 1920S. Kern's always had an eye toward the future, and in 1939, the entire second floor was gutted to create a new Floor for Youth. It was hailed as "the most unique young people's department in America!" Kern's management included parents, teachers, and students in the planning process. Even the fixtures were scaled down and youth advisors selected colors to create a cheerful environment. (Courtesy Detroit Historical Museum.)

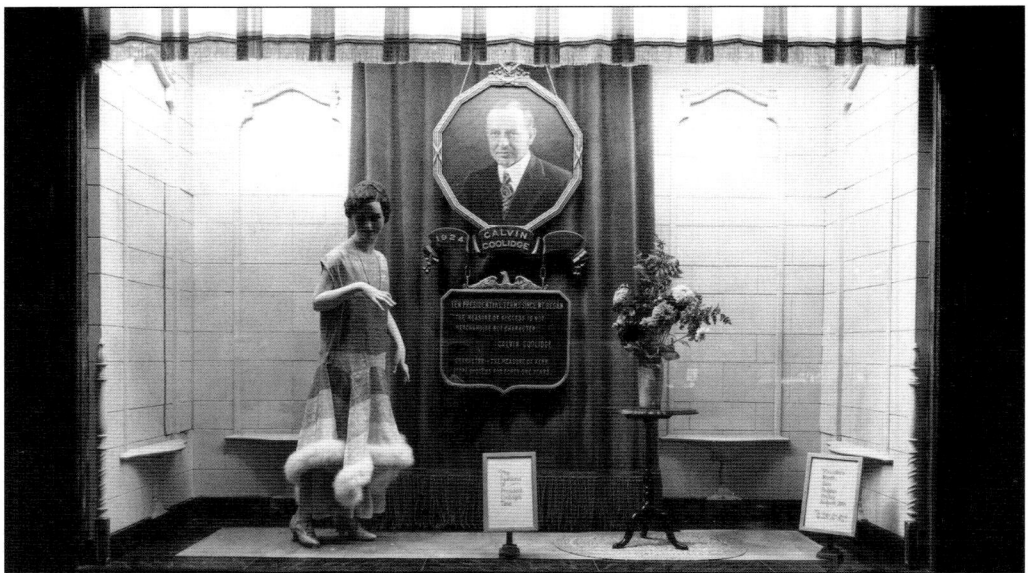

DISPLAY WINDOW TRIBUTE TO CALVIN COOLIDGE, 1924. In 1957, Kern's was sold to Sattler's Department Stores of Buffalo, New York. Otto Kern wanted to be relieved of the responsibility of running a large store. By this time, Kern's occupied over 200,000 square feet on 10 selling floors. Kern also cited a lack of parking, emerging suburban shopping centers, and the inability of Kern's to establish branch stores, as looming problems to be dealt with. (Courtesy Detroit Historical Museum.)

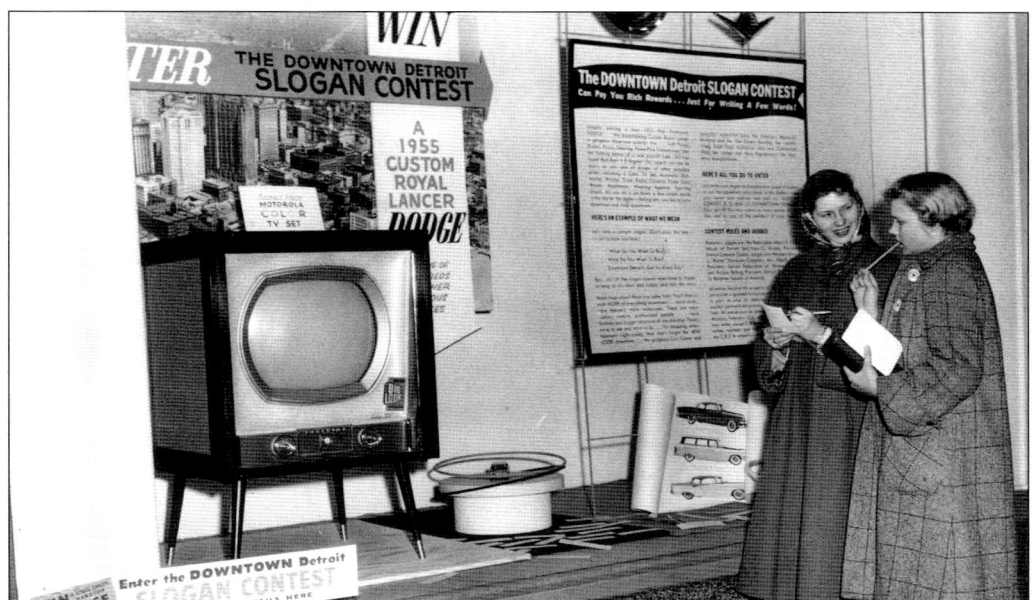

DOWNTOWN SLOGAN CONTEST, 1950S. In 1959, barely 20 months after the sale to Sattler's, Kern's again found a new owner. Benjamin Goldstein, a former Winkelman's executive, purchased the store and promised branch stores, upgraded merchandise, and a modernized physical plant. However, cash flow problems quickly arose, and the store closed its doors as its famous clock struck midnight on December 23, 1959. (Courtesy Central Business District Foundation.)

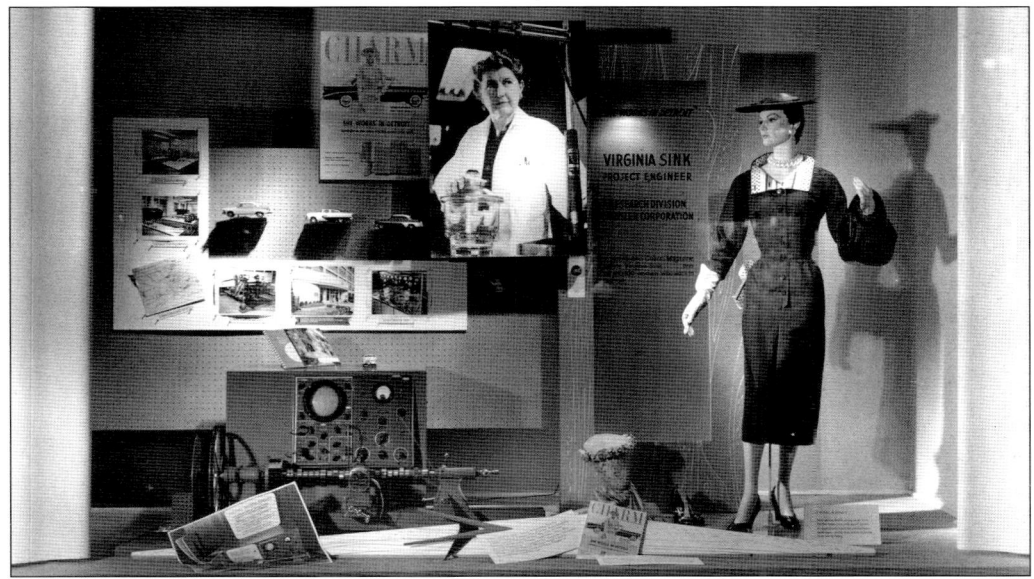

KERN'S AND CHARM MAGAZINE COLLABORATION, 1956. This display window features a salute to the 400,000 women who worked in Detroit at the time. Virginia Sink is feted as the only female chemical engineer at Chrysler Corporation. Kern's entire bank of windows on Woodward and Gratiot Avenues, planned in collaboration with the Central Business District Association, were devoted to this unique promotion of women in business. Other tie-in events included luncheons, fashion shows, and educational programs. (Courtesy Central Business District Foundation.)

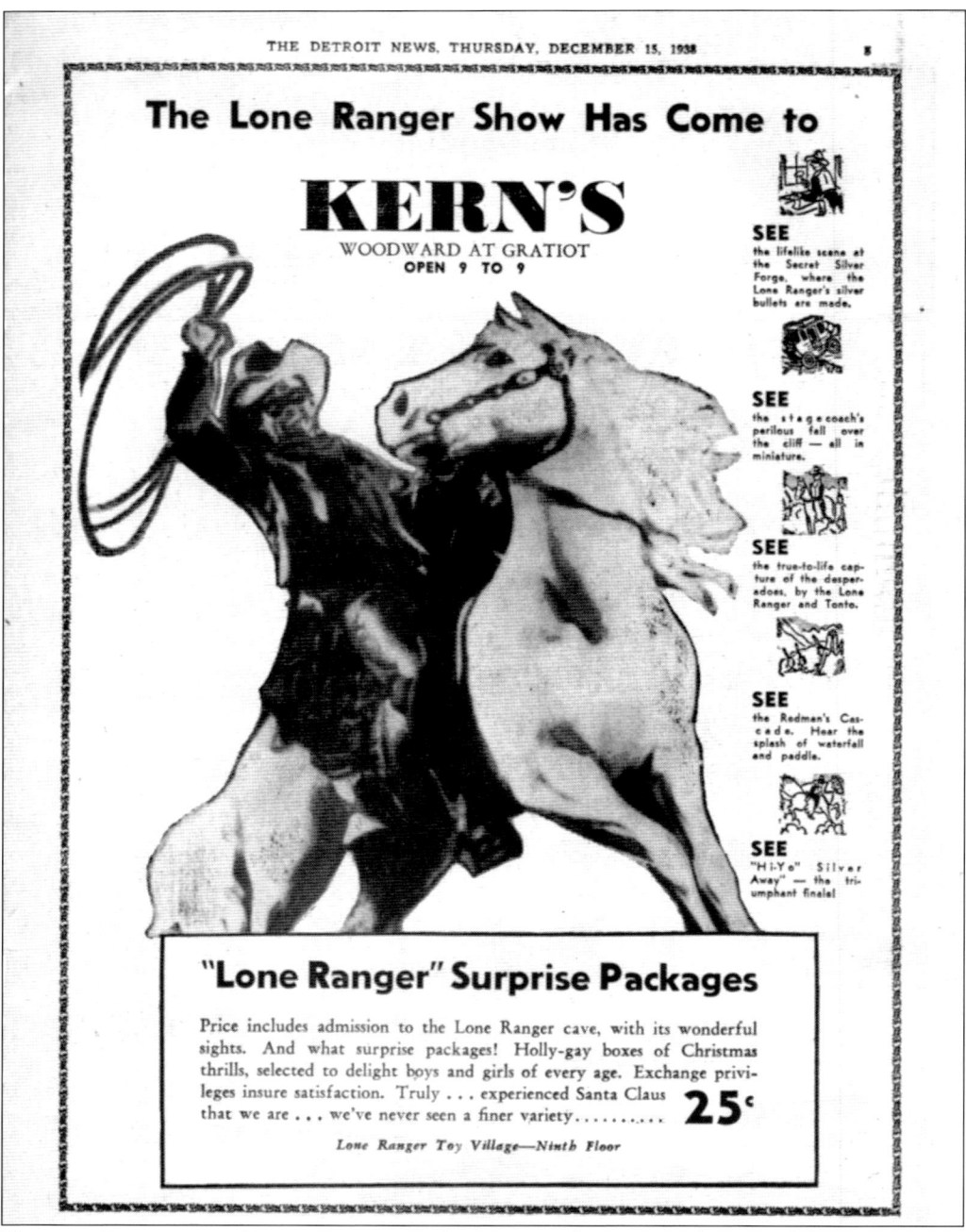

HOLIDAY EVENTS FOR CHILDREN AT KERN'S, 1938. In the 1920s and 1930s, children could not wait to ascend to Kern's ninth-floor toyland. A new theme was implemented every several years. In the 1930s, it was the Lone Ranger, and in the 1940s, it was Disney's Dumbo. Offerings included a free book from Santa, merry-go-round rides for 5¢, and surprise packages for 25¢. In later years, the toyland was expanded and moved to the fourth floor. (Courtesy Michael Hauser.)

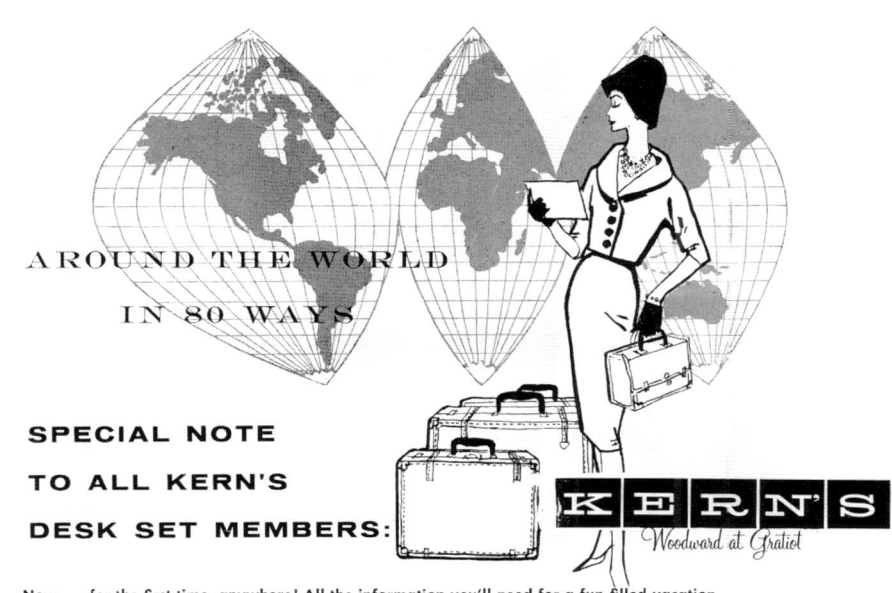

SPECIAL EVENTS AT KERN'S, 1959. Many special events such as the Desk Set initiatives to attract career women were held in the fourth-floor auditorium of Kern's. Kern's made this special area of the store available to nonprofit and community-oriented groups. The store also presented luncheon fashion shows each Wednesday in the casino at the Sheraton Cadillac Hotel, highlighting fashions and trends of the season. (Courtesy Central Business District Foundation.)

A NEW SHOPPING SERVICE FOR YOU THE WORKING GIRL

THE Desk SET

it's new... it's exciting... it's at the new Kern's!

It's Easy to Join

THE DESK SET . . .

Just fill out the coupon and mail to Kern's. There's no obligation. Tell your friends. They'll appreciate it, too.

THE DESK SET solves the problems of the working girl who must shop and eat on her limited lunch hour. It keeps her posted on services, fashions and private sales. There are no dues, no membership fees or other obligations.

DESK SET MEMBERSHIP CARD

provides you with these and many other services.

Fast efficient service

Quick service snack bar, now under construction.

Fashion shows, luncheons, career clinics, monthly newsletters.

Charge account plate identification.

One-stop service desk: shoe tinting, jewelry, handbags, etc.

KERN'S
Woodward at Gratiot

THE DESK SET
KERN'S
Woodward at Gratiot
Detroit 26, Michigan

Please enroll me as a member of THE DESK SET and send me a membership card.

Name_____

Home Address_____

City_____ Zone____ State____

Business Assoc._____

Business Address_____

3-3-58

THE DESK SET, 1958. Diane Edgecomb, of the Central Business District Association, pondered various ideas on how to reach Detroit's career women, who seemed to be forgotten by retailers. Kern's picked up her idea and implemented the Desk Set program in 1958. It included fashion shows, personal assistance, special sales, and interior design clinics. It also made charge accounts easier to obtain. Over 4,000 female professionals signed up for the program in its first year. (Courtesy Central Business District Foundation.)

ERNST KERN COMPANY PERSONALLY SALUTES

CKLW's Mary Morgan

Mary Morgan, CKLW's fashion and beauty editor, is the Ernst Kern Company's choice among the eight women saluted in Detroit's "Women Who Work Week", March 17 through 22.

An entire window display picturing Miss Morgan and the latest authentic Ladies' fashions has been devoted to her during Salute week.

CKLW radio 800 on the dial

GUARDIAN BLDG., DETROIT
RADIO and TV

KERN'S SALUTES MEDIA PERSONALITY MARY MORGAN, 1958. In conjunction with the Central Business District Association's Salute to Women Who Work Week, Kern's celebrated the career of Detroit and Windsor media personality Mary Morgan. Known as "the most beautiful woman on local radio," Morgan was one of CKLW's most high-profile personalities. Besides being the fashion and beauty editor for CKLW Radio, Morgan also hosted movies and interviewed celebrities on CKLW Television. (Courtesy Central Business District Foundation.)

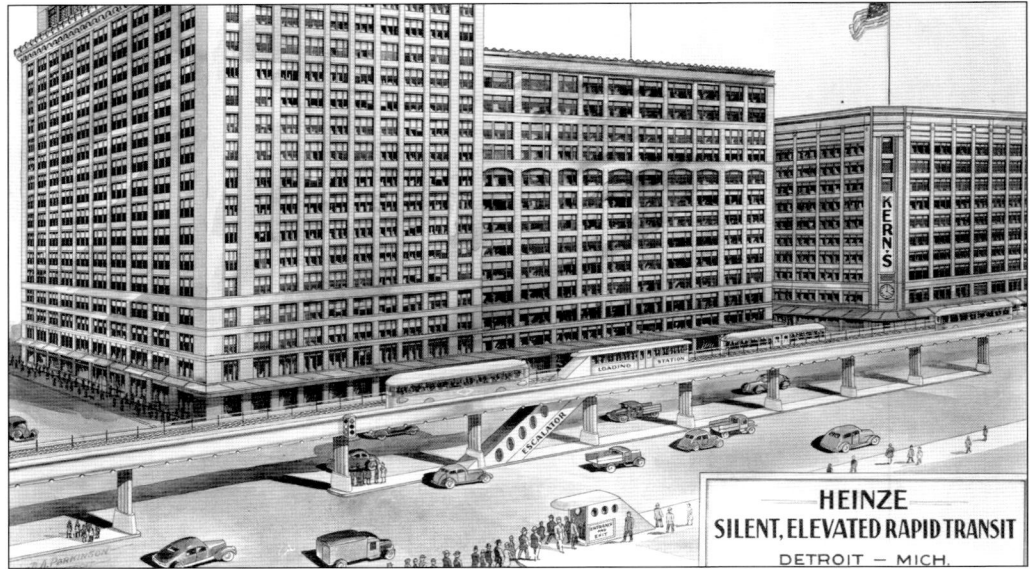

PROPOSED RAPID TRANSIT STOP AT KERN'S FRONT DOOR, 1947. Yet another proposal for rapid transit appeared as Detroit's population approached two million residents. This "silent" streamlined elevated system was 29 feet wide and supported by a single row of piers in the center of the street. The proposed route ran 13.75 miles from downtown, out Grand River Avenue to Seven Mile Road. This route was selected because there was no parallel artery at the time to relieve congestion. (Courtesy Central Business District Foundation.)

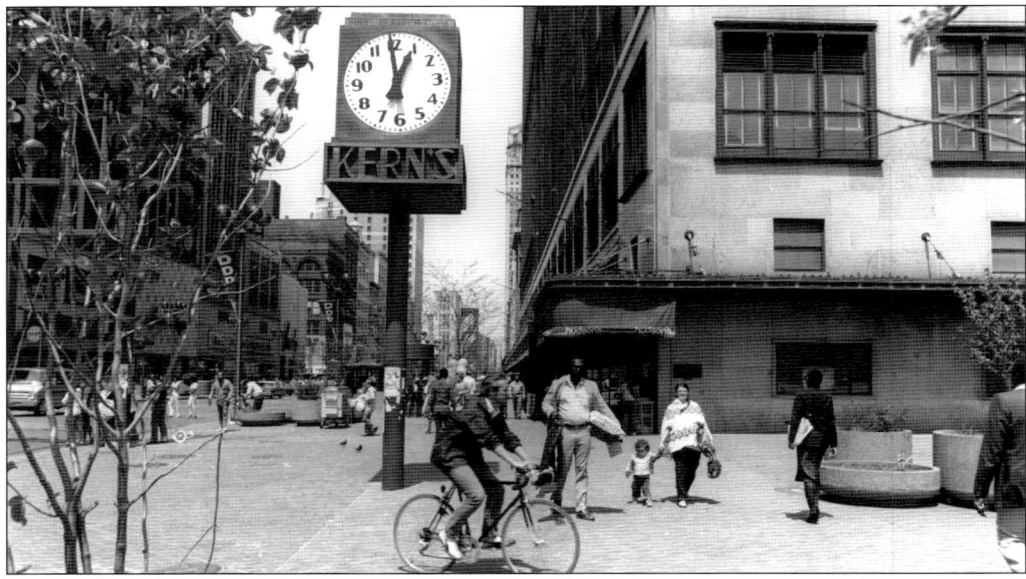

KERN'S CLOCK ON WOODWARD AVENUE, 1981. The Kern's clock that had adorned the store since 1933 was removed in 1966 and placed in storage. The Junior League of Detroit led a campaign to restore the two-ton clock in the late 1970s and in 1980 rededicated the icon at Woodward and Gratiot Avenues. The clock was removed in 1998 for the demolition of Hudson's and once again placed in storage. Compuware Corporation, which built its headquarters on the site of Kern's, restored the clock and rededicated it in 2003. (Courtesy Central Business District Foundation.)

Seven
SPECIALTY STORES AND SERVICES

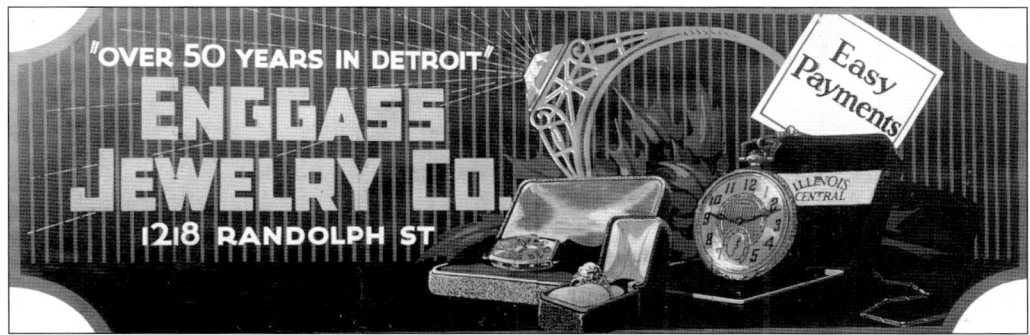

ENGGASS JEWELRY BILLBOARD, 1924. Enggass Jewelry Company was founded in 1865 and served patrons for a century. Originally on Randolph Street, the firm later moved to a more lucrative location next to the downtown Crowley's store on Monroe Street at Farmer Street. The store slogan was Where Grandma and Grandpa Bought! (Courtesy Detroit Historical Museum.)

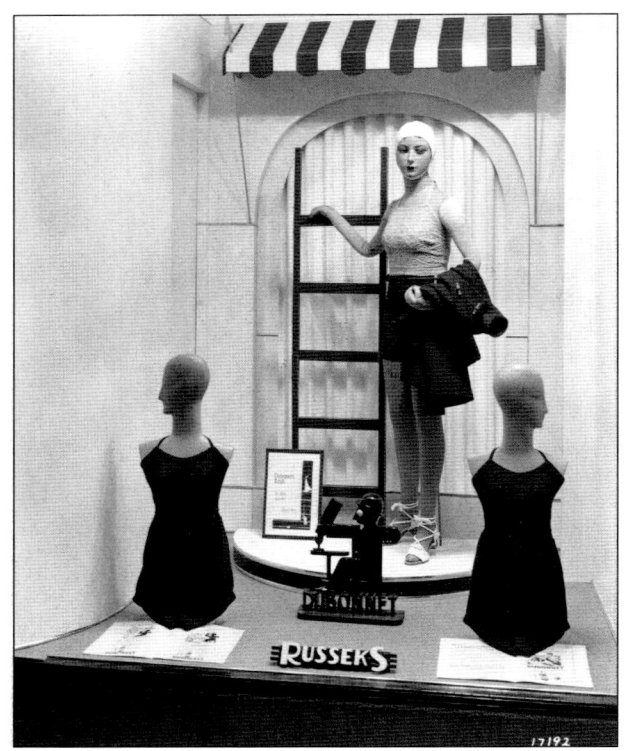

Russek's Window Featuring Dubonnet Swimwear, 1930s. Russek's was an upscale women's apparel retailer founded in 1922. "The shop of original modes" at 1448 Woodward Avenue also featured a stylish I. Miller Shoe Salon on the second floor. In 1956, following the demise of Russek's, Winkelman Brothers leased this building for its first downtown store. (Courtesy Detroit Historical Museum.)

Cast-Iron Exterior of B. Siegel Company, 1920. Benjamin Siegel was a German immigrant who founded the B. Siegel Company in 1881. It was located on Woodward Avenue, north of State Street. Siegel's became known as *the* place to purchase cloaks, suits, and furs. By 1904, the growing business moved to its landmark structure at 1075 Woodward Avenue. (Courtesy Walter P. Reuther Library, Wayne State University.)

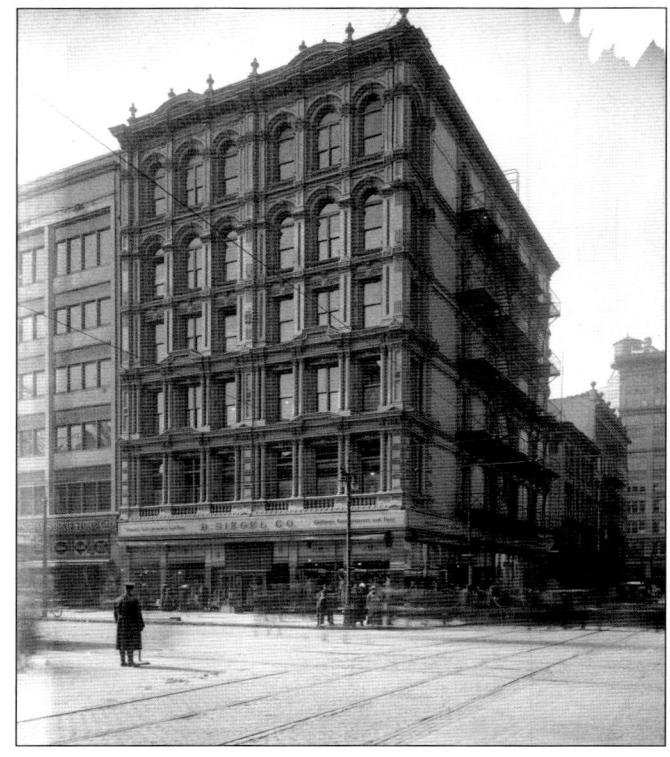

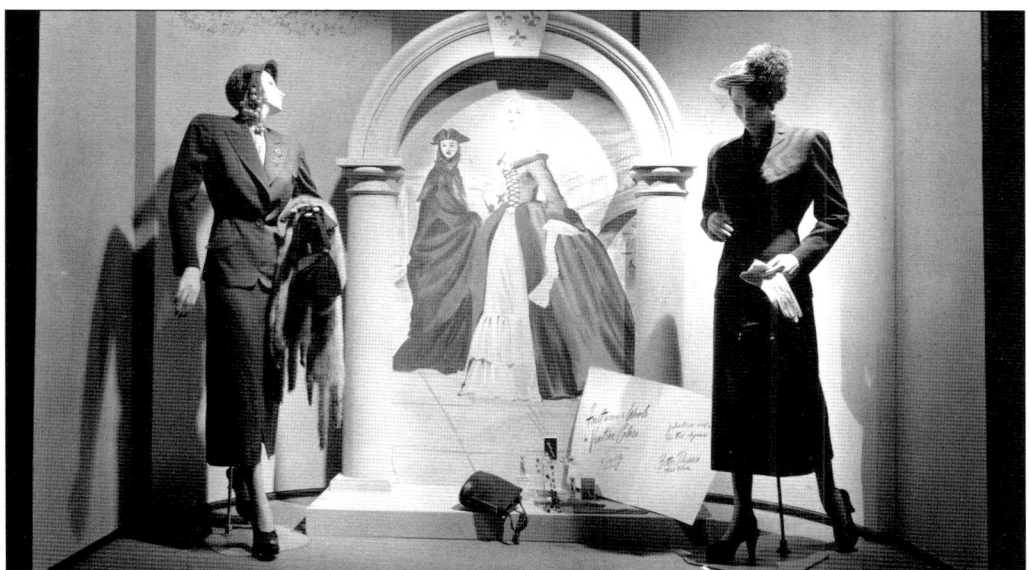

BETTER DRESS DEPARTMENT WINDOW DISPLAY AT B. SIEGEL'S, 1930S. Siegel's was one of the first retailers in the nation to specialize exclusively in women's wear. Children's furnishings were added later, and the store was known for providing each newborn in Detroit with a pair of baby shoes. The downtown store featured 42,000 square feet of fashion on six floors. Many receptions and fashion shows were staged in the upscale French Room. (Courtesy Detroit Historical Museum.)

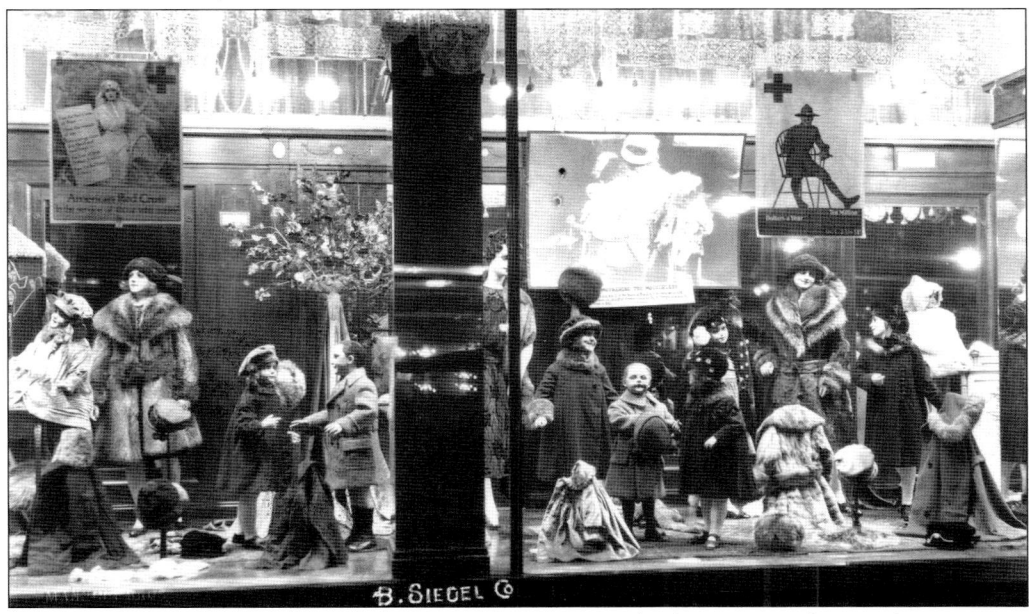

RED CROSS WINDOW DISPLAY AT B. SIEGEL'S, 1921. Siegel's slogan was Where Fashion Reigns, and the store was continually upgrading itself with major renovations in 1962, 1972, 1977, and 1979. Changing tastes, however, forced Siegel's to declare bankruptcy in 1981, and the company was sold to local investors who kept Siegel's alive until 1985. In 1990, a three-alarm fire destroyed the vacant store. (Courtesy Detroit Historical Museum.)

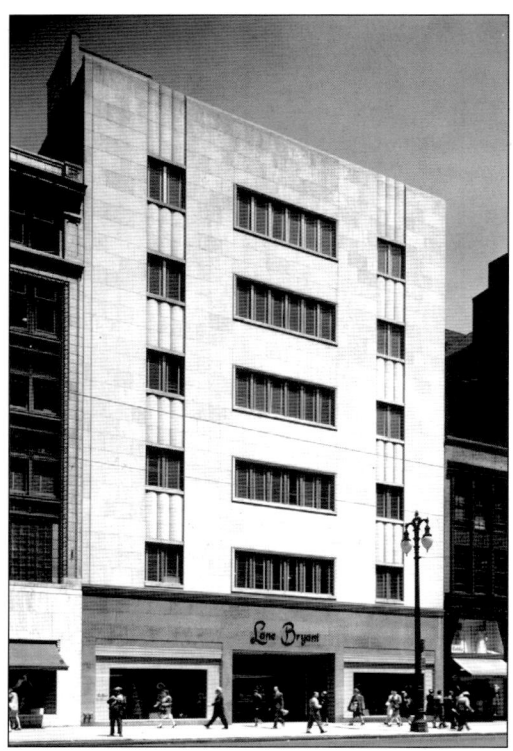

Lane Bryant, 1514 Woodward Avenue, 1947. Lane Bryant has been the leading national specialty store for plus-size women's fashions since the early 20th century. Its first Detroit store opened in 1916, near Hudson's. In 1945, the chain moved to a renovated art moderne structure on Woodward Avenue that was designed by Detroit architect Charles N. Agree. Opening festivities included an appearance by opera star Dorothy Sarnoff. The store closed in 1982 and was converted to a Smart Size outlet. (Courtesy Burton Historical Collection, Detroit Public Library.)

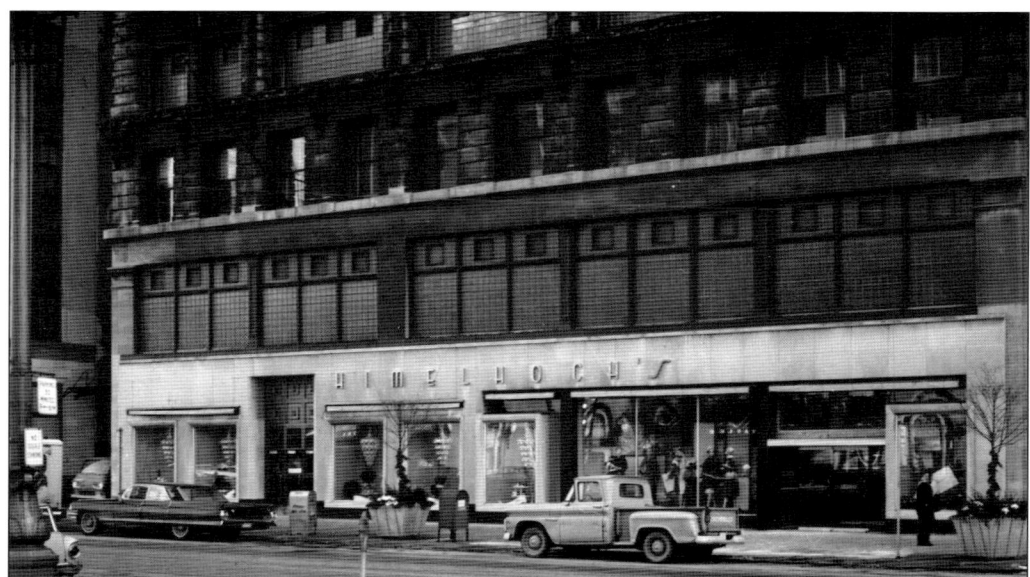

Himelhoch's Washington Boulevard Facade, 1960s. This upscale women's apparel retailer was founded in the 1870s by four Himelhoch brothers in Caro. The store moved to 1545 Woodward Avenue in 1907, with an additional entrance on Washington Boulevard. This handsome structure was designed by the prominent architectural firm of Donaldson and Meier. At its peak in 1957, the downtown store employed 600 people. (Courtesy Walter P. Reuther Library, Wayne State University.)

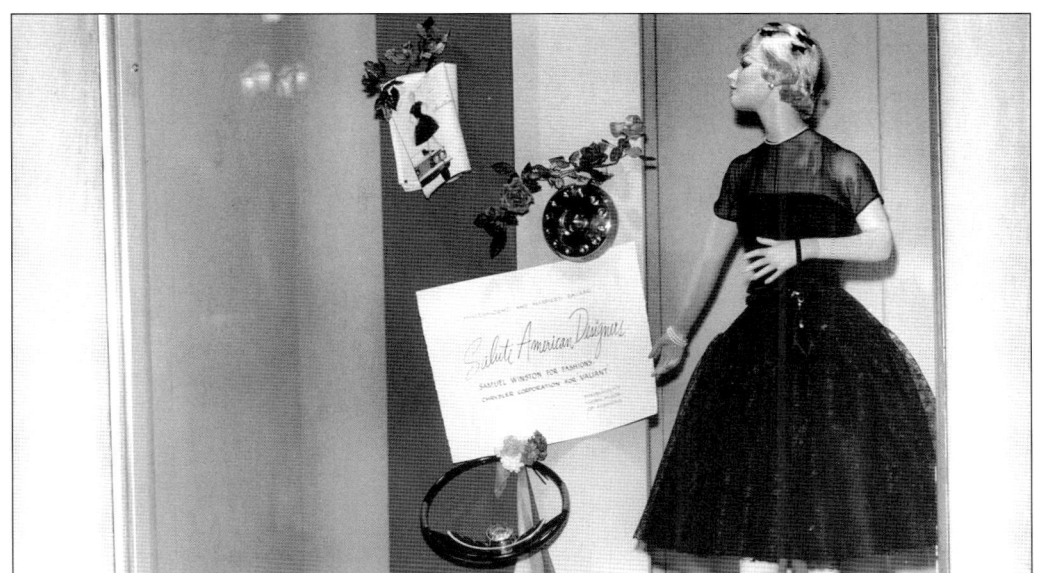

HIMELHOCH'S SALUTES AUTOMOBILE AND FASHION DESIGNERS, 1960. Himelhoch's and *Harper's Bazaar* joined forces to salute American design. The stylish Samuel Winston fashions in the window display above are augmented with steering wheels and hubcaps from Chrysler Corporation's Valiant division. Evolving lifestyles caught up with Himelhoch's, and the company filed for bankruptcy in 1978. The building was later converted to senior housing. (Courtesy Central Business District Foundation.)

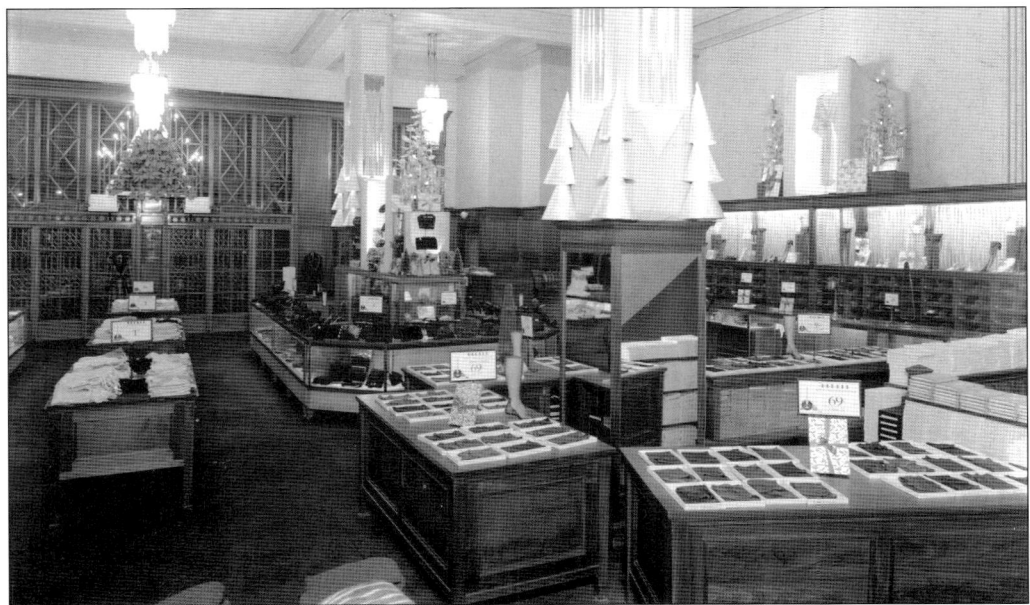

STYLISH ART DECO INTERIOR AT BEDELL OF NEW YORK, 1923. Bedell was a women's clothing chain based in New York with branches in major American cities. The company specialized in upscale fashions at moderate prices and prided itself on training local sales associates. The store at 1249 Woodward Avenue featured merchandise on 10 floors. This location later became Woolworth's. (Courtesy Detroit Historical Museum.)

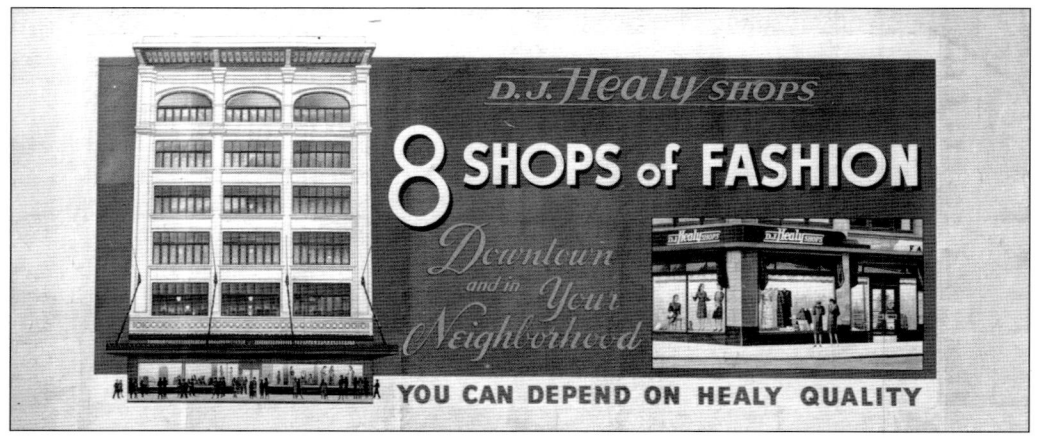

D. J. HEALY SHOPS BILLBOARD, 1944. D. J. Healy Shops was founded by Daniel Joseph Healy and Mary Kennedy in 1882 as a feather-cleaning shop. The first shop was located on the site of the David Whitney Building, with subsequent moves to locations on Woodward Avenue. In 1911, the Chicago architectural firm of Postle and Mahler designed a six-story edifice for the retailer. (Courtesy Detroit Historical Museum.)

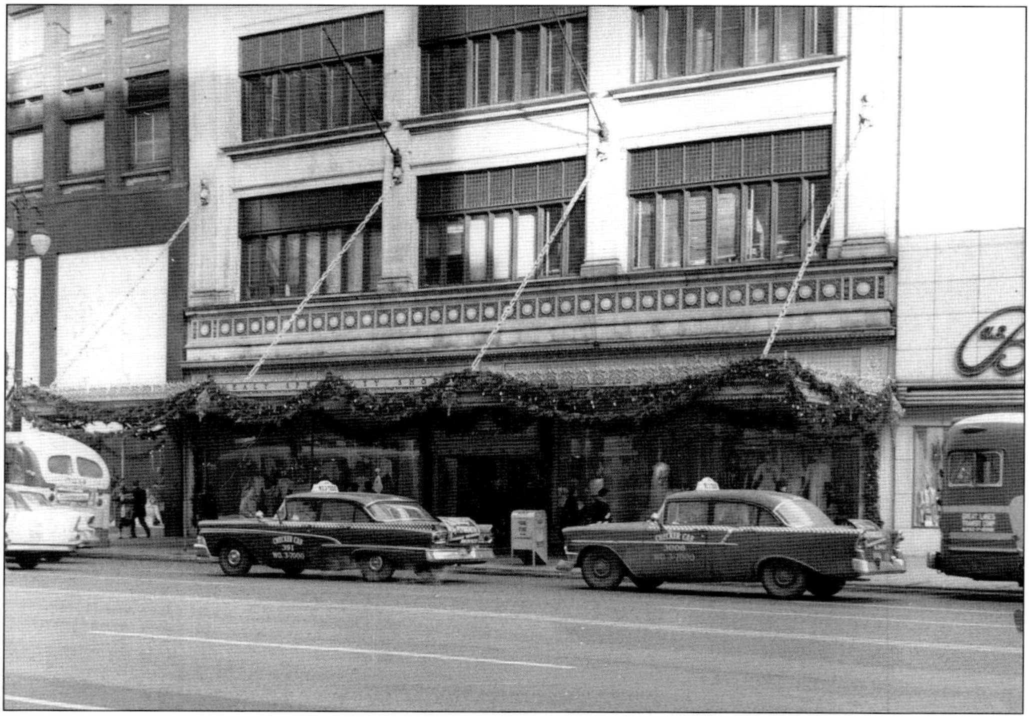

EXTERIOR OF D. J. HEALY SHOPS, 1426 WOODWARD AVENUE, 1958. Healy's was the first Detroit retailer to make European buying trips. One of the company's innovations for the new Woodward Avenue store was the shop-within-a-shop floor plan. Company troubles began in 1959 when Healy's filed for involuntary bankruptcy. The company was sold in 1960 to De Hayes Brothers, which held the firm together until 1962 when high operating costs forced the closing of the retailer. (Courtesy Central Business District Foundation.)

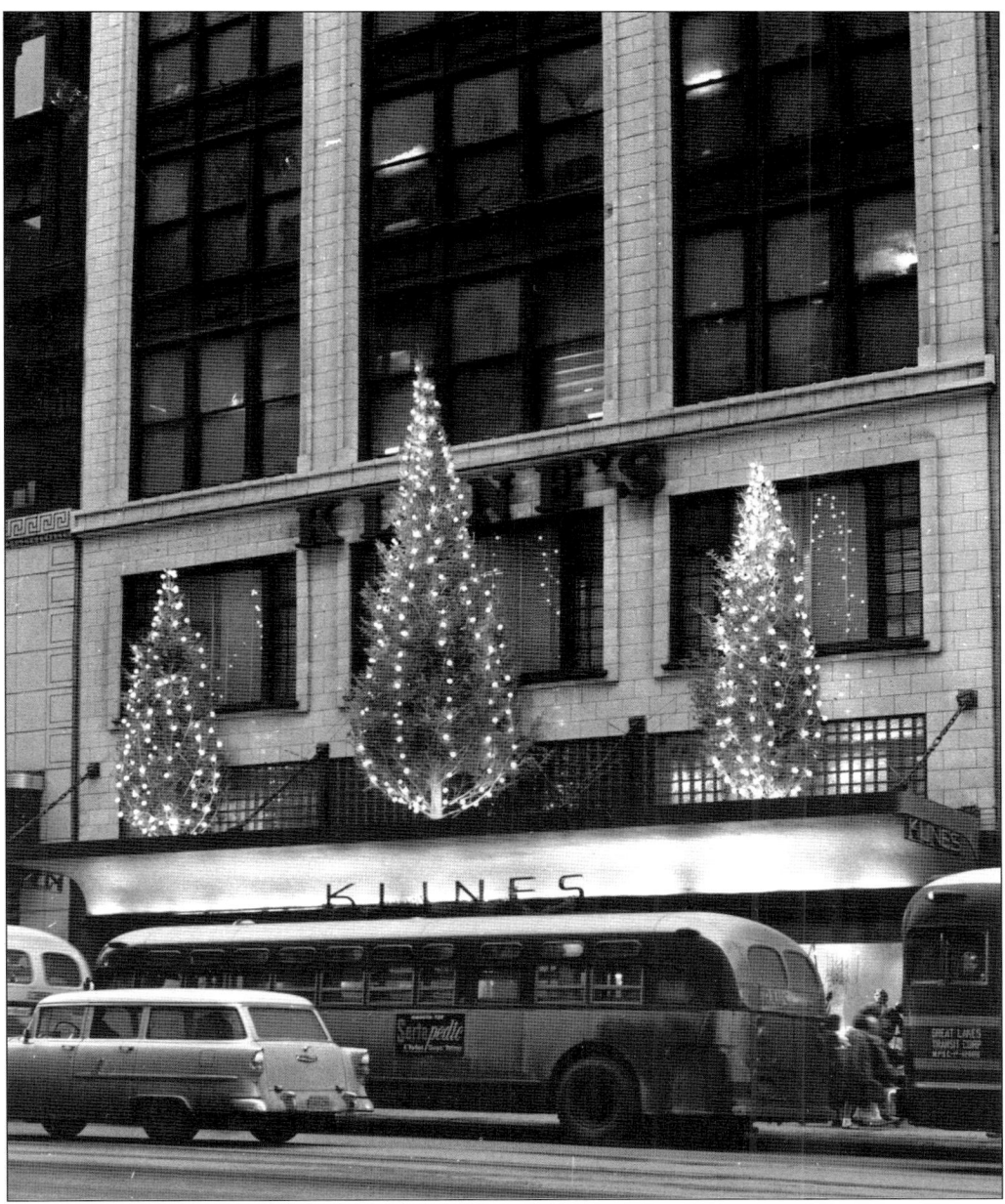

EXTERIOR OF KLINE'S WOMEN'S FASHIONS, 1958. Kline's was founded by Eugene B. Kline in 1911 at 1225 Woodward Avenue. With a streamlined entrance and display windows under a gleaming marquee, it was called the most modern store in the country in 1940. Merchandise was housed on eight floors. In 1958, Kline's was acquired by City Specialty Stores, operators of Franklin Simon Stores. Many shoppers found outstanding bargains during Downtown Detroit Days in the famous Franklin Simon Attic on the sixth floor. The store closed in 1977 and was succeeded by Pam's Fashions and later a beauty supply store. (Courtesy Central Business District Foundation.)

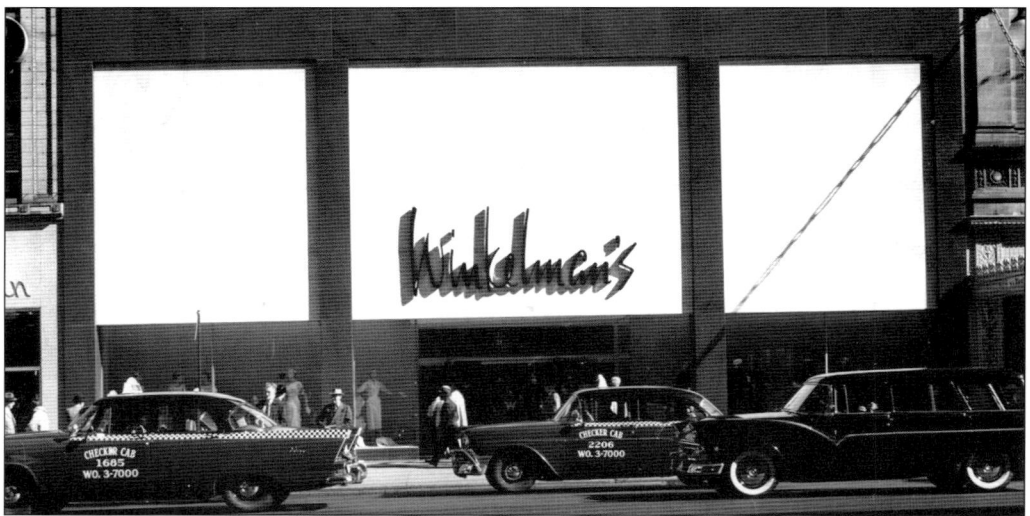

EXTERIOR OF WINKELMAN BROTHERS' NEW DOWNTOWN STORE, 1956. Winkelman's was founded in 1928 by brothers Leon and Isadore, who pioneered the concept of neighborhood specialty stores. By 1956, the company felt the timing was right to open a downtown store on Woodward Avenue. A total of $500,000 was spent to renovate the former Russek's location into a six-story pleasure dome of fashion. Winkelman's strength was serving 25-to-45-year-old career women. In 1984, New Jersey–based Petrie Stores acquired the company; however, Petrie filed for bankruptcy and closed all Winkelman's locations by 1998. (Courtesy Burton Historical Collection, Detroit Public Library.)

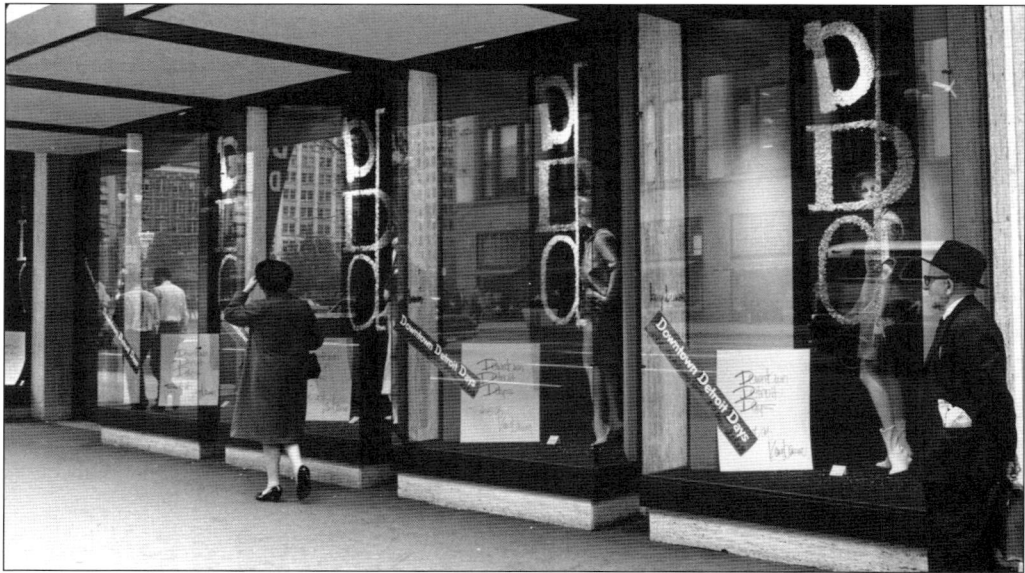

KAY BAUM WOMEN'S FASHIONS, 1966. Kay Baum was founded in 1937 by five brothers from metropolitan Detroit's Kershenbaum family. Following successful suburban expansion, the retailer opened a downtown store on Woodward Avenue in 1965. Kay Baum was the retailer of choice in the 1960s and 1970s for young women who sought the preppy look. The store failed to change quickly enough to keep up with consumer tastes, and by 1988, all stores were shuttered. (Courtesy Central Business District Foundation.)

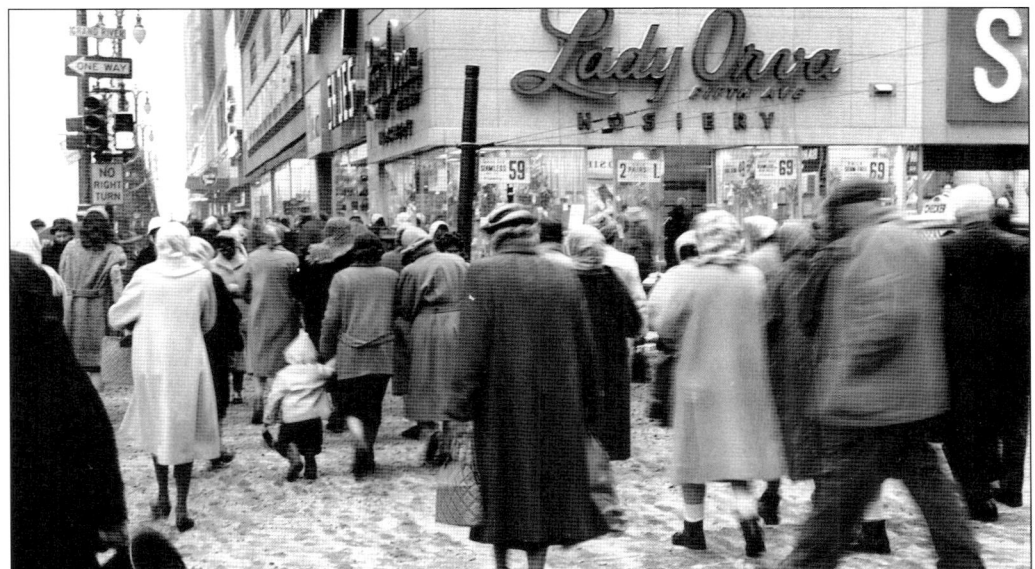

LADY ORVA HOSIERY, 1281 WOODWARD AVENUE, 1961. Lady Orva was a New York–based retailer founded in 1944 by Joseph Aizer. Its Woodward Avenue outlet opened in the late 1950s and was one of 20 stores the firm operated in major eastern cities. The chain specialized in hosiery, dance wear, and casual sportswear. Wigs were added in the late 1970s, but the store closed in the late 1980s as mainstream retailers could not exist without the traffic that had been generated by Hudson's. (Courtesy Central Business District Foundation.)

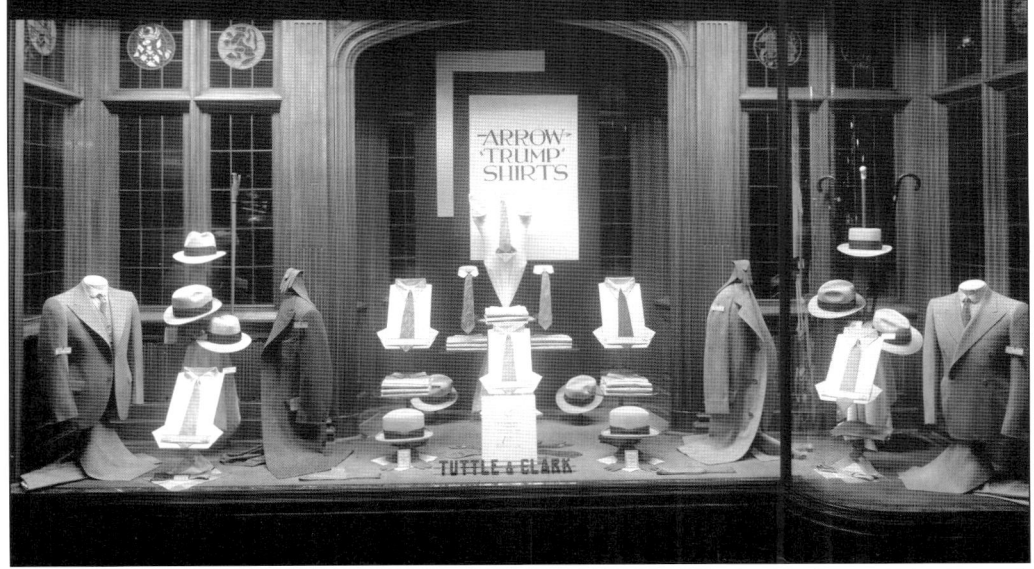

TUTTLE AND CLARK WINDOW DISPLAY, 1930S. Tuttle and Clark, founded in 1877 by Benojah Tuttle, began as a harness manufacturer. Tuttle partnered with John G. Clark in 1895 to form Tuttle and Clark. By 1913, Elmer E. Tuttle, son of the founder, joined the firm and is credited with diversifying the company by selling home furnishings and clothing. In 1915, an eight-story, 50,000-square-foot building was constructed at 1525 Woodward Avenue to house the firm. The downtown store closed in 1942. (Courtesy Detroit Historical Museum.)

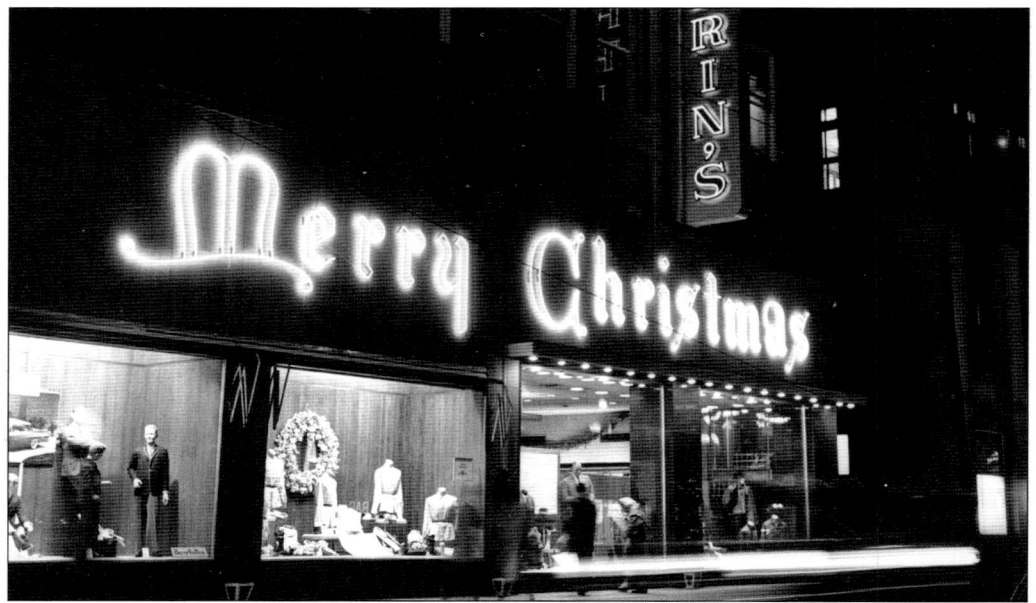

HARRY SUFFRIN'S, 1133 SHELBY STREET, 1958. Suffrin's began in 1922 and for many years proclaimed itself Detroit's largest men's clothier. The store was known not only for its vast selections but for its customer service, including free alterations. Newspaper taglines for the store read, "You know, some of the nicest people I met were at Harry Suffrin's!" The firm was acquired by Hughes and Hatcher in 1959. (Courtesy Central Business District Foundation.)

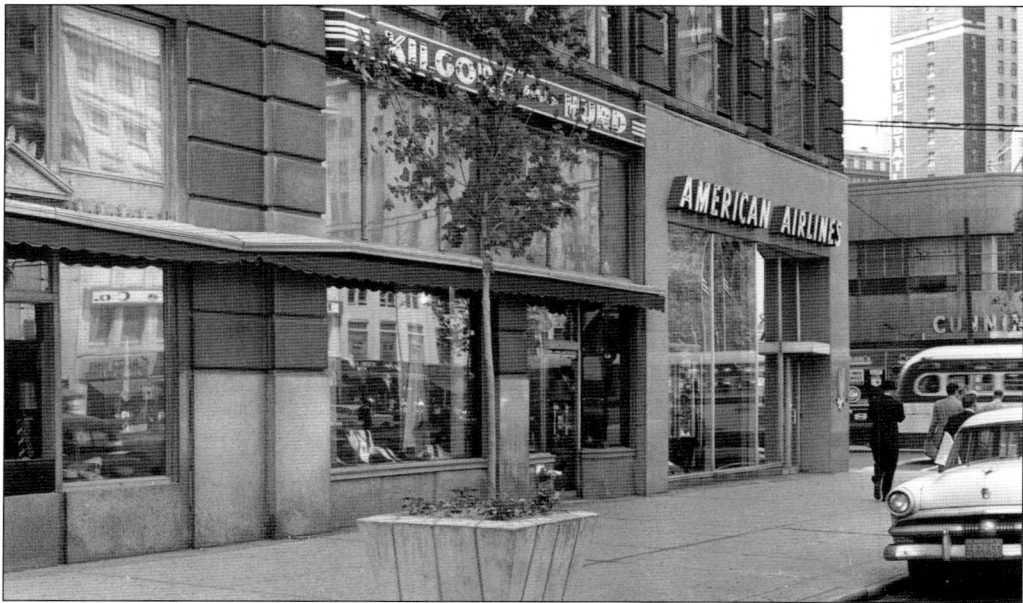

EXTERIOR IMAGE OF KILGORE AND HURD, 1959. Kilgore and Hurd was located at 1255 Washington Boulevard in the Book Building. The company was founded in 1937 by Red Kilgore and Delmar Howard Hurd. The store prided itself on selling "gentlemen's attire." The popular retailer was not able to renegotiate a lease with the building owner, and the doors closed in 1970. (Courtesy Central Business District Foundation.)

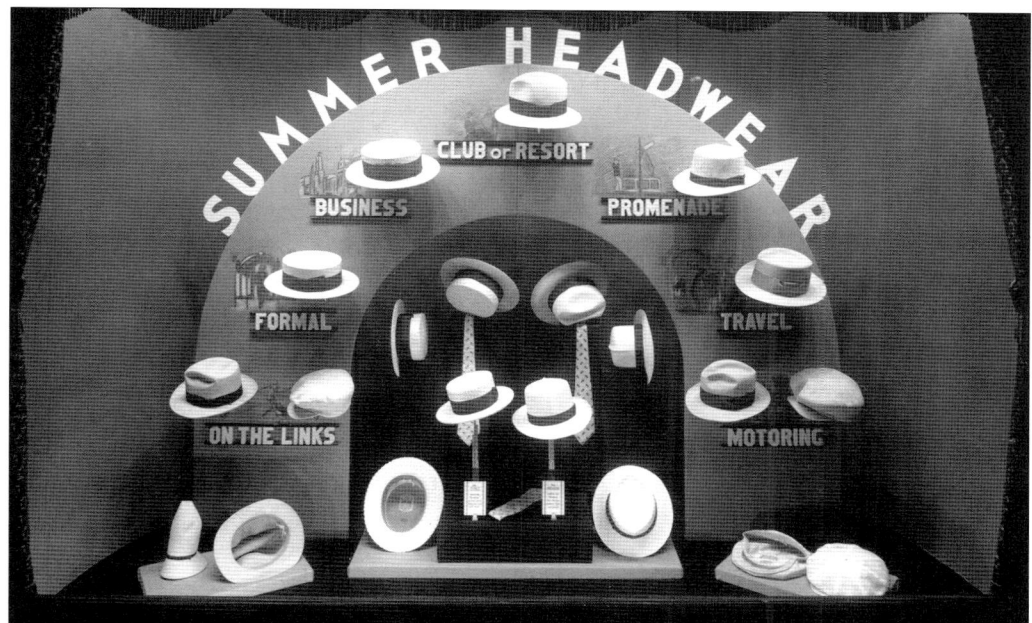

S. L. Bird and Sons Window Featuring Society Brand Clothing, 1920s. Bird's was founded in 1890 by R. H. Traver at 1219 Woodward Avenue. By 1903, S. L. Bird, father of the brothers who operated the business, partnered with Traver. The company billed itself as "Detroit's largest clothier" with four branch locations. (Courtesy Detroit Historical Museum.)

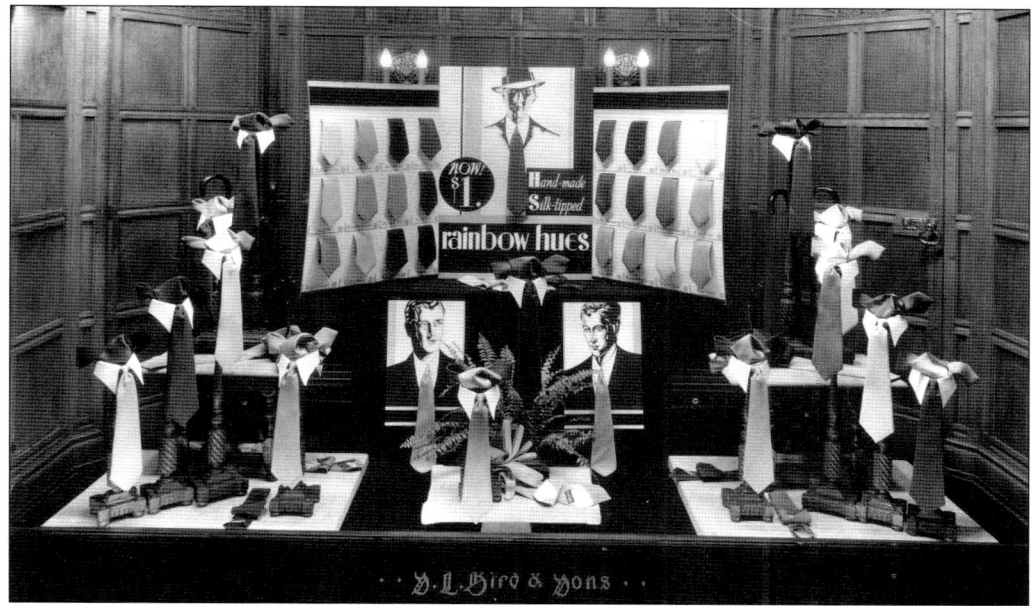

Stylish S. L. Bird Window Display for Neckties, 1920s. In 1937, Bird's stunned the retail community by announcing that it would be leaving its prominent home on Woodward Avenue and moving west to Washington Boulevard. The firm spent $150,000 to renovate the seven-story Stevens Building, which afforded it the opportunity to add women's fashions. In 1952, Bird's was purchased by the B. R. Baker Company of Toledo. (Courtesy of Detroit Historical Museum.)

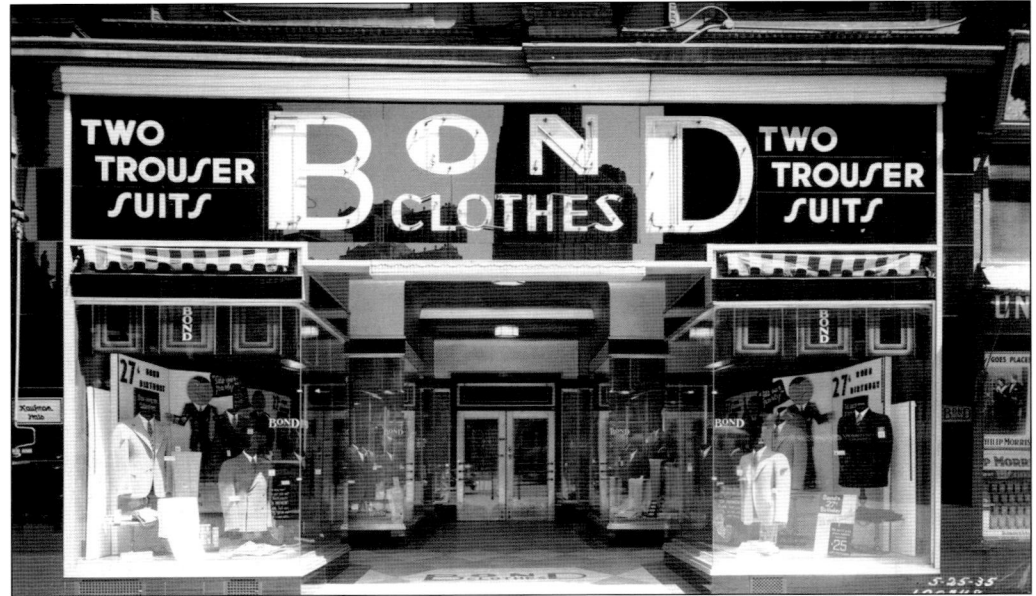

BOND CLOTHIERS ON CAMPUS MARTIUS, 1935. Bond Clothiers' first Detroit store was located at 37 Campus Martius, adjacent to the Detroit Opera House. New York–based Bond's became the largest retail chain of men's clothing in the country. It was best known for selling two trouser suits and for its 10-payment plan whereby a customer could pay weekly or twice a month. (Courtesy Detroit Historical Museum.)

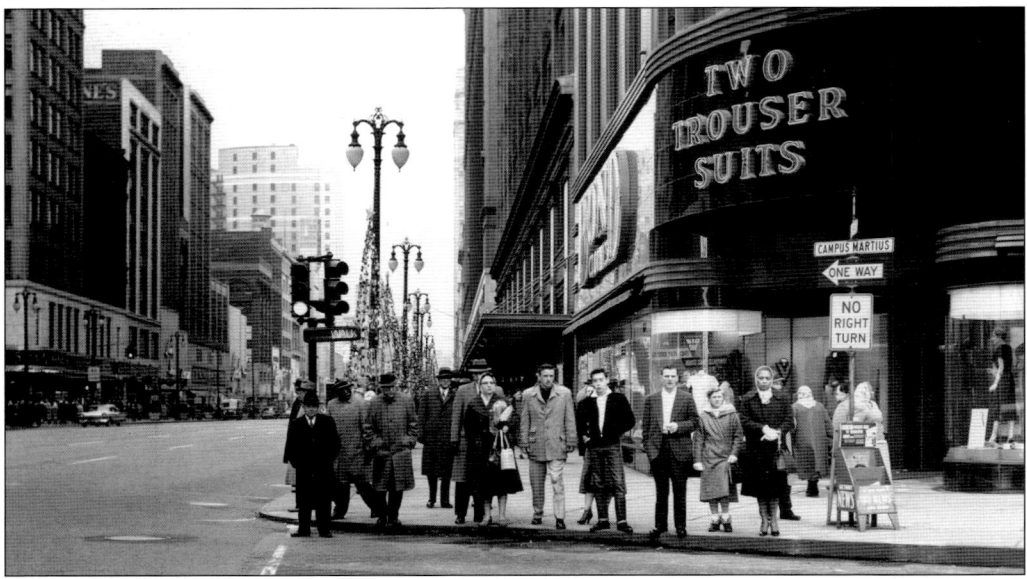

BOND'S WOODWARD AVENUE STORE, 1959. In 1937, Bond's moved to the northeast corner of Woodward Avenue and Campus Martius, next to the Ernst Kern Company. Chicago architects Lachenko and Esser designed a stunning six-story art moderne structure that housed Bond's on the first four floors with Kern's housing various departments in the basement and on remaining floors. When this block was demolished in 1966, Bond's moved to 1525 Woodward Avenue, where the firm stayed until closing in 1977. (Courtesy Central Business District Foundation.)

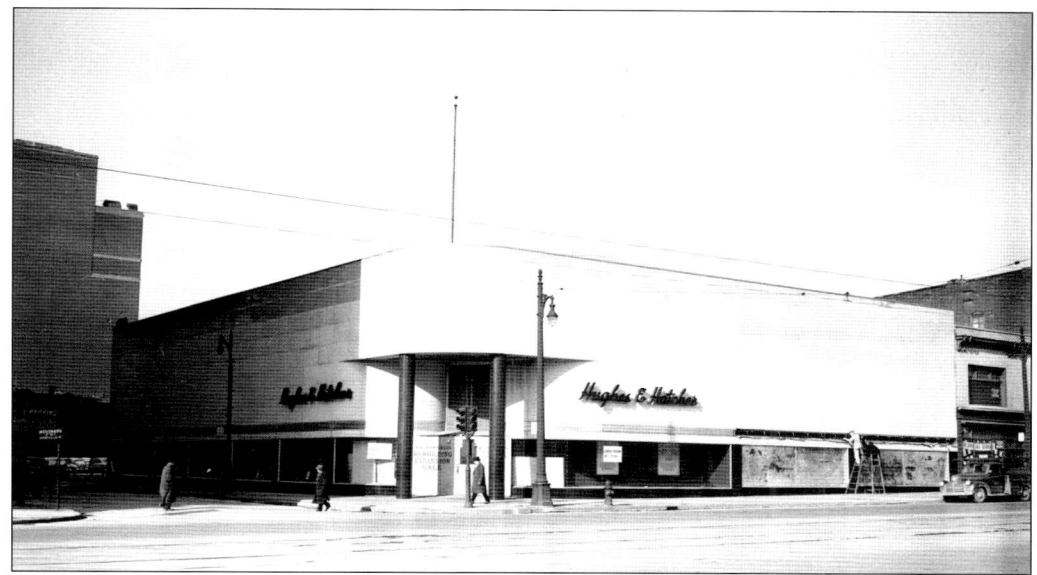

HUGHES AND HATCHER, 2305 WOODWARD AVENUE, 1940. Hughes and Hatcher was founded in 1910 by Fred Hughes and Leslie Hatcher as a fine menswear retailer. The move to Woodward Avenue and Montcalm Street in 1911 followed an earlier location farther uptown. The streamline-style store was designed by Detroit's C. Howard Crane architectural firm, which also designed the 1939 and 1949 additions to the store. (Courtesy Walter P. Reuther Library, Wayne State University.)

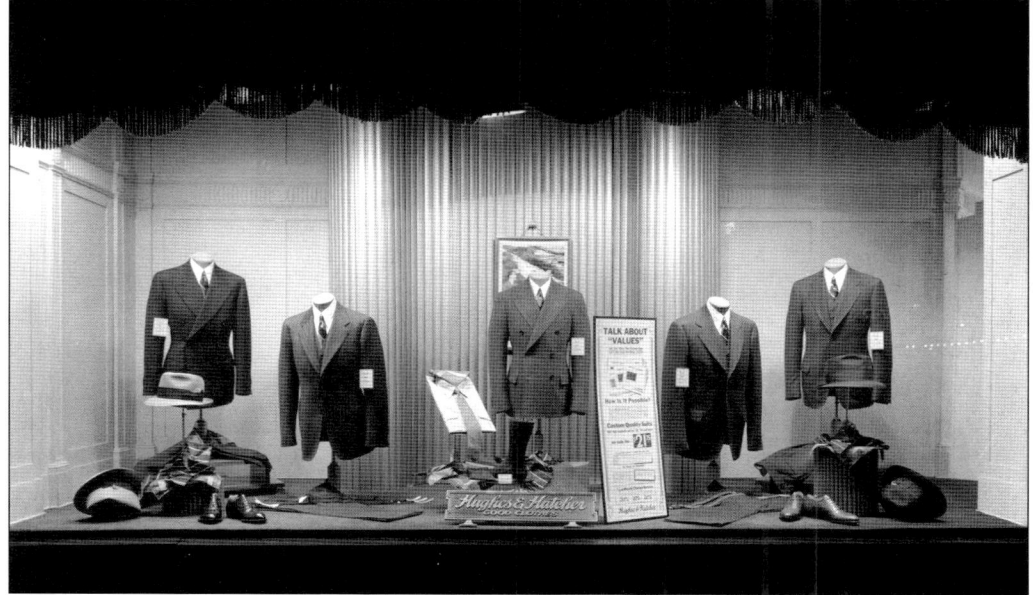

HUGHES AND HATCHER VALUE-ORIENTED WINDOW DISPLAY, 1930S. Slogans through the years included Everything a Man Will Wear! and Detroit's Accepted Style Corner. Women's fashions were added in 1944. With the 1949 addition, the 40,000-square-foot Montcalm Street store featured the largest fluorescent-lit interior in the country and the largest display windows in Detroit. (Courtesy Detroit Historical Museum.)

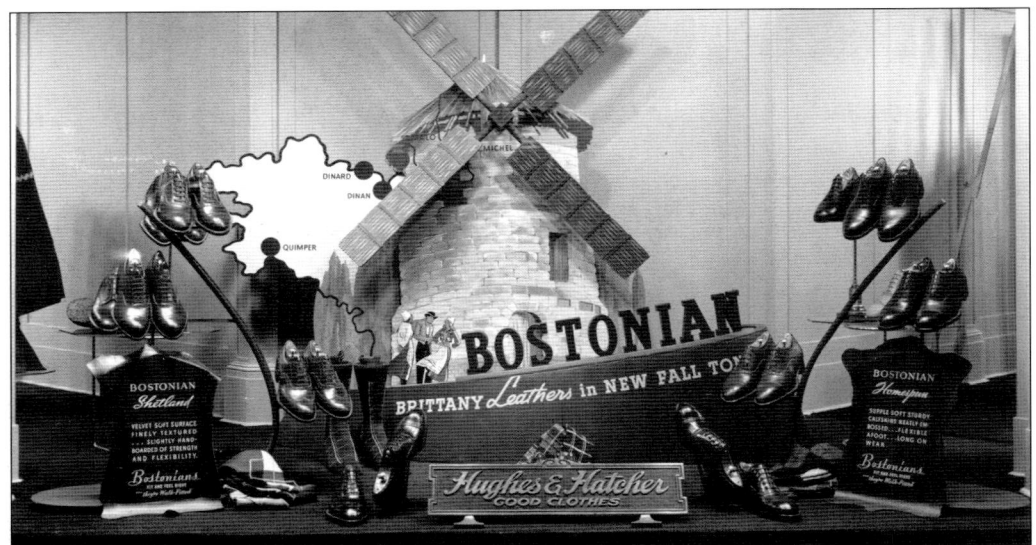

HUGHES AND HATCHER BOSTONIAN SHOE DISPLAY, 1930S. In 1966, Hughes and Hatcher purchased two structures at 1059 and 1065 Woodward Avenue. They were demolished to construct a new five-story flagship store across the street from Hudson's. The company survived several ownership changes in the 1970s and 1980s. Due to slumping sales, the Montcalm Street store was closed in 1981, and shortly thereafter, the company filed for bankruptcy. The Montcalm store was later renovated into what is today the Hockeytown Café and City Theatre. (Courtesy Detroit Historical Museum.)

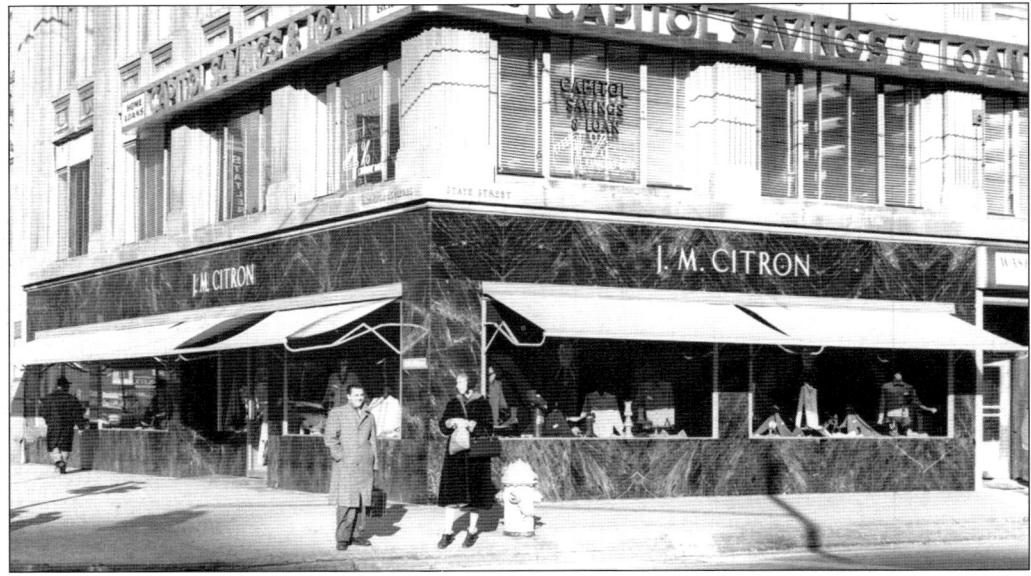

J. M. CITRON MEN'S FURNISHINGS, 1200 WASHINGTON BOULEVARD, 1960. J. M. Citron was a long-standing men's clothier on Washington Boulevard. Because of the store's location, there was much foot traffic from the nearby Statler Hilton and Sheraton Cadillac Hotels. A complete renovation in 1960 prolonged the life span of the retailer into the early 1980s. By then, the once elegant Washington Boulevard was all but deserted of retail, hotels, and restaurants. (Courtesy Central Business District Foundation.)

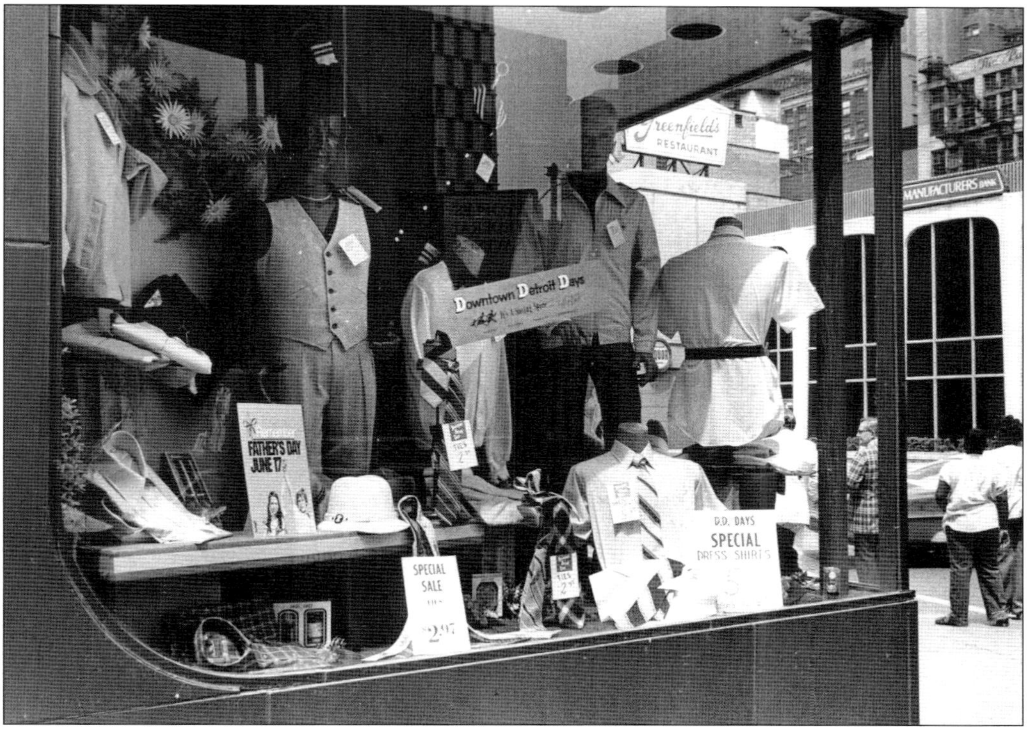

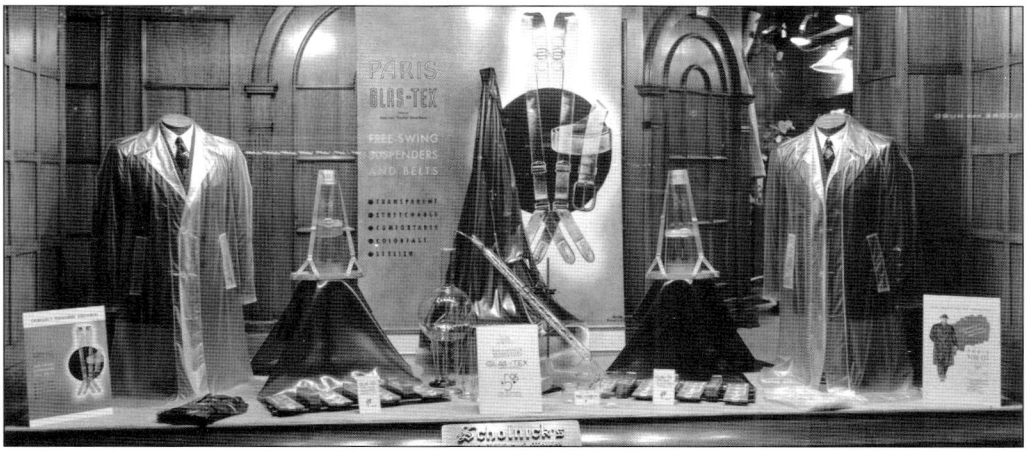

UNITED SHIRT DISTRIBUTORS, 107 MICHIGAN AVENUE, 1979. United Shirt was a local chain of men's clothing stores with 40 locations, including four downtown stores. United was one of the earliest retailers to stay open every evening. The chain was purchased by Interco Industries in 1974. By 1991, Interco had overexpanded and began divesting its holdings, including United Shirt, which closed later that year. (Courtesy Central Business District Foundation.)

SCHOLNICK'S IMPORTERS, 1400 WASHINGTON BOULEVARD, 1940. Scholnick's was a local men's clothier. The display window above is promoting Paris Glas-Tex accessories, which were transparent, stretchable, comfortable, and colorfast. The store was known as being the "style center for men." In 1982, a designer shoe salon for men and women was added. The continued decline of Washington Boulevard forced the store to close by 1990. (Courtesy Detroit Historical Museum.)

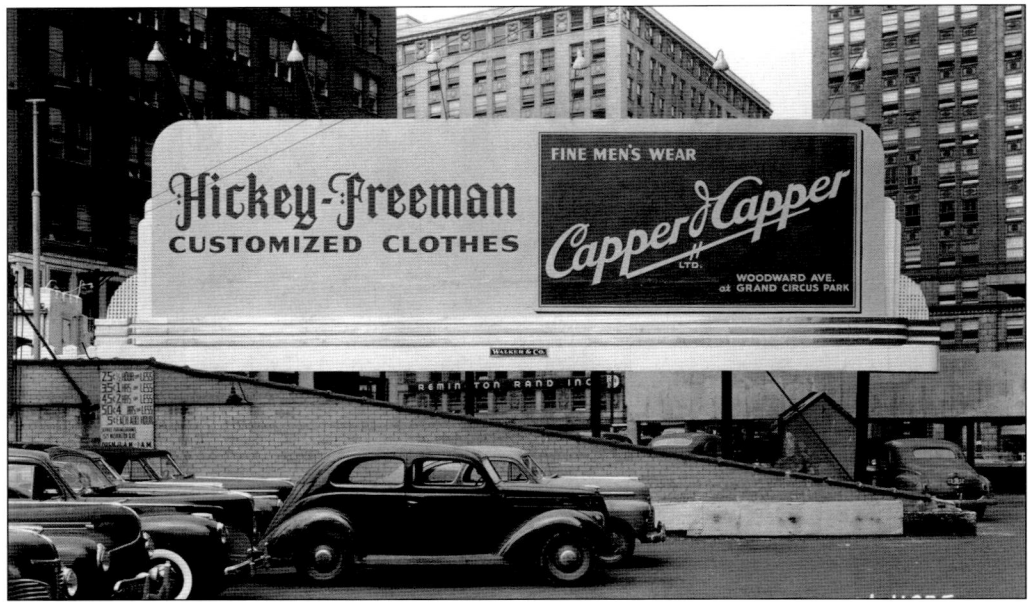

BILLBOARD FOR CAPPER AND CAPPER, 1946. Capper and Capper was a fine men's clothing store located on the main floor of the David Whitney Building. It was the exclusive Detroit retailer for Hathaway dress shirts and Hickey Freeman suits. As the tenant roster of the Whitney Building declined, the store was forced to close its doors in the late 1980s. (Courtesy Detroit Historical Museum.)

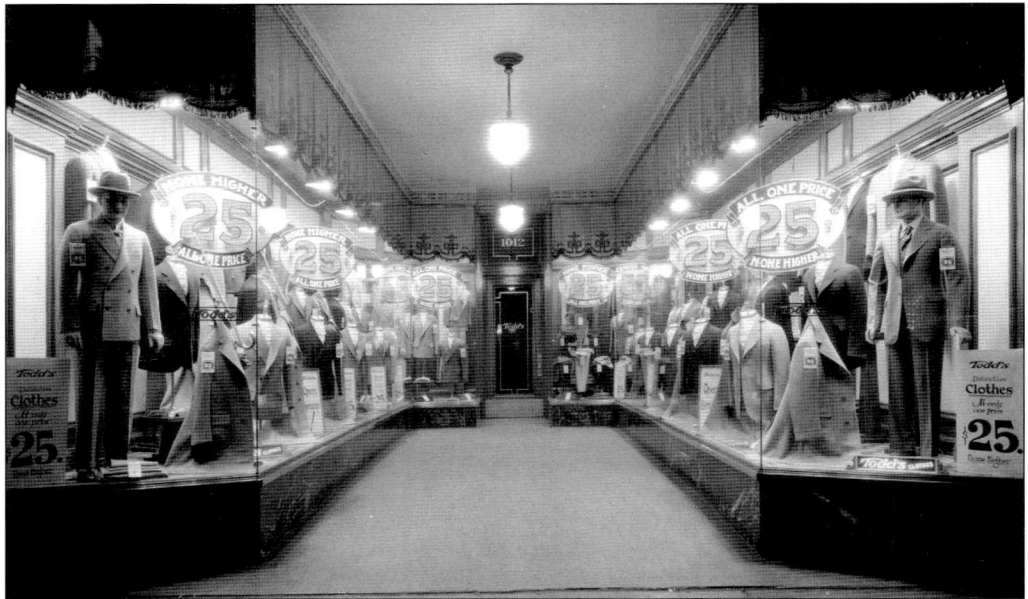

TODD'S MEN'S CLOTHING, 1012 RANDOLPH STREET, 1930S. Todd's, founded by Nathan Elkus in 1933, was located at Randolph and Monroe Streets on the ground floor of the former 1874 Odd Fellows temple. Todd's distinguished itself from competitors by offering all of its distinctive clothing at "just one price, $25, none higher." The store closed in 1975 and was replaced by Classic Men's Wear, which flourished until 2006. (Courtesy Detroit Historical Museum.)

WHALING'S MENS WEAR, MID-1960S. Whaling's began in 1905 near Jefferson and Woodward Avenues. Through the decades, Whaling's made several moves between the 500 and 600 blocks of Woodward. The downtown store relocated to the Renaissance Center in 1979. (Courtesy Central Business District Foundation.)

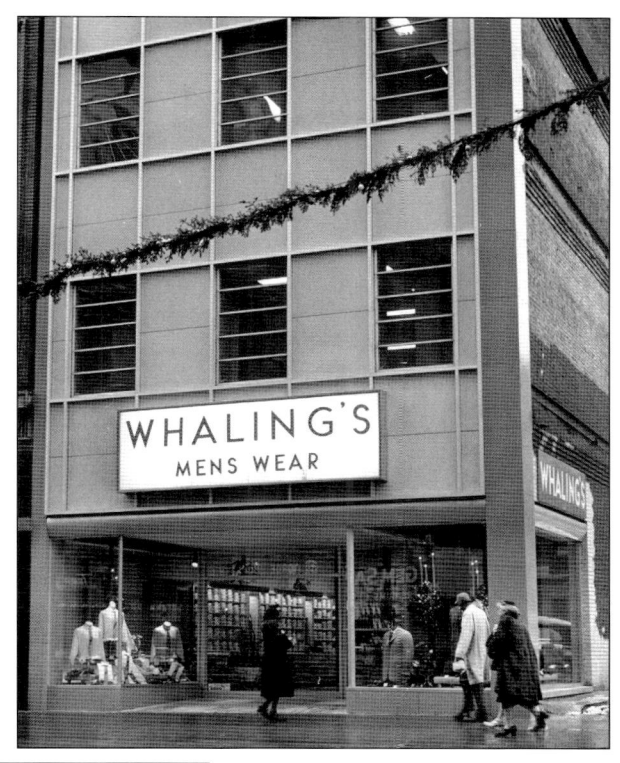

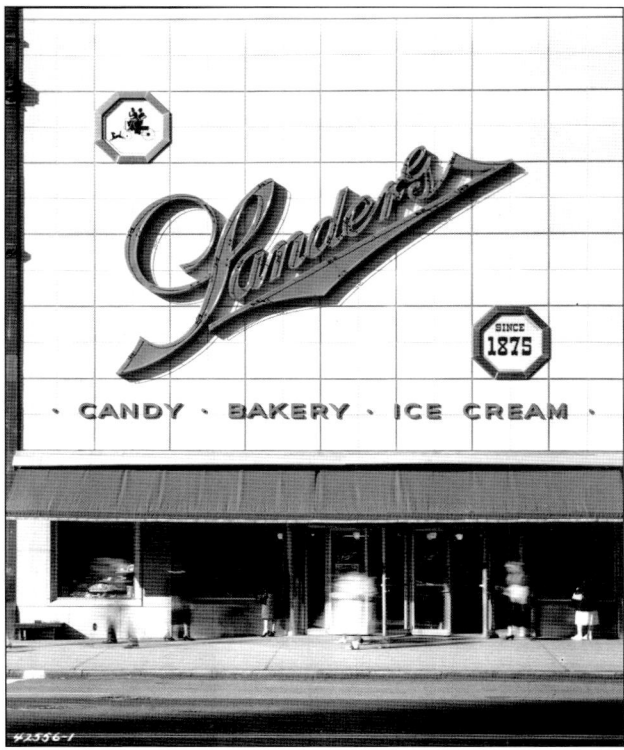

SANDERS CONFECTIONERY, 1037 WOODWARD AVENUE, 1957. Sanders was founded by German-born Frederick Sanders Schmidt in 1875 at Woodward and Gratiot Avenues. Following several moves along Woodward, Sanders settled in at 1037 Woodward Avenue by 1897 and in 1912 added baked goods to its offerings. Sanders was famous for inventing the ice-cream soda, hot fudge dessert topping, bumpy cake, and almond tea rings. Financial problems began in the 1970s, and in 1981, the firm filed for reorganization. A succession of owners, including present owner Morley Brands, LLC, has kept the firm alive. (Courtesy Burton Historical Collection, Detroit Public Library.)

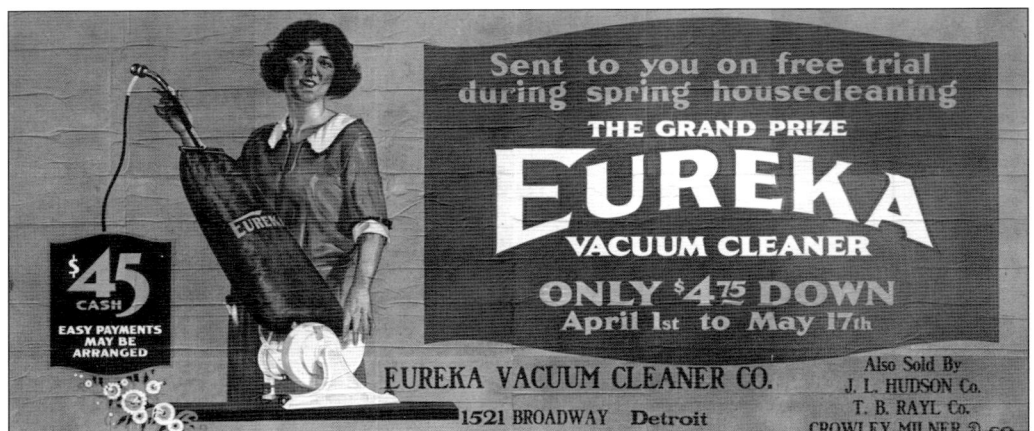

BILLBOARD FOR EUREKA VACUUM CENTERS, 1920s. Many folks are unaware that the Eureka Company had its origins in Detroit. In 1909, real estate auctioneer Fred Wardell acquired a number of patents for vacuum cleaner technology and opened a large factory on Hamilton Avenue. Subsequent retail stores were opened in major cities, including a multifloor outlet at 1521 Broadway, which today houses Small Plates and Eureka Lofts. (Courtesy Detroit Historical Museum.)

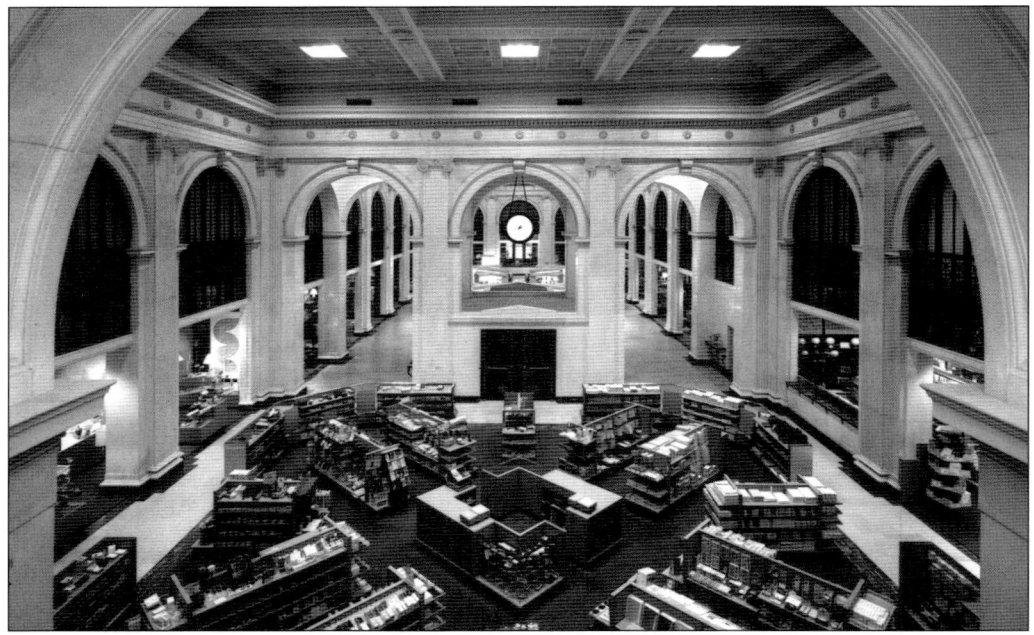

INTERIOR OF SILVER'S, 151 WEST FORT STREET, 1980. Silver's Office Furnishings was founded in 1947 by Ira G. Silver. The firm purchased the former State Savings Bank in 1979. This spectacular neoclassical structure was designed in 1898 by the renowned New York architectural firm of McKim, Mead and White. Silver's restored the building in 1980 as its flagship store. The popular 151 Gift Shop was later added as was Britt's Café. Office Depot bought the firm in 1994 and closed the retailer. (Courtesy Central Business District Foundation.)

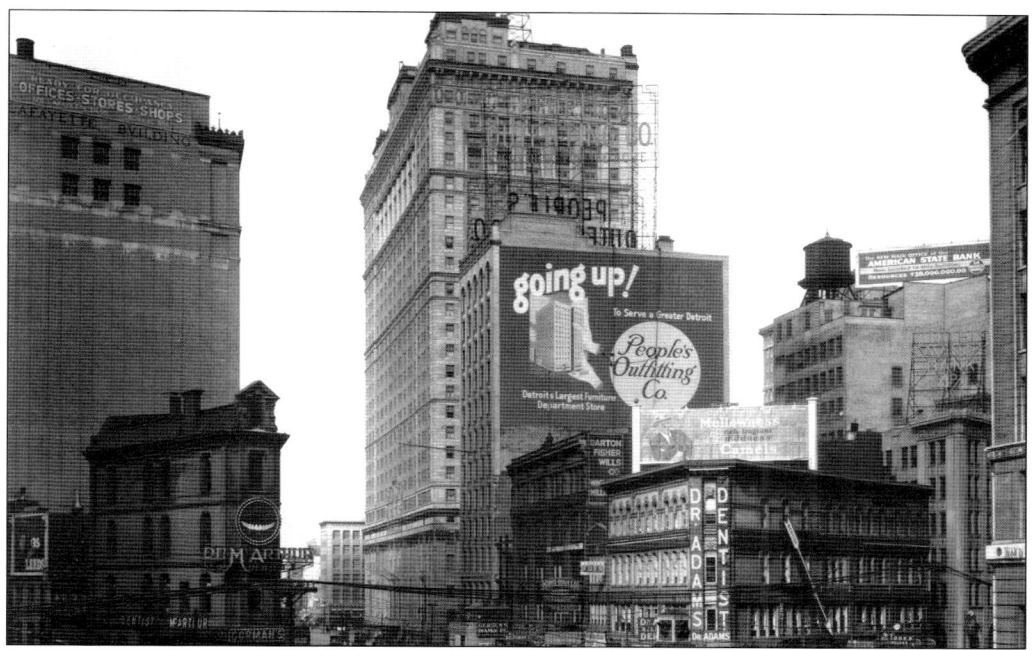

PEOPLE'S OUTFITTING ON MICHIGAN AVENUE, 1925. People's Outfitting was founded in 1893 by Leopold Wineman and opened in modest quarters on Michigan Avenue. Following years of growth and additions, People's built its landmark 12-story, 125,000-square-foot store at 150 Michigan Avenue in the mid-1920s. People's was the first large retail concern to extend credit at retail. (Courtesy Manning Brothers Historical Collection.)

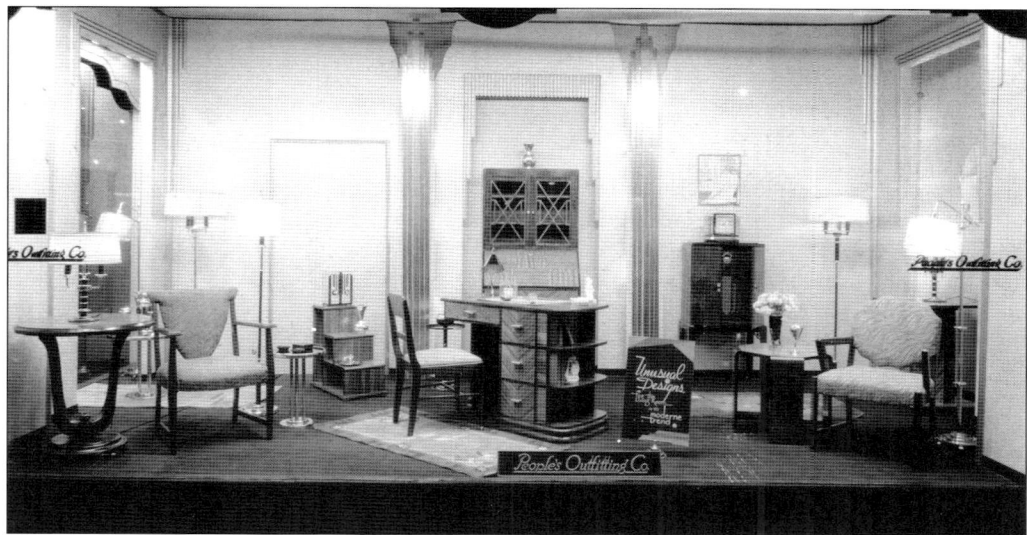

PEOPLE'S WINDOW DISPLAY PROMOTES MODERN DESIGNS, 1940S. People's mantra was simple: "to have what you want, when you want it, lower prices than you had expected, and available to you on easiest credit terms without interest or carrying charges!" In 1959, People's merged with State Sample, a nearby competitor. By 1969, People's was forced into receivership. The store closed and was renovated for office space. The building was demolished in 2007 for a parking garage to service the renovated Book Cadillac Hotel. (Courtesy Detroit Historical Museum.)

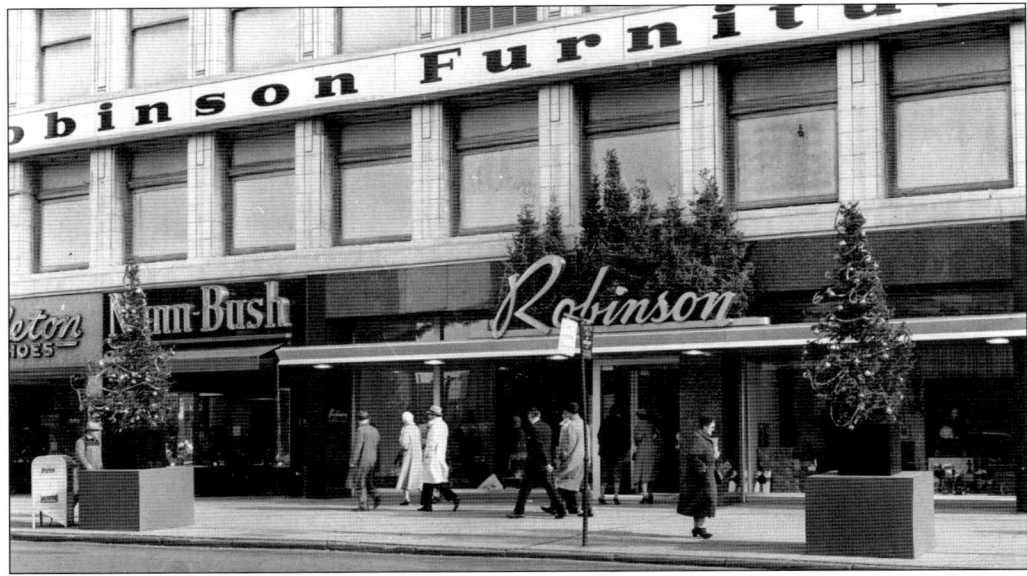

ROBINSON FURNITURE ON WASHINGTON BOULEVARD, 1958. David Robinson immigrated to the United States in 1888 and opened Robinson's in 1910 with his business partner and son, Louis. In 1960, the store was completely renovated. Robinson's was known for having the largest selections, reasonable prices, complimentary decorating advice, and multiple payment plans. The store closed in the late 1970s and was replaced by Gardner and Schumacher home furnishings. (Courtesy Central Business District Foundation.)

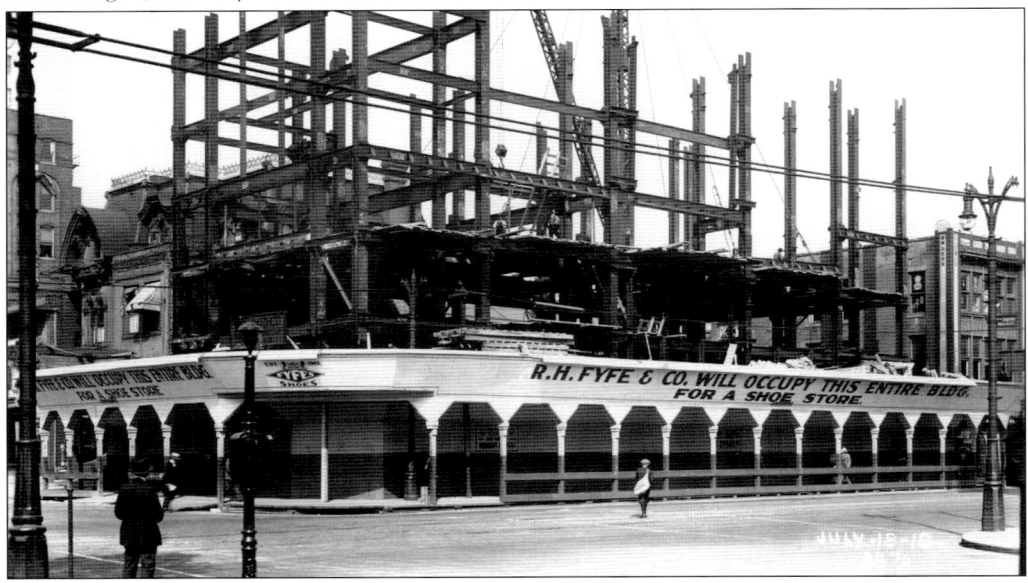

FYFE'S SHOES CONSTRUCTION, WOODWARD AVENUE AT ADAMS STREET, 1918. R. H. Fyfe and Company was founded in 1865 by Richard H. Fyfe. Prior to relocating to 10 West Adams Street (above), the firm leased space at four previous locations on Woodward Avenue. Fyfe's catered to the fashion-minded as well as budget conscious customers. Designed by Smith, Hinchman and Grylls architects, this neo-Gothic structure was completed in 1919. (Courtesy Manning Brothers Historical Collection.)

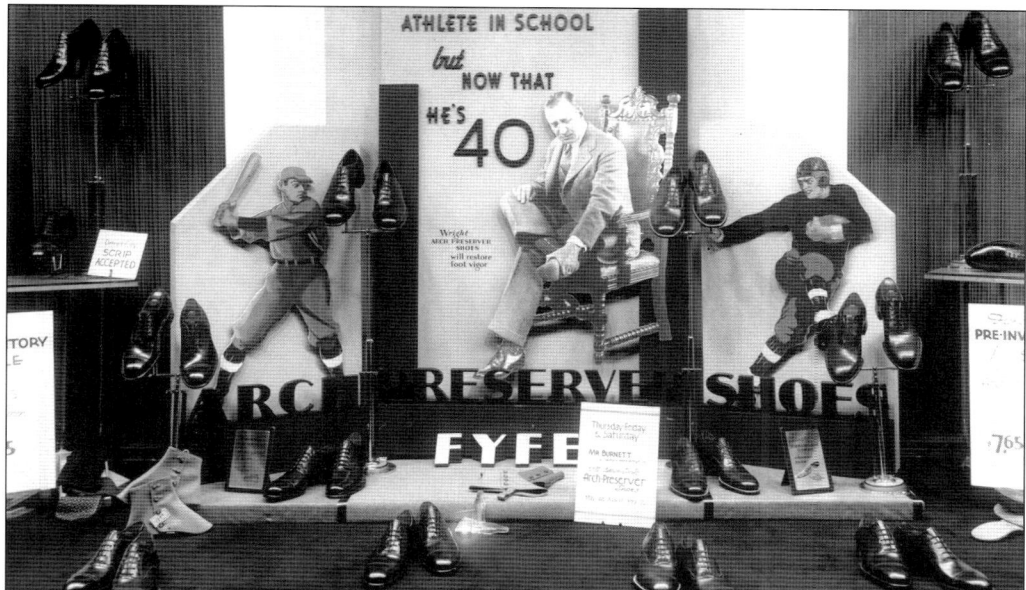

FYFE'S WINDOW DISPLAY FOR ARCH PRESERVER SHOES, 1930. Fyfe's opened the world's largest shoe store in 1919. The building included 10 floors of shoes and services, four mezzanines, and two basements. Men's shoes were located on the main floor because management felt that male shoppers would not travel to another floor to make a purchase. One attraction designed to guarantee traffic flow was a miniature golf course on the fifth floor. (Courtesy Detroit Historical Museum.)

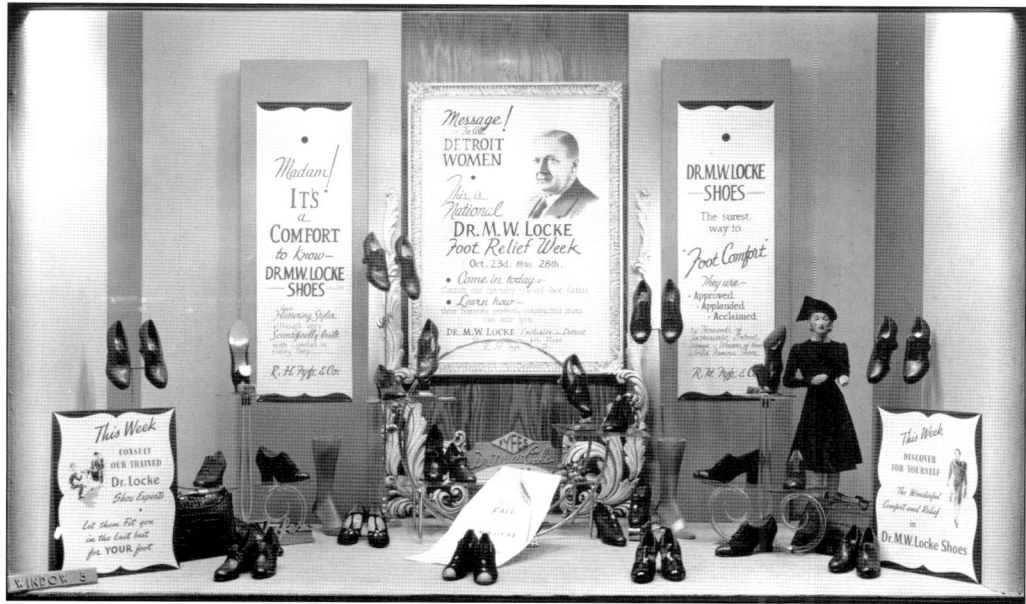

FYFE'S WINDOW DISPLAY PROMOTING DR. LOCKE SHOES, 1930S. Fyfe's became known as the "temple of shoes." At its peak in the 1940s, the store stocked 150,000 pairs of shoes and employed 150 associates. Millinery was added to the merchandise mix in 1956. The store also offered a shoe-shining parlor on the sixth floor and a full-time chiropodist. (Courtesy Detroit Historical Museum.)

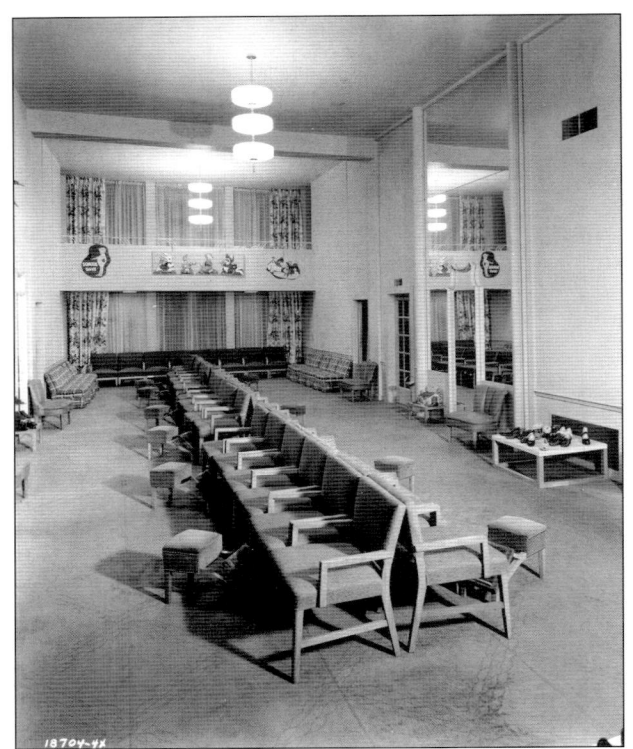

CHILDREN'S SHOE SALON AT FYFE'S, 1950S. Young people were treated as special guests at Fyfe's. Their department on the second floor included a merry-go-round and a children's barbershop. Women's shoes were in the first basement, men's on the main floor and mezzanine, slippers on the 3rd floor, specialized shoes on the 4th floor, an auditorium on the 5th floor, repair and rebuilding on the 6th floor, telephone and mail order on the 7th floor, offices on the 8th floor, and stock on the 9th and 10th floors. (Courtesy Detroit Historical Museum.)

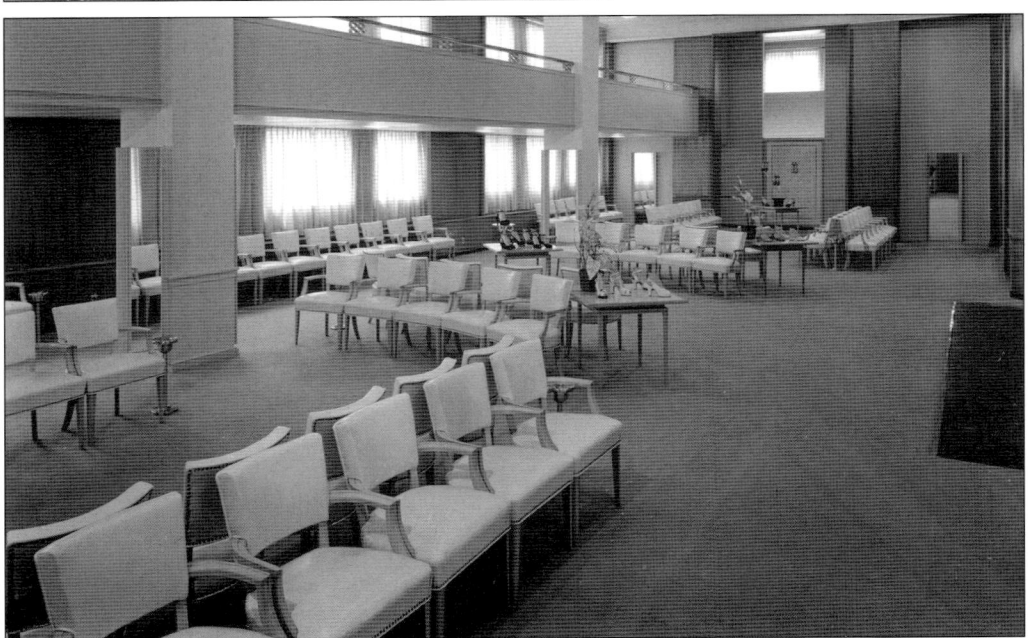

TYPICAL SHOE SALON AT FYFE'S, 1950S. Fyfe's boasted spacious, comfortable rooms that were colorful and featured large windows. Fyfe's was a pioneer in the sale of rubber boots and became the largest customer of the United States Rubber Company. Fyfe's was also a large exporter, shipping hundreds of shoes daily to all parts of the world. (Courtesy Detroit Historical Museum.)

PROMOTIONAL POSTCARD FROM FYFE'S, 1950s. With only one store and no suburban branches, time caught up with Fyfe's. The firm filed for bankruptcy and closed in 1971. The building was later converted to 65 residential units. The main floor again housed a shoe store in 1988 when Sibley's shoes moved its store to this location from the Fox Building. With the demise of Sibley's in 2001, the space became a martini bar called Proof. (Courtesy Michael Hauser.)

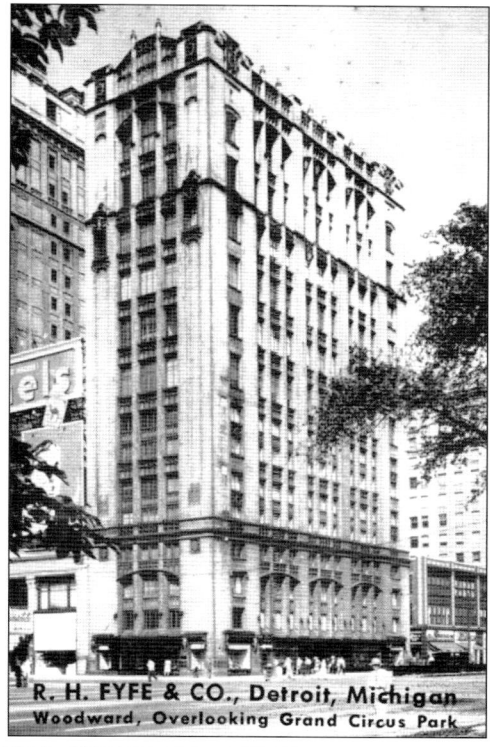

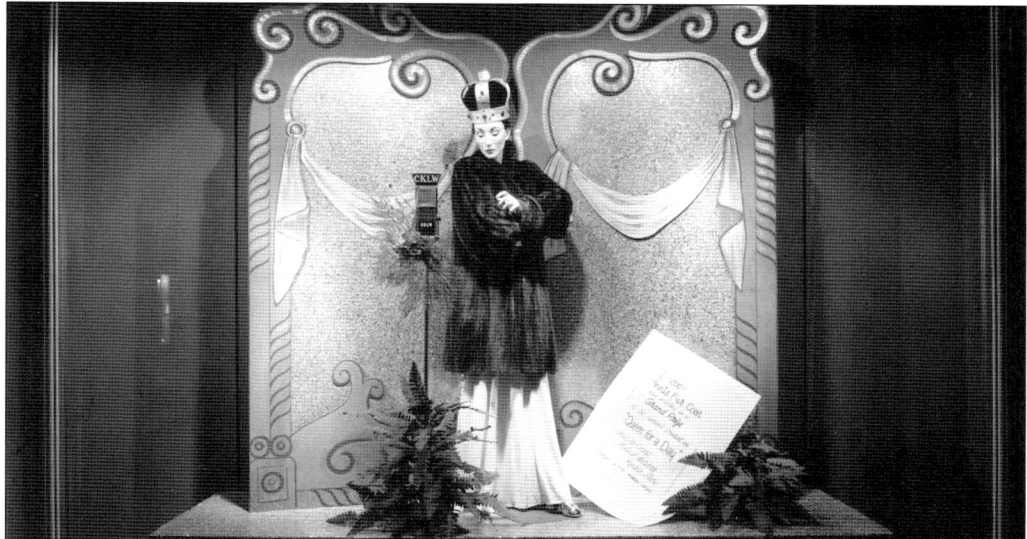

ANNIS FURS WINDOW PROMOTING "QUEEN FOR A DAY," 1940s. Annis Furs, founded in 1887 by Newton Annis, was located on Woodward Avenue. In 1895, the firm moved to Woodward Avenue and Clifford Street. Needing to expand, in 1931, it moved to the former home of L. B. King China, at 1274 Library Street. This six-story terra-cotta structure was designed by Detroit architects Rogers and MacFarlane. Changing tastes in the 1970s forced Annis to scale back and move to the Penobscot Building in 1983. It closed permanently in 1985. (Courtesy Detroit Historical Museum.)

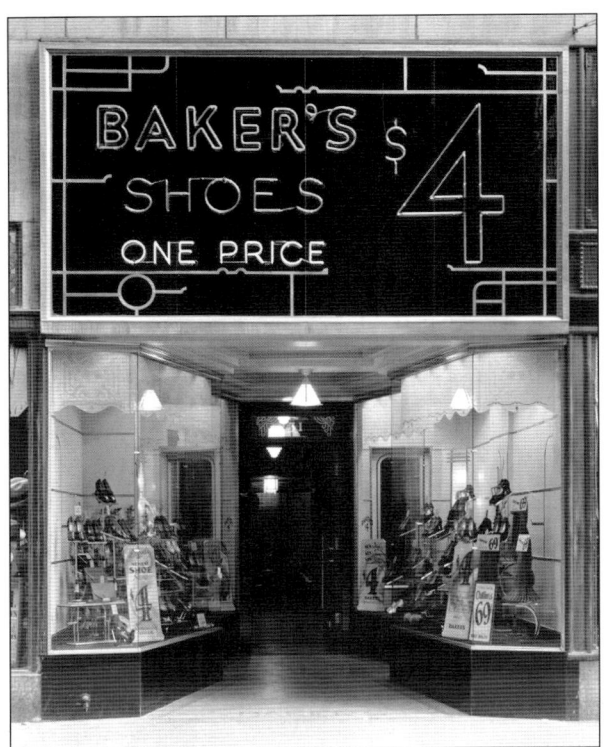

BAKER'S SHOES' FIRST DETROIT STORE, 31 STATE STREET, 1932. Baker's Shoes was part of the St. Louis–based Edison Brothers chain of shoe stores, founded in 1923 by five of the Edison brothers. Baker's became the leading specialty retailer of moderately priced fashion footwear for women. The store later moved to 1413 Woodward Avenue and flourished until the lease ran out in 1987. (Courtesy Detroit Historical Museum.)

BURT'S SHOES, 1247 WOODWARD AVENUE, 1937. Burt's, another division of the Edison Brothers chain of shoe stores, began in 1930. Burt's specialized in a less-expensive line of women's shoes. (Baker's sold shoes for $4 a pair, while Burt's featured shoes for $2.88 a pair.) Burt's was located on Woodward Avenue across from Hudson's. The chain was phased out by Edison Brothers in the early 1980s. (Courtesy Detroit Historical Museum.)

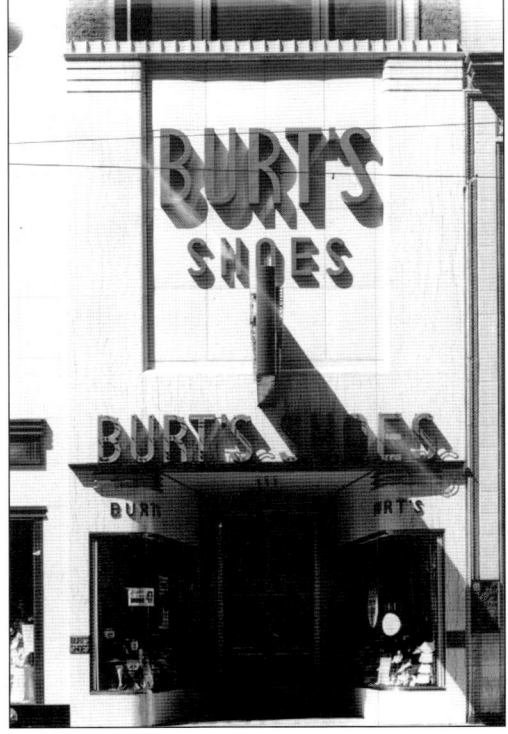

EVENING VIEW OF WISE SHOES, 1936. Wise Shoes was a national chain of women's shoe stores founded in the 1920s. The store was located in a prime spot at 1059 Woodward Avenue, opposite the Ernst Kern Company. It was known for its guaranteed footwear policy. This location and the adjacent Cunningham's Drugs were demolished in 1966 to construct the new flagship store for Hughes and Hatcher. (Courtesy Detroit Historical Museum.)

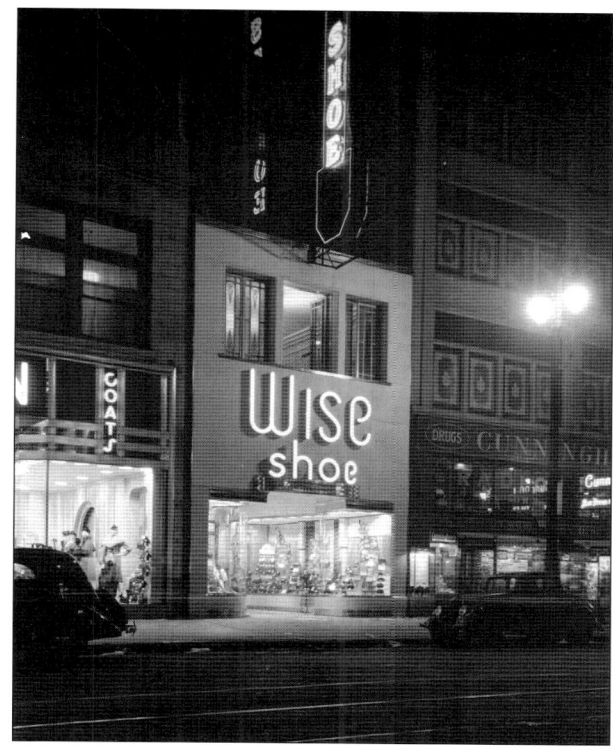

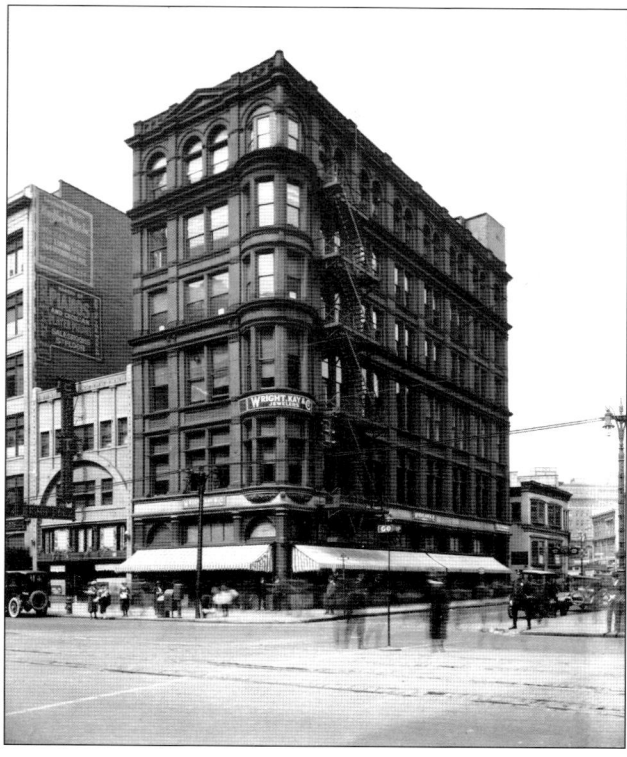

WRIGHT KAY JEWELERS, 1500 WOODWARD AVENUE, AROUND 1910. Wright Kay was established in 1861 by R. J. F. Roehm. Henry W. Wright became a partner in 1872. Roehm sold his share of the business to John Kay in 1886. Following several successive moves on lower Woodward Avenue, the firm moved to the former Schwankovsky's Music House in 1920. In 1954, the firm was acquired by American Music Stores. The downtown store closed in 1978 and in later years the building was home to House of Fabrics, RadioShack, and a nightclub. (Courtesy Walter P. Reuther Library, Wayne State University.)

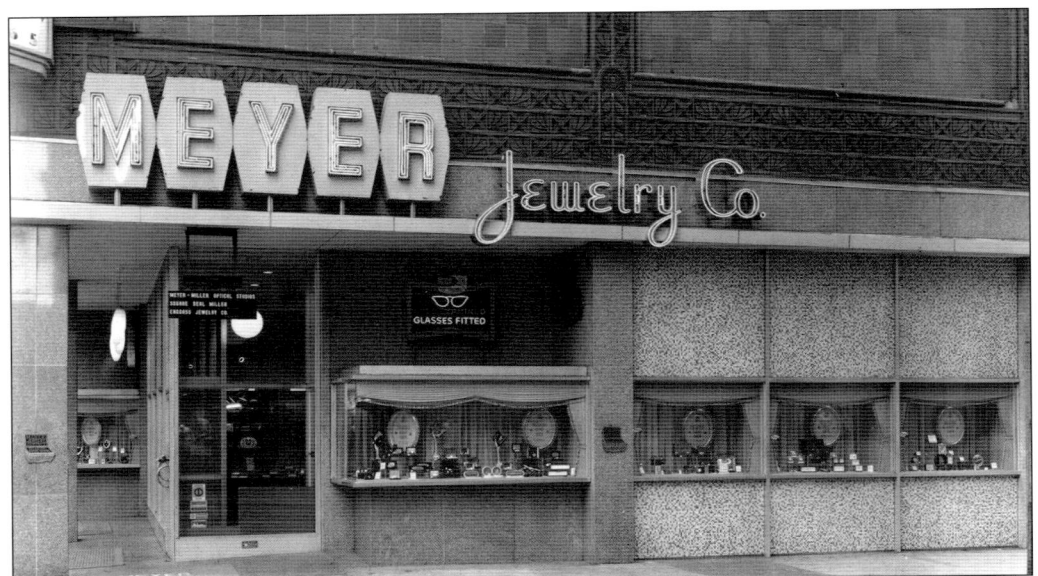

EXTERIOR OF MEYER JEWELERS, WOODWARD AT GRAND RIVER AVENUES, 1950S. Meyer was founded in 1920 by Meyer Rosenbaum. Its first downtown store opened in 1936 in the Eaton Tower (today's David Broderick Tower). The firm remained there until it purchased the former T. B. Rayl building in 1956. This nine-story Sullivanesque structure, constructed in 1915, was designed by the architects Baxter, O'Dell and Halpin. Previous tenants besides Rayl's included Liggett's Drugs and Robinson's department store. (Courtesy Detroit Historical Museum.)

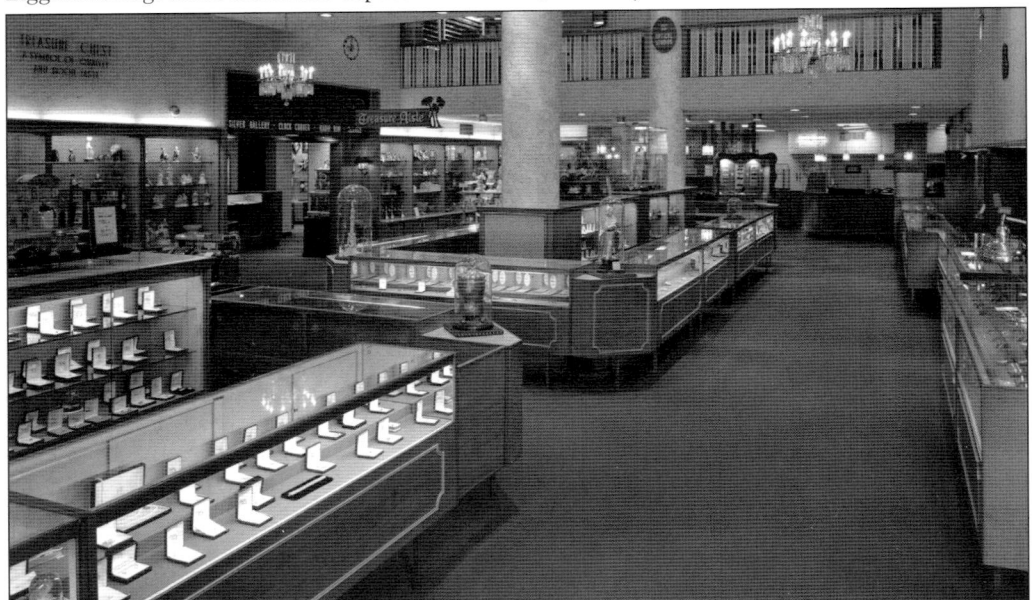

MAIN FLOOR AND MEZZANINE OF MEYER JEWELERS, 1950S. Meyer spent $2 million to purchase and renovate this landmark 60,000-square-foot structure for its flagship store and corporate headquarters. The new location offered customers a greatly expanded silver and gift gallery and a spacious new optical studio. The entire Meyer chain folded in 1983. Today the main floor houses Eastern Wigs. (Courtesy Detroit Historical Museum.)

POSTCARD VIEW OF GRINNELL BROTHERS MUSIC STORE, 1921. Grinnell's was founded by Ira L. Grinnell in 1872 in Ann Arbor. In 1882, Ira and his younger brother Clayton opened their first Detroit store. Following several moves on Woodward Avenue, the firm opened its landmark eight-story store in 1908 at 1515 Woodward Avenue. Grinnell's piano factories were located on Cass Avenue in Detroit and later moved to Holly. (Courtesy of Michael Hauser.)

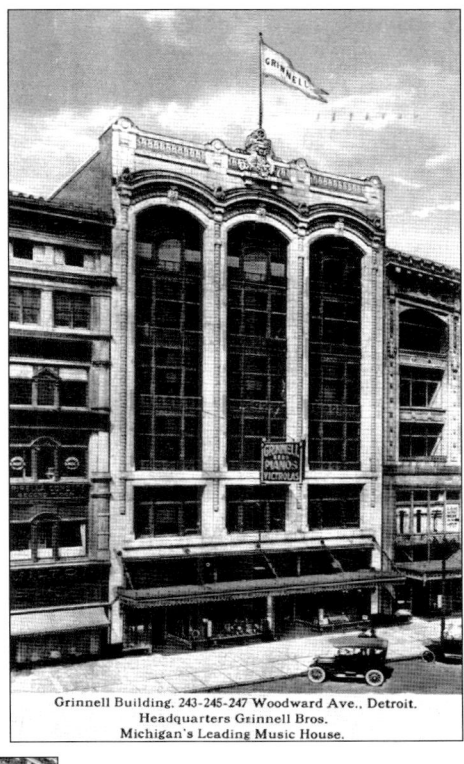

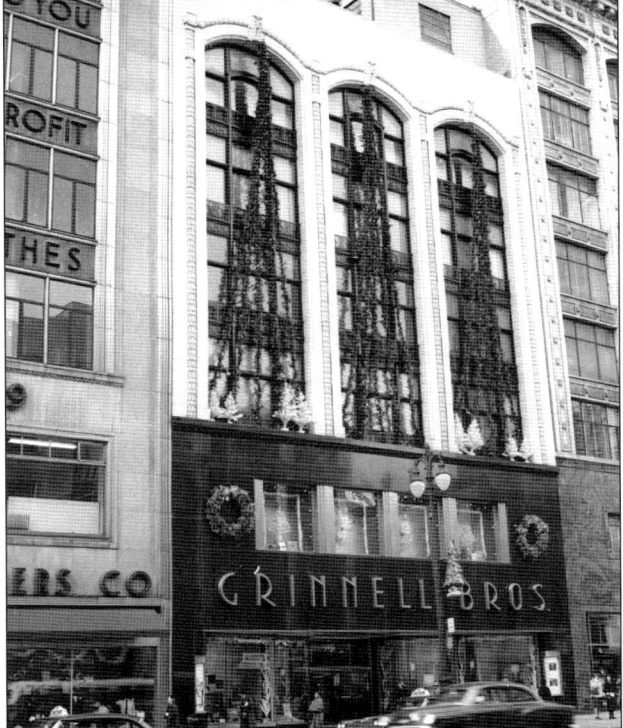

GRINNELL'S HOUSE OF MUSIC ON WOODWARD AVENUE, 1958. The Woodward Avenue store, besides selling musical instruments, featured a large sheet music department, a lending library, and an entire floor devoted to classical music. The company motto was Everything in the Realm of Music. By 1920, the firm had 20 stores in Michigan, Ohio, and Ontario and had become one of the nation's largest distributors and manufacturers of pianos. (Courtesy Central Business District Foundation.)

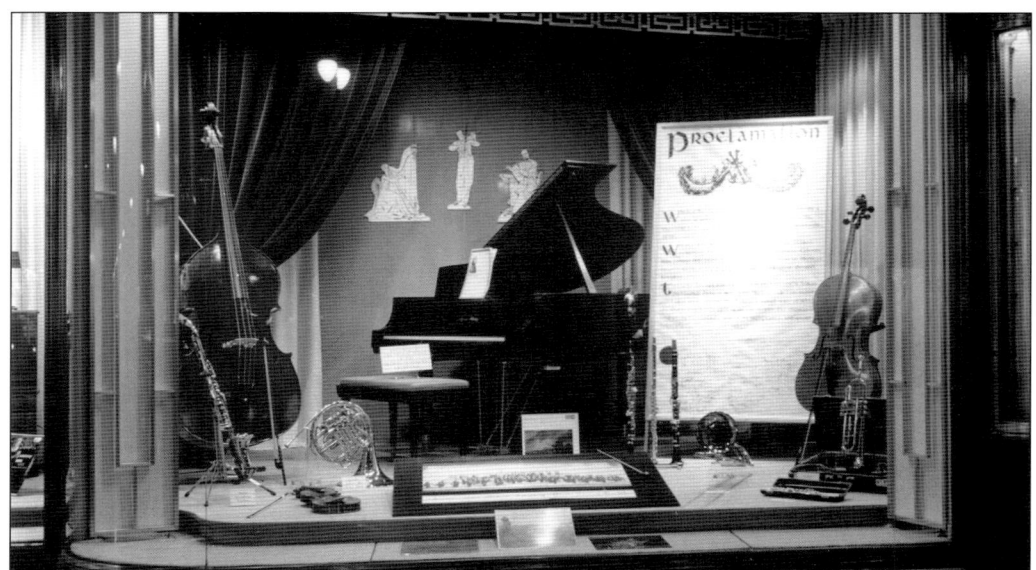

GRINNELL'S WINDOW DISPLAY SALUTES THE DETROIT SYMPHONY ORCHESTRA, 1950S. This window features a Steinway piano surrounded by an array of musical instruments. An enlarged proclamation from the mayor salutes Detroit Symphony Week. Grinnell's regularly sponsored The Grinnell Symphony Hour on WJR Radio each Sunday evening. This sponsorship reinforced the fact that when Detroiters thought of music, they immediately thought of Grinnell's. (Courtesy Central Business District Foundation.)

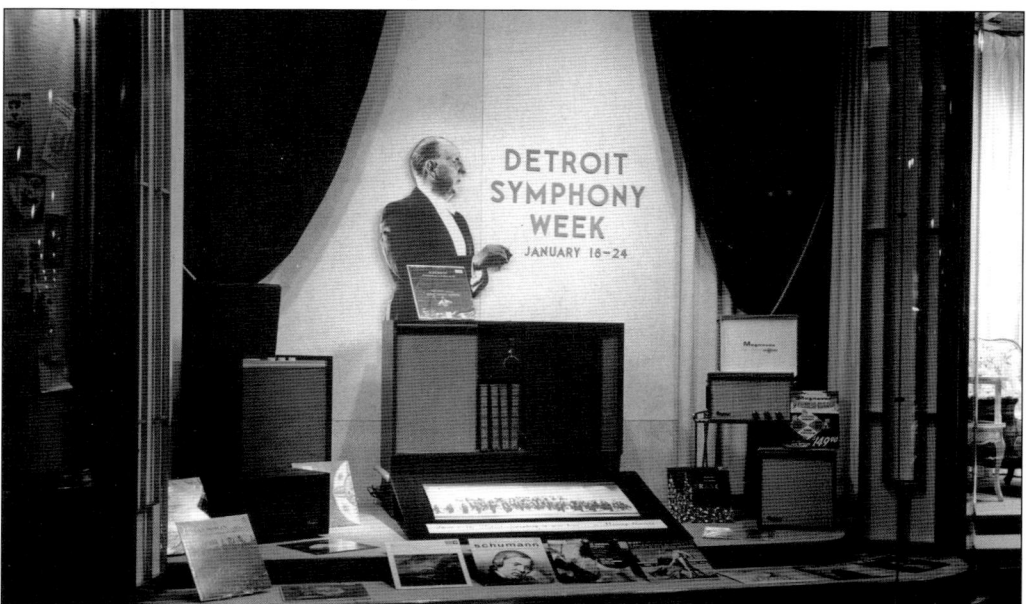

GRINNELL'S WINDOW DISPLAY PROMOTING STEREO-RAMA, 1950S. This window display features a life-size figure of Paul Paray, the popular conductor of the Detroit Symphony Orchestra. He is flanked by the latest Magnavox stereophonic system and Mercury high-fidelity. Doomed by new technology, foreign competition, and demographic changes, Grinnell's declared bankruptcy and closed in 1981. (Courtesy Central Business District Foundation.)

Eight
VALUE MERCHANTS

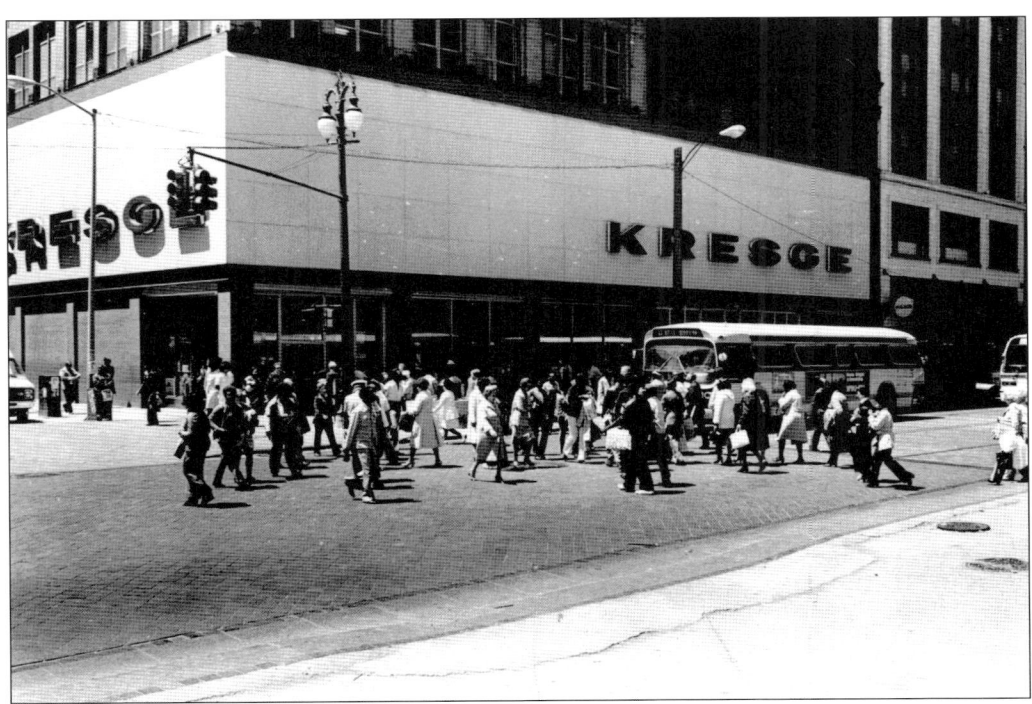

KRESGE'S, WOODWARD AVENUE AT STATE STREET, 1979. The Detroit-based S. S. Kresge Company was founded in 1899 by Sebastian Spering Kresge and Charles J. Wilson. Kresge's became one of "the big three" of the dime store industry. In 1962, Kresge changed retail history forever with the debut of Kmart. The variety store format had now morphed into a discount department store. (Courtesy Central Business District Foundation.)

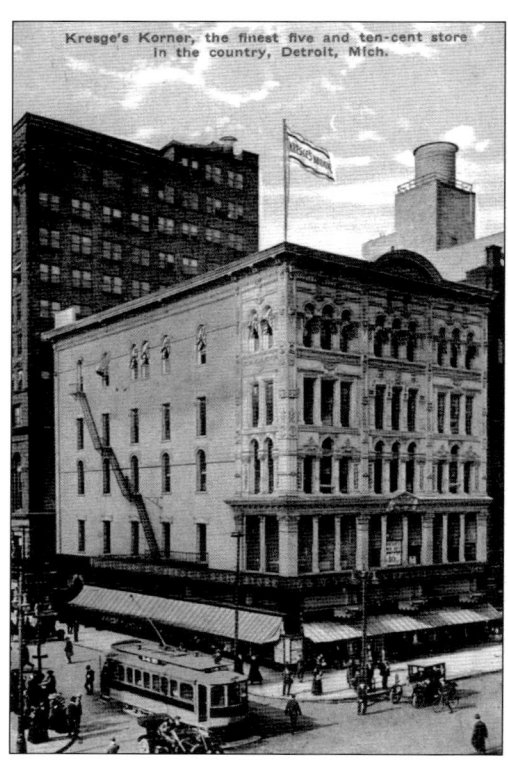

POSTCARD OF KRESGE'S, 1201 WOODWARD AVENUE, 1915. Store No. 1 of the Kresge chain was located on the west side of Woodward Avenue, halfway between State Street and Grand River Avenue. The store was four stories tall, with retail on the first two floors and the balcony. A large exterior sign proclaimed, "Nothing Sold over 10 Cents in This Store!" Store No. 1 moved to State and Woodward in 1909 in a building that was constructed in 1880 for Elliott Taylor-Woolfenden Dry Goods. (Courtesy Michael Hauser.)

KRESGE'S LUNCHEONETTE SPECIAL, 1940S. Most Kresge stores featured snack bars or luncheonettes. Store No. 1 on Woodward Avenue had a snack bar on the main floor and luncheonettes in the basement and on the main floor. Kresge's prided itself on serving thousands of fresh, home-cooked meals daily. Many Detroiters remember popping a balloon for a free banana split or hot fudge sundae. The luncheonettes featured marble-top counters, red swivel stools, and the whirl of overhead ceiling fans. (Courtesy Michael Hauser.)

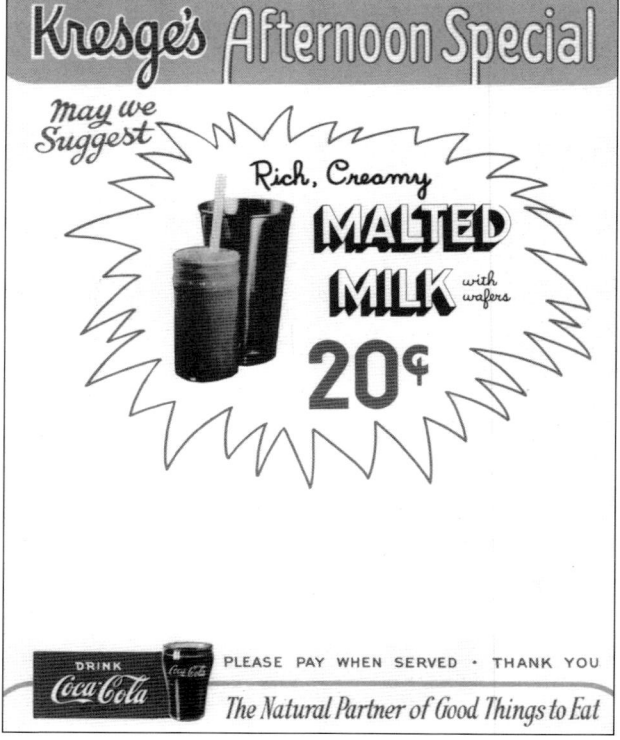

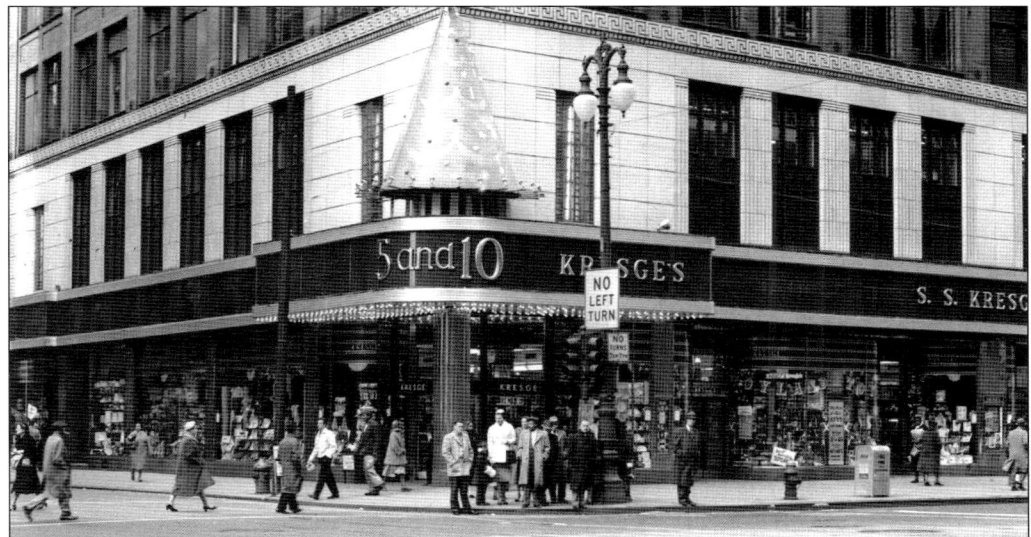

KRESGE'S STORE NO. 1 ON WOODWARD AVENUE, 1958. Prior to 1919, this site was replaced with a new nine-story facility. During construction, signs proclaimed, "Watch the krowds at Kresge korner!" In 1937, Kresge's doubled the size of the store by acquiring the adjacent former home of S. L. Bird and Sons. The store then featured eight entrances, a beauty salon, a bakery, and two luncheonettes. Store No. 1 received another face-lift in 1959. Kresge's sold its remaining variety stores to McCrory's in 1987, which operated at this location until 1994. (Courtesy Central Business District Foundation.)

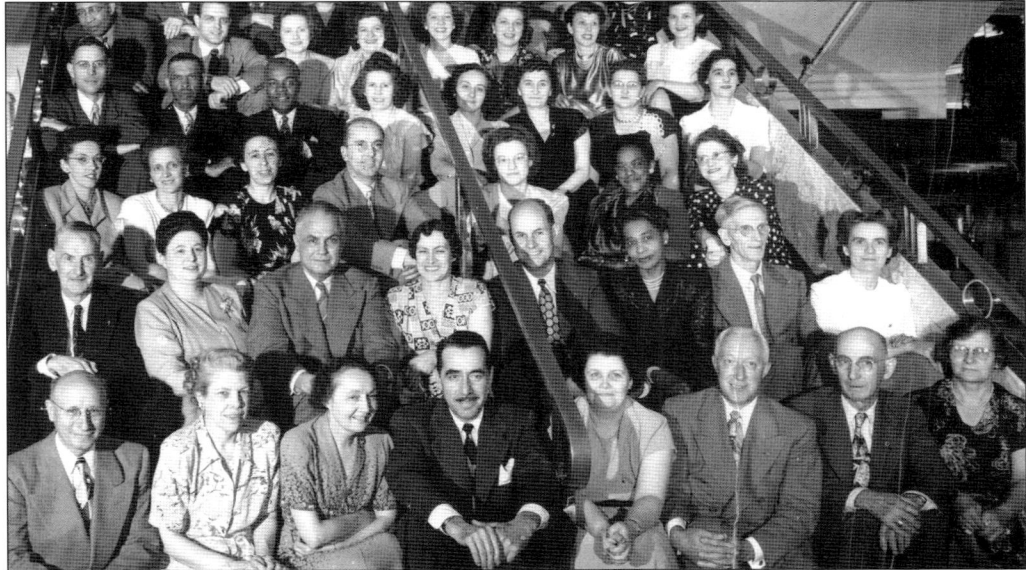

STORE NO. 1 KRESGE EMPLOYEES. The era of five-and-dime items ended in 1917 when Kresge's was forced to raise prices to 15¢. By 1920, Kresge's opened "green front" stores that sold items ranging in price from 25¢ to $1. (Traditional Kresge variety stores were known as "red front" stores.) Detroit's first green front, at Woodward and Grand River Avenues, closed in 1959. In 1952, Kresge's began converting stores to a checkout operation rather than having registers in each department. (Courtesy Detroit Historical Museum.)

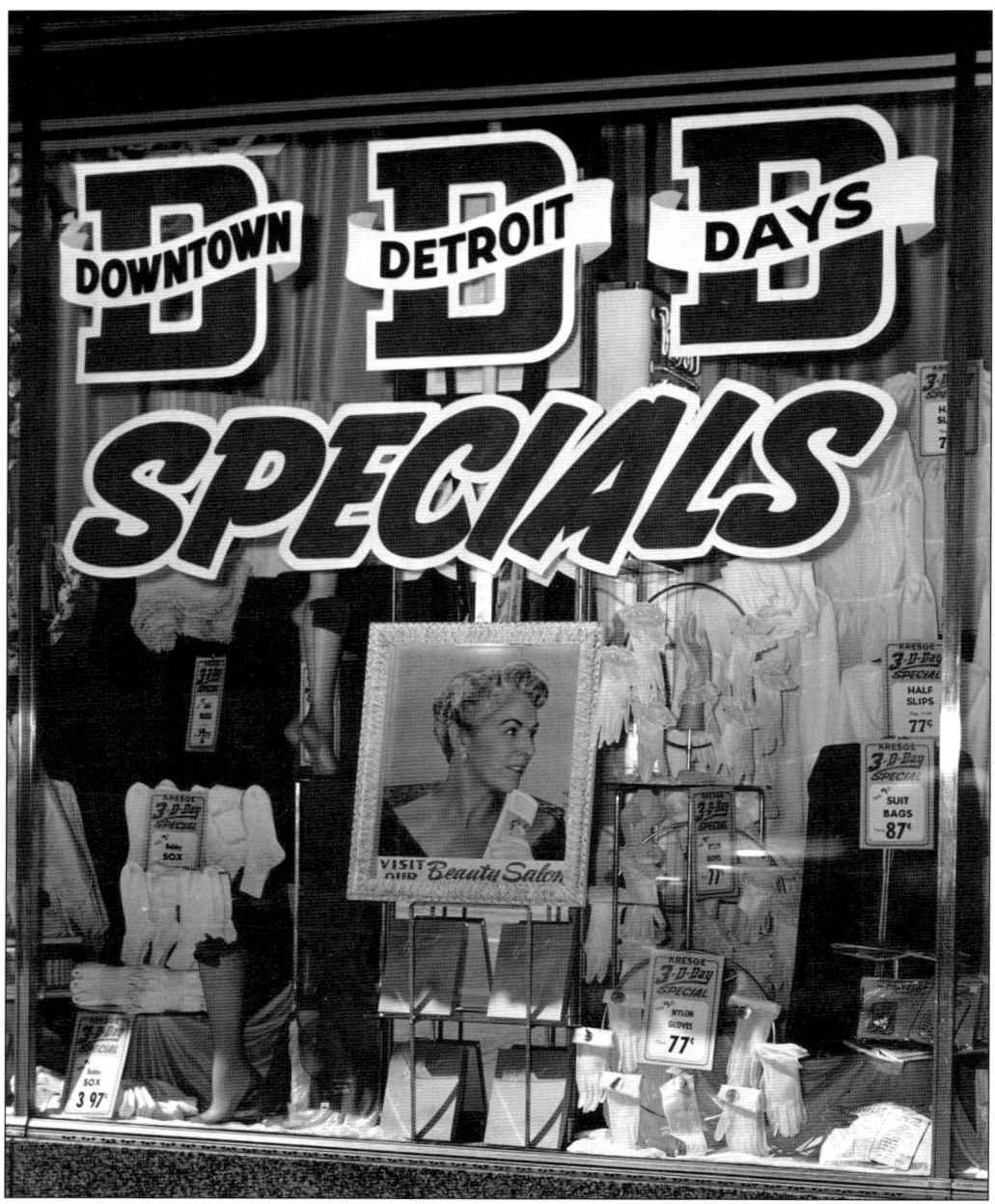

KRESGE STORE NO. 1 WINDOW DISPLAY, 1950S. Whether it was peanut clusters, transistor radios, nylons, parakeets, or spray snow, Kresge's strongly believed in visuals and promotions. Memorable slogans through the years include "Shop Kresge's every week . . . you'll save, save, save!" and "Every day more people are awakening to Kresge values!" In its prime, Kresge's operated three downtown stores on Woodward Avenue: State Street (red front), Clifford Street (red front), and Grand River Avenue (green front). (Courtesy Central Business District Foundation.)

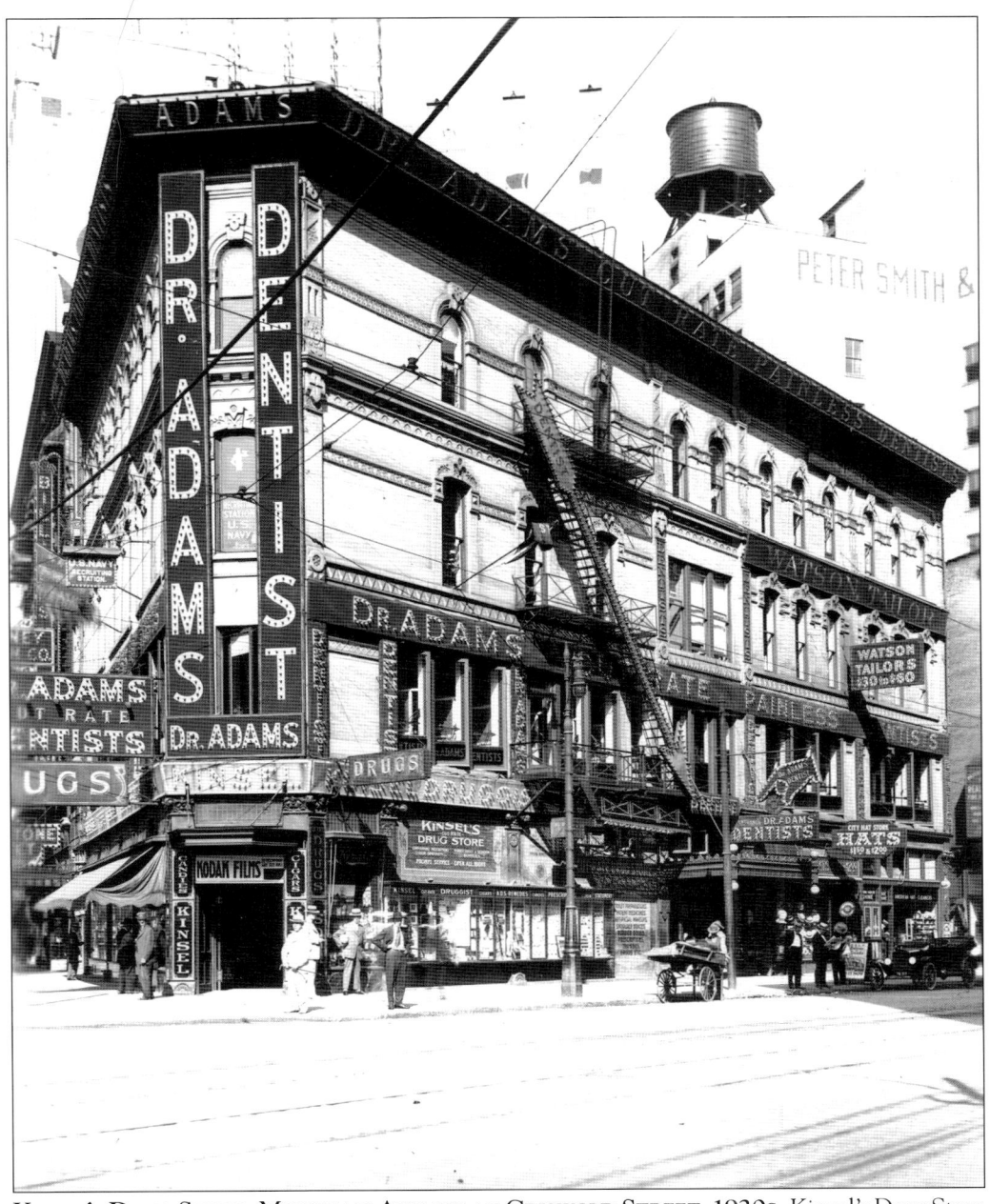

KINSEL'S DRUG STORE, MICHIGAN AVENUE AT GRISWOLD STREET, 1920S. Kinsel's Drug Store was founded in 1893 by Edward Kinsel. The retailer is credited with several firsts, including being the city's first 24-hour retailer and the first discount drugstore. During its 80-year history, Kinsel's closed temporarily only for World War I and II celebrations, for Edward Kinsel's funeral, and following a fire in 1947. The store was sold in 1958 to Cunningham's Drugs, which operated Kinsel's until 1981. Paul's Cut Rate Drugs leased the space from 1981 to 1985. For a short time, it became a Taco Bell, only to be demolished in the late 1990s. (Courtesy Manning Brothers Historical Collection.)

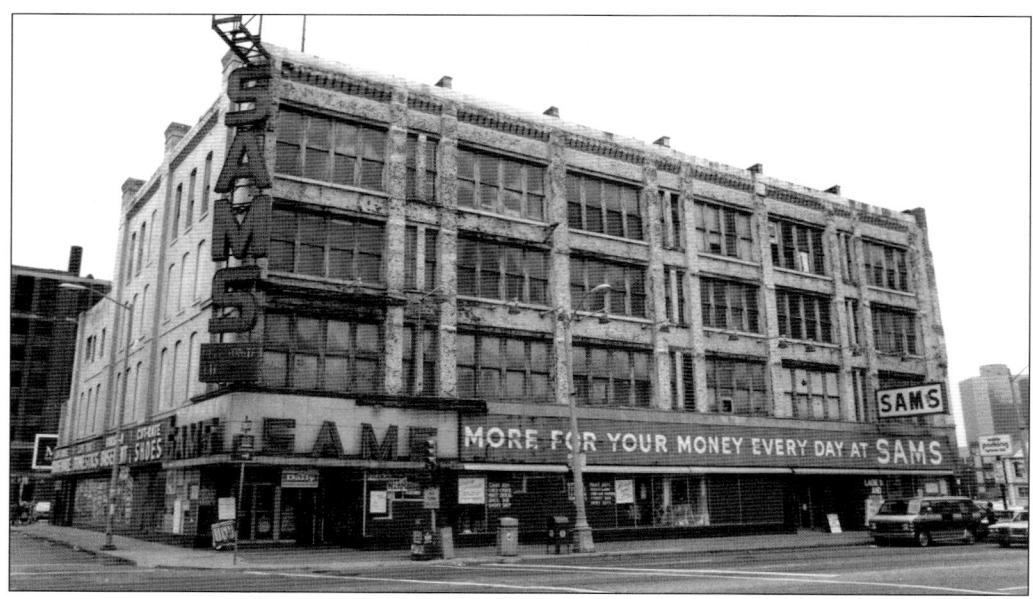

EXTERIOR VIEW OF SAMS, 1056 RANDOLPH STREET, 1970. Sams Cut Rate Department Store, founded by Russian émigré Sam Osnos, began as a cigar store on Monroe Street in 1917. The Randolph Street store was located in a building constructed in 1885. Sams occupied this site from 1925 to 1985. The store was enlarged in 1933 by acquiring the adjacent La Salle Theatre. By 1940, Sams had expanded to three downtown locations. (Courtesy Michael Hauser.)

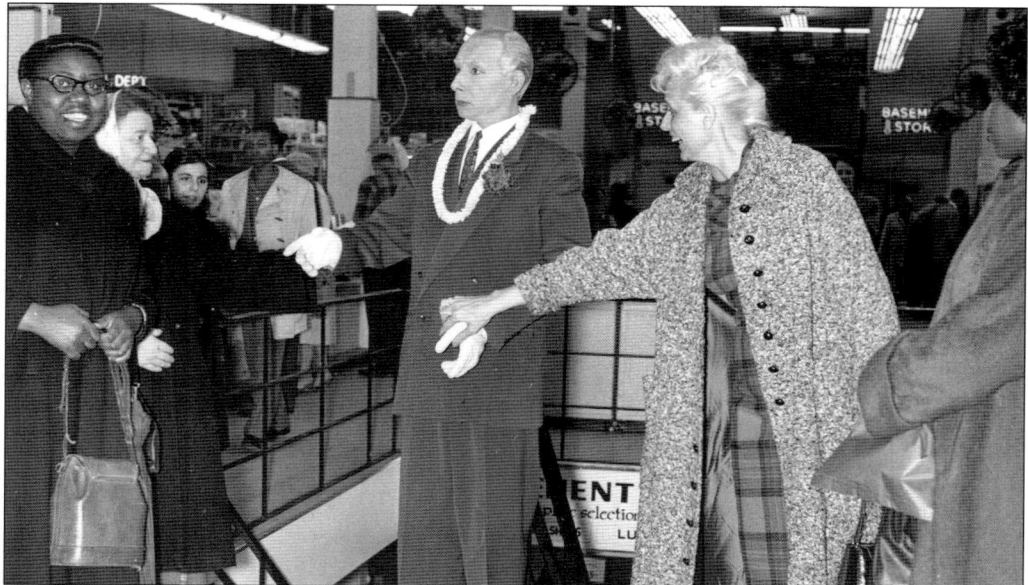

RENE THE ROBOT VISITS SAMS, 1959. Rene was a "mechanical man" in Sams display window as part of a Downtown Detroit Days promotion. In reality, he was a former Parisian ballet dancer. Sams was Detroit's discount department store pioneer. Sam Osnos's secret was to cut his markup to 25 percent rather than the usual 40 percent. This obviously cut into the sales at Hudson's, which fought back by creating its own lower-priced basement store in the 1920s. (Courtesy Central Business District Foundation.)

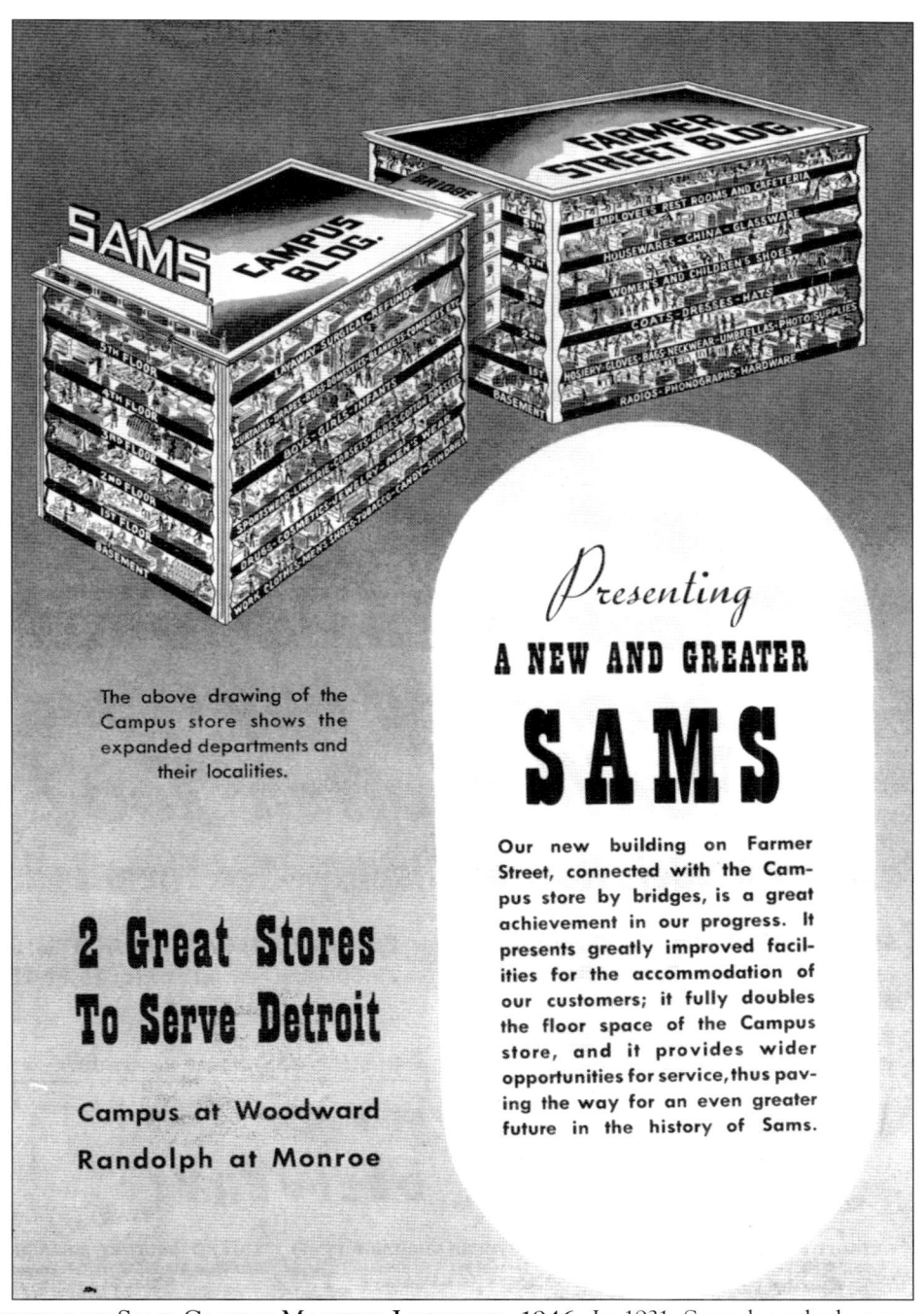

CUTAWAY OF SAMS CAMPUS MARTIUS LOCATION, 1946. In 1931, Sams leased what was the Detroit Opera House, located at 13–27 Campus Martius. By 1944, with business booming, the firm constructed a four-level bridge across an alley to connect a new six-story addition at 1127 Farmer Street. Sams was the only unionized department store downtown. In 1952, Sams became downtown's first major retailer to integrate its sales staff by hiring African American associates. (Courtesy Michael Hauser.)

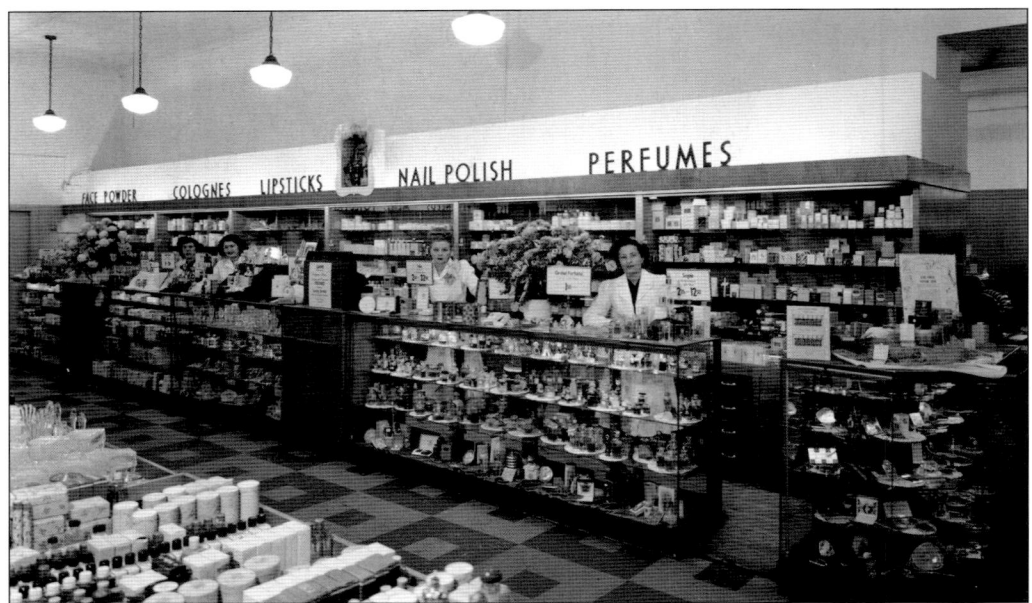

SAMS CUT RATE COSMETICS DEPARTMENT, 1948. Sams was one of the first large retailers that encouraged customers to cash their paychecks. The store sponsored numerous radio programs and outreach initiatives through the years. Memorable store slogans include Sams Always Means Savings!, We Keep Detroit Prices Down, and Sams . . . the Talk of the Town! (Courtesy Detroit Historical Museum.)

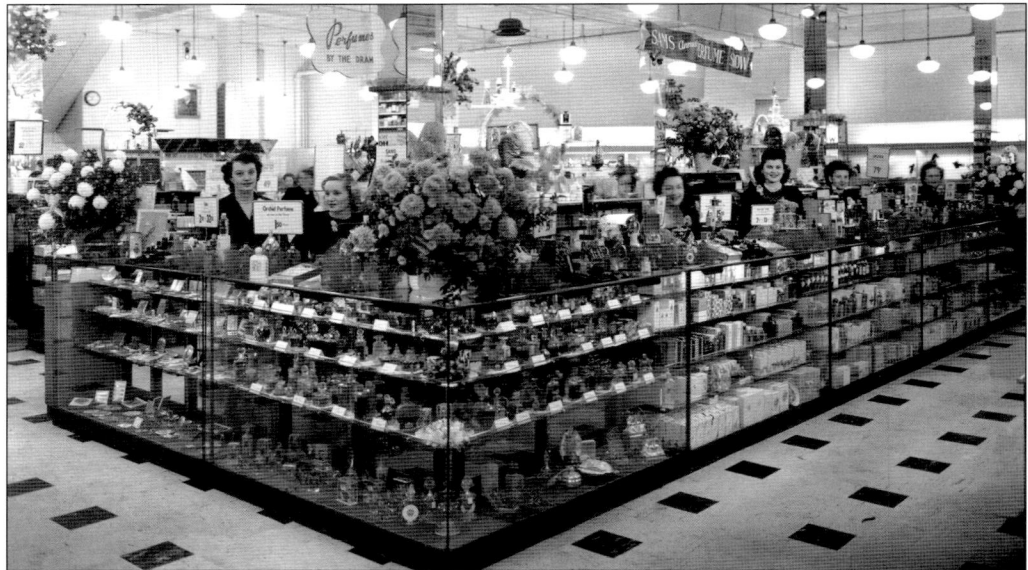

PERFUME COUNTER AT SAMS CUT RATE, 1948. By 1960, Sams operated 13 stores in metropolitan Detroit, employing 3,000 associates. However, competition from new discounters, rising costs, and credit issues forced the firm into receivership for a time. The Campus Martius store closed in 1965 and was demolished. In 1971, the Osnos family sold the firm. The Randolph Street store closed in 1985 as the result of a rent dispute and was demolished for a parking garage. (Courtesy Detroit Historical Museum.)

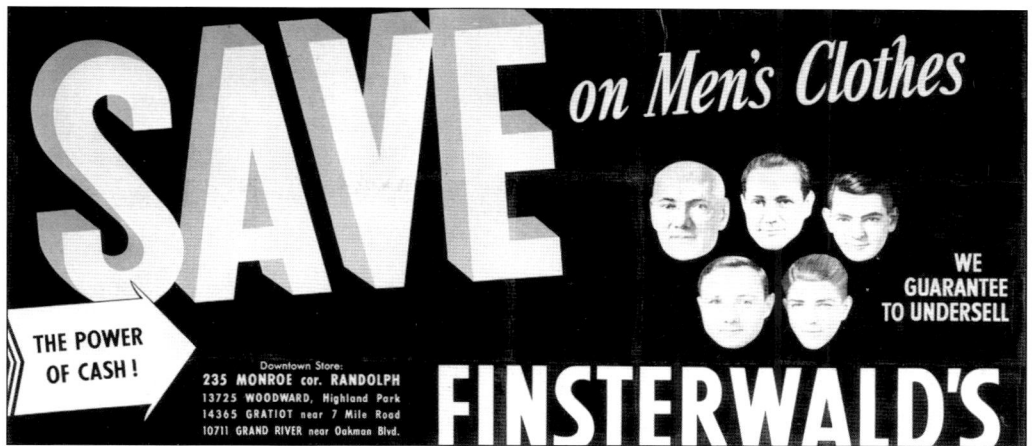

BILLBOARD FOR FINSTERWALD'S CLOTHIERS, 1940S. Finsterwald's downtown store was located on Monroe Street at Randolph Street, near Crowley's. This popular-priced men's clothing retailer aggressively promoted its thrifty payment plan. The plan enabled a customer to take advantage of the cash price and divide the cost into 10 weekly or 5 semimonthly payments. Imagine offering this service today for only $1! (Courtesy Detroit Historical Museum.)

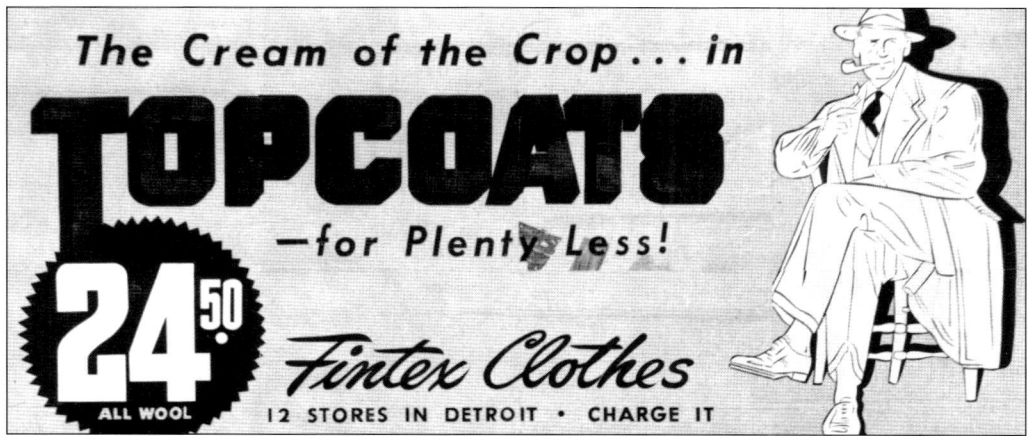

BILLBOARD FOR FINTEX CLOTHING COMPANY, 1945. Fintex Clothing Company was a national chain that pioneered the idea of a one-price suit. Its original downtown store was located at Griswold Street and Grand River Avenue. In 1945, the firm moved to 1457 Griswold Street, at Clifford Street, offering four floors of popular-priced fashions for men and women. The store prided itself in being only 51 seconds from Woodward Avenue and 49 seconds from Washington Boulevard. (Courtesy Detroit Historical Museum.)

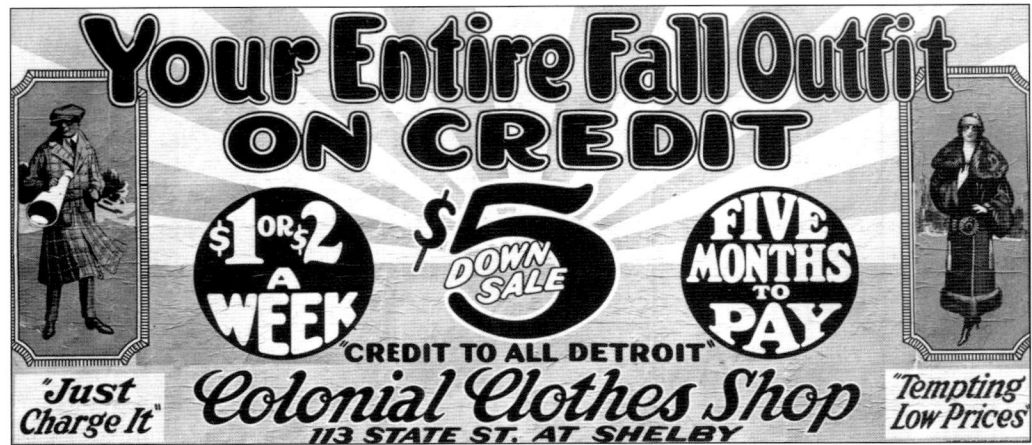

BILLBOARD FOR COLONIAL CLOTHES, 1923. The Colonial department store opened at 25 State Street in 1919. Customers could purchase home furnishings, guns, and even musical instruments on credit for as little as $1 down on purchases up to $50. During the Depression, the firm advertised that it would exchange clothing for farm produce. With no scrip available to stimulate trade, the retail business plummeted. (Courtesy Detroit Historical Museum.)

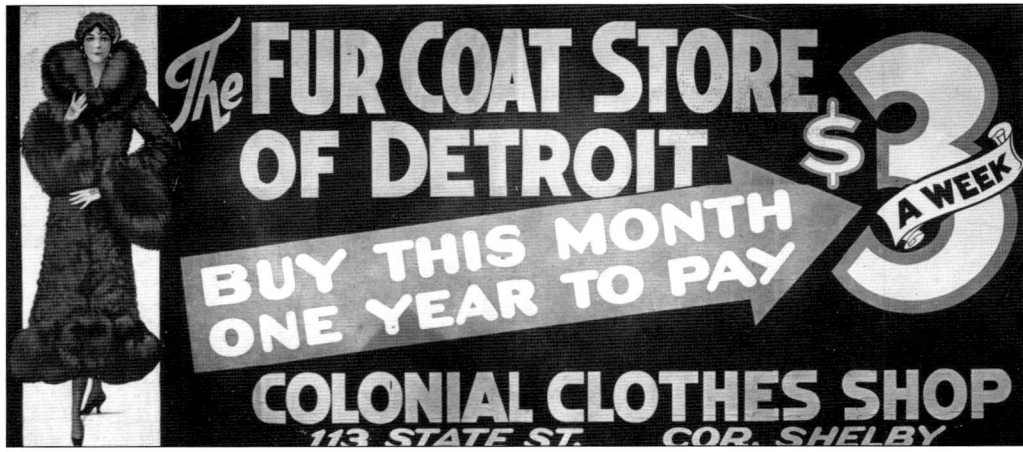

BILLBOARD FOR COLONIAL CLOTHES, 1924. Colonial featured merchandise on all six floors of its landmark art deco building. The store was open every evening until 9:00 and adopted the motto "Avoid downtown crowds . . . shop the easy way at Detroit's leading credit store!" After it closed in 1962, a new firm, Colonial Merchandise Mart, emerged and survived until 1990 but as only a shadow of its former self, selling $1 items. (Courtesy Detroit Historical Museum.)

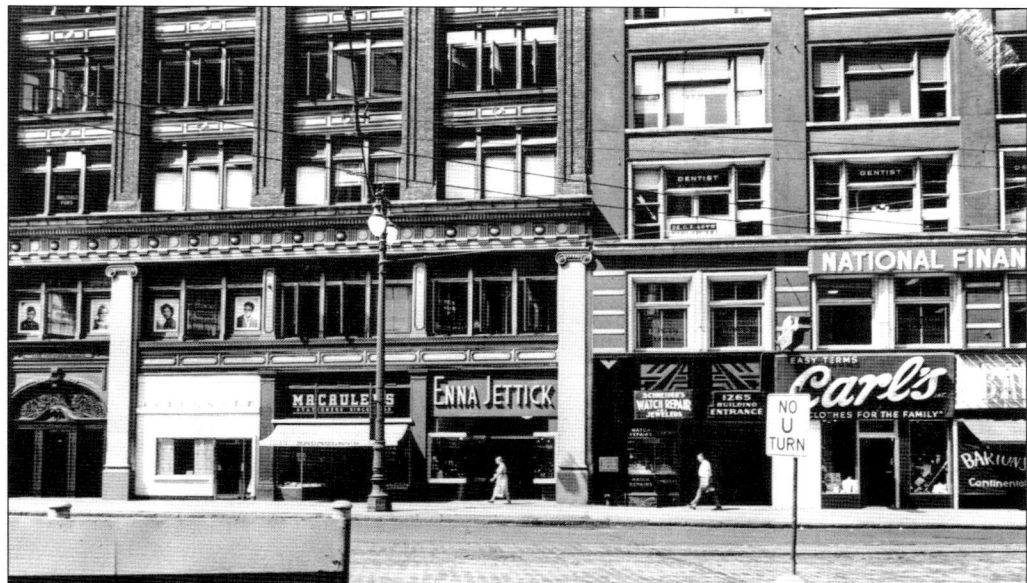

Capitol Park Retailers on Griswold Street, 1950s. Many of downtown's secondary arteries such as Griswold Street were home to a mix of unique merchants. Shown above is Macauley's Office and Stationery Store, founded in 1869 by James Macauley. Also shown is Enna Jettick Shoes, a national chain that flourished from the 1930s through the 1950s and was touted as offering "America's smartest walking shoes!" (Courtesy Manning Brothers Historical Collection.)

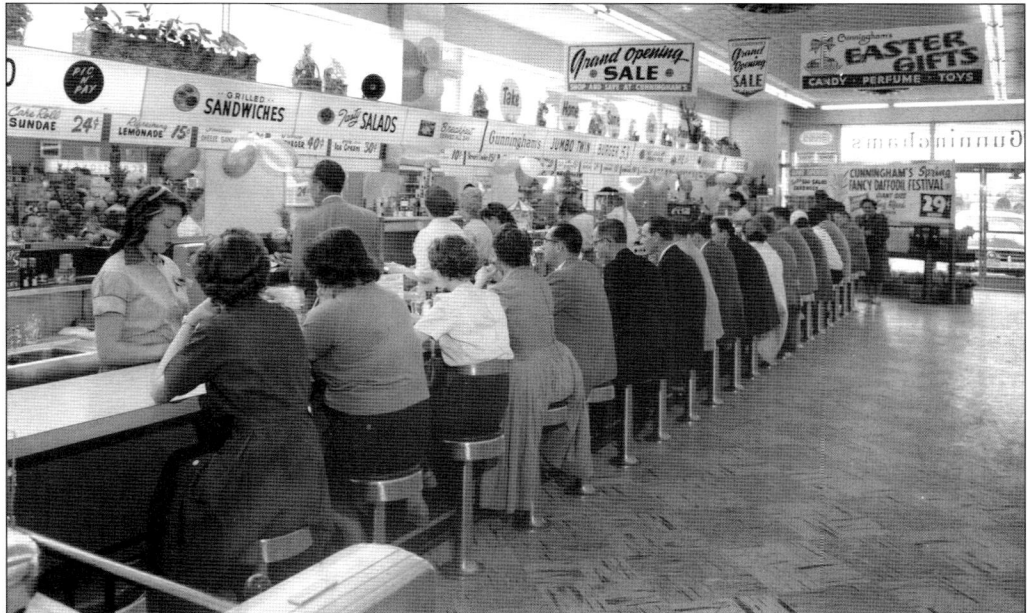

Luncheonette at Cunningham's Drugs, 1957. Cunningham's Drugs was founded by Andrew Cunningham. In 1931, the firm merged with Economical Drugs, founded in 1918 by Nathan Shapero. At its peak, the Detroit-based chain included 167 stores. A succession of new owners in the 1980s, combined with changes in the chain drug industry, paved the way for the demise of this once proud company. (Courtesy Burton Historical Collection, Detroit Public Library.)

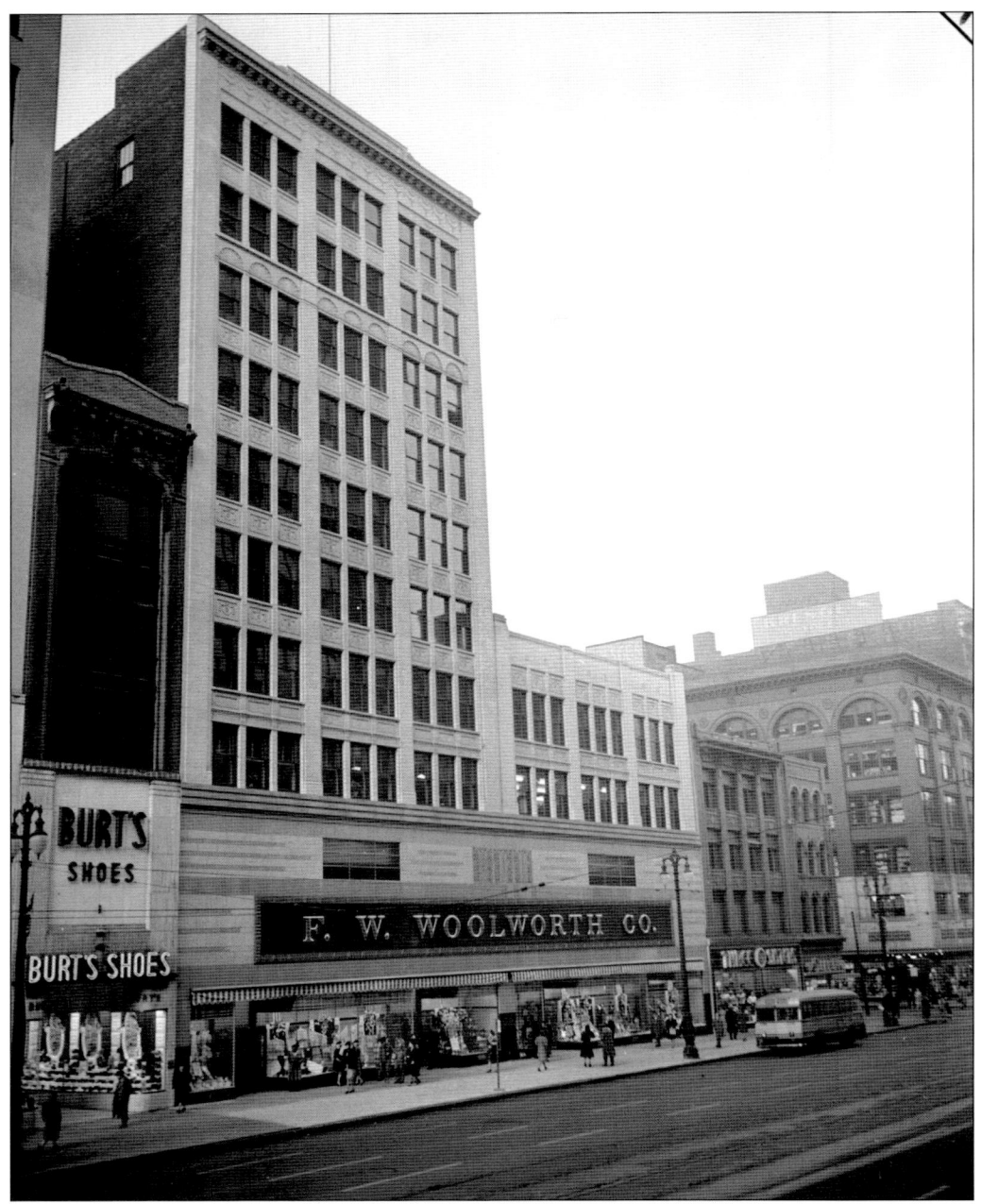

EXTERIOR VIEW OF F. W. WOOLWORTH, 1249 WOODWARD AVENUE, 1950. F. W. Woolworth's first downtown store opened in 1930. In 1940, the New York–based firm leased the former 10-story Bedell building at 1249 Woodward Avenue. It also demolished its former three-story home next door and rebuilt that portion so the floor plates conformed with the 1249 building. The new store contained 36,000 square feet of selling space, had 500 employees, and featured three restaurants. (Courtesy Walter P. Reuther Library, Wayne State University.)

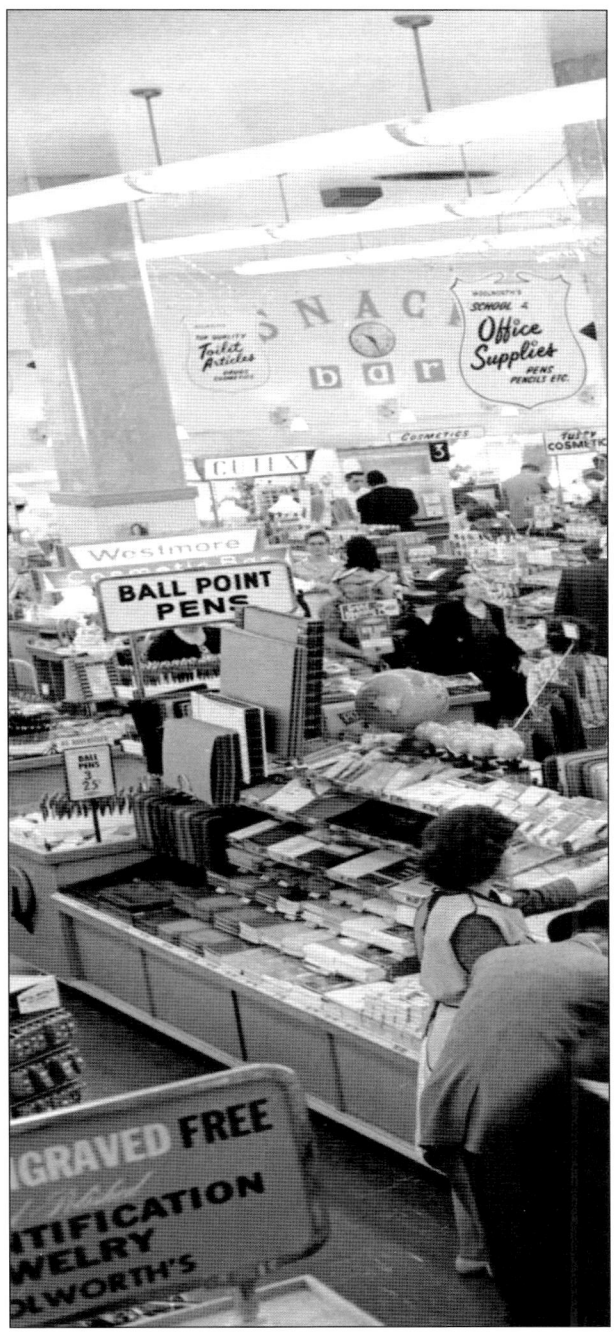

INTERIOR OF DOWNTOWN WOOLWORTH'S, 1960. In 1960, the firm again spent six figures to update the store and add large display windows, new signage, and new display cases. It was also the first in the chain to offer furniture, sporting goods, appliances, and toys in renovated space on the eighth and ninth floors. Despite being one of Woolworth's top performers for many years, the lease was not renewed and the store closed in 1985. The structure today is a part of the Lofts of Merchant's Row residential project. (Courtesy Walter P. Reuther Library, Wayne State University.)

Across America, People are Discovering Something Wonderful. Their Heritage.

Arcadia Publishing is the leading local history publisher in the United States. With more than 3,000 titles in print and hundreds of new titles released every year, Arcadia has extensive specialized experience chronicling the history of communities and celebrating America's hidden stories, bringing to life the people, places, and events from the past. To discover the history of other communities across the nation, please visit:

www.arcadiapublishing.com

Customized search tools allow you to find regional history books about the town where you grew up, the cities where your friends and family live, the town where your parents met, or even that retirement spot you've been dreaming about.

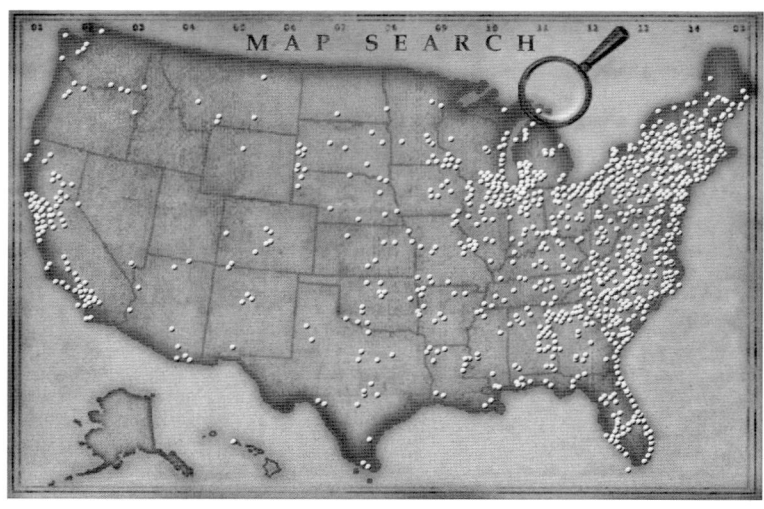